The Book of Crafts

The Book of Crafts

Edited by Henry Pluckrose

Evans Brothers Limited London

Published by Evans Brothers Limited
Montague House, Russell Square,
London, WC1

First published 1971

Phototypeset in Univers by Filmtype Services Limited, Scarborough, Yorkshire
Printed in Great Britain by Hazell Watson & Viney Limited, Aylesbury, Bucks.

237 35185 4   PR 1592

Contents

Acknowledgements   6
Introduction by Henry Pluckrose   7

Materials
Cane, Rushes and Raffia   E. H. Blakeman   11
Clay and Synthetic Modelling
Materials   Alan Lewis   17
Foil   Leon Metcalfe   44
Glass   Peter Tysoe   46
Leather   Dorothy Wright   51
Metalwork   L. A. G. Howard   59
Natural Materials   Derek Waters   71
Paper   Michael Grater   75
Plastics   John Lancaster   80
Wood   Michael Laxton   84

Methods
Basic Sewing   Irene Barker   101
Bookbinding   H. A. de Coverly   114
Brass Rubbing   Mark Haeffner   121
Collages   Eugenie Alexander   123
Copper Enamelling   Elizabeth Carpreau   126
Fabric Printing   Mary Oliver   132
Gem-cutting and Polishing   Gemrocks Ltd.   139
Glovemaking   Dorothy Wright   142
Improvising Dolls   Mabs Tyler   145
Mobiles   Elizabeth Holder   154
Model Making   G. Roland Smith   159
Modern Embroidery   Lavinia Everard   163
Musical Instrument Making   William Prince   184
Plaster and Polystyrene Plaques Leon Metcalfe   191

Printmaking   Gerald Woods   193
Puppets, Masks and Model Theatres   Stuart Robinson   202
Sculpture in Various Media   Glenn Hellman   220
Spinning and Weaving   Mary Barker   231
Tie-and-Dye   Anne Maile   238

Bibliography   245

Materials and Suppliers   246

Index   252

Acknowledgements

The Editor's grateful thanks are due to the experts who wrote the articles and who, unless otherwise acknowledged in the text, provided or found illustrations, besides giving freely of advice; Mary Driscoll for the drawings and Maurice Brownfoot for the diagrams; G. D. Hales who took many of the photographs, some of them under anything but ideal conditions; the staff of museums and galleries and librarians who gave such willing assistance and took such an interest; the manufacturers and suppliers of materials whose staff answered numerous letters and patiently dealt with queries. In particular, Mrs. V. Ellis and Mr. Barlow of the Singer Sewing Machine Company, Mr. B. H. Lewis of Enamelaire Ltd. and Mr. L. S. Ansell of Gemrocks Ltd. Their help has made the preparation of this book a much easier task than it might otherwise have been.

I should like to record my thanks for all the help given by Mrs. Margaret Rivers in the compilation of this anthology.

H.P.

Introduction

Some time ago I was fortunate enough to be able to go to the United States to observe recent developments in the field of art education. I remember in particular one conversation I had with a professor whose first love was physics and whose sole aim in life seemed to be to make the non-scientific (of whom I am one) better aware of the fascination of Newton's law, the significance of light years and the wonder of magnetic fields. The conversation was somewhat one sided, although finally I did manage to make the point that my interest was in the graphic arts. 'Forgive me,' he said, 'I also care about the Arts. I believe that our education system is too geared to technology. We tend to forget that while new industrial processes give man greater freedom by reducing mechanical toil, our educational programmes will need to prepare our people to use their leisure purposefully. No, we must never forget the vital part that the Arts still have to play in our lives.'

A significant remark, I thought, for one whose life has been spent helping to produce a generation of technocrats who can put man on the moon, a space ship round Mars, replace a man's heart or send coloured T.V. pictures across the world. Wherever future developments may be in any of the many fields of human endeavour, man, because he is what he is, will always need to make, to fashion, to build, to create . . . and the implications of all this is that the child of today will have far more leisure time when he reaches adulthood than ever we thought possible a decade ago. Compare the lot of the Detroit car workers who hope to work a fifteen hour week, with that of many of our industrial workers, for whose parents a sixty or seventy-two hour week was commonplace!

Educating for leisure, however, is no easy thing. The mass communications business — television, radio, piped music, tabloid newspapers — make it easy for us to sit back and do nothing until we become little more than automatons, working for the scientists who create the machines. If leisure is to be used purposefully, then from a very early age, children should be encouraged to develop their own skills and have interests of their own. These interests and skills will be quite different, even within the same family — for each of us is unique.

There has been, over the past twenty years, a growing awareness on the part of educationalists as to the vital part which the Arts can play in helping a child discover himself — by handling materials, by fashioning things like cane, clay and wood, by struggling to master the subtle skill of twisting a spindle so that the yarn grows like gossamer from the finger tips . . .

Yet it is not only the young child who grows through activities of this sort. The adolescent, the young mum, imprisoned with her brood, the middle-aged housewife, the retired bank clerk — all gain an intangible something from struggling to master techniques which were evolved at the dawn of civilisation. Many of the techniques remain unaltered, though the materials have become easier to handle. (We no longer need to dig our own clay, it comes pre-packed; we no longer even need to fire it, if we buy it suitably prepared.)

The purpose of a book such as this is not simply to encourage everyone who dips into it to try working in glass or to fill their kitchen with empty detergent packs so that an army of dolls may be made for the next missionary sale at St. Dominics. Rather, we have tried to prepare a handy reference book for all who feel that crafts have a vital part to play in our own lives — and in the lives of those with whom we work.

Teachers in schools, colleges and evening institutes, youth club leaders, guiders and scouters will find much in this volume which bears upon their work.

Of course, purists may look at the contents and express surprise that this and that process has been omitted or is only referred to in passing. It is, however, quite impossible to include everything or every craft. Our aim has been to provide essential starting points from which a more detailed study of a particular medium can grow.

Rebecca West wrote 'Art is nothing less than a way of making joys perpetual'. Art is certainly joyful and if the joys so gained are intensely personal, does that really matter?

Henry Pluckrose

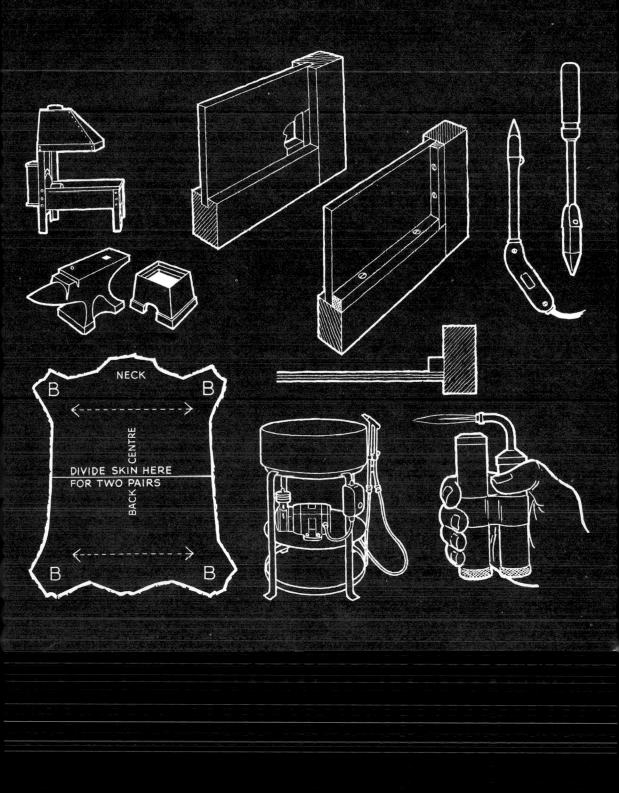

NECK

B   B

DIVIDE SKIN HERE
FOR TWO PAIRS

CENTRE

BACK

B   B

Cane, Rushes and Raffia

E. H. Blakeman

Canework

Canework, as practised at home, in schools and adult education centres, is generally known as 'Basketry' and, as the name implies, refers mainly to smaller baskets of all kinds used in the home, but also includes mats, trays and other articles made by the same methods.

Materials The material used for this type of work is called 'pulp cane' or 'centre cane'. It is chiefly obtained from the core of the rattan palm which grows in tropical forests of the East Indies, although there are a number of suitable substitutes. The outer bark is stripped off (this is made into 'chair cane' or 'flat glossy lapping cane') and the remainder is cut by machine to various thicknesses which are referred to by numbers; the smaller the number the thinner the cane, e.g. No. $2 = 1\frac{7}{8}$ mm., No. $15 = 4\frac{1}{2}$ mm. For use in hospitals and by the disabled, there are certain types of cane which have been 'bleached' after machining, thus making them more pliable and easier to work. There is another type of cane which is used in workshops for the blind and by professional basket makers. This is known as 'willow' and requires more treatment than can usually be given either at home or in school. This cane is used for dog baskets, laundry hampers and other containers which need to be ridged and durable.

Tools For the beginner wishing to start on something simple the following tools are the most necessary:

1 pair 5 in. side cutters
1 pair round-nosed pliers
1 small bodkin
1 long ruler

It also helps the beginner to have an empty jam jar or similar type of container available (the use of which will be explained later).

A basket being made of the thicker cane used by professionals and in blind workshops.

As most students do not have a work board to fasten the work to, it is necessary to provide some kind of weight to hold the work steady. This can be an old brick wrapped in paper or a piece of material. For smaller items, a kitchen weight, suitably covered so as not to damage the work, is satisfactory.

There are a number of technical terms which are useful to know as they save a lot of explanation when making a basket. The principal ones are as follows:

Stakes These are always the thicker of the two

or more different sizes of cane used in making a basket. They form the uprights round which the finer canes are woven.

Bye-stakes These are placed on the right-hand side of the stakes, after the upsetting has been completed, and add strength to the stakes.

Foot-trac Denotes the method of fastening the stakes after placing them into the holes of a wooden base.

Weavers This is the finer cane which is woven in various ways round the stake canes.

Upsetting This is the method of using three weaving canes, worked alternately, and as the name implies 'sets' the work up to the correct shape required. It is therefore most important that it should be done correctly.

Randing Weaving with one cane.

Pairing Weaving with two canes worked alternately.

Waling This is exactly the same as upsetting, and is done at different intervals in a basket to give added strength and rigidity to the work.

Border The means of finishing off the stakes after the basket has been made to the required shape and size.

Making a basket Having decided on the type of article to be made, the next thing to decide is how long the stakes should be. This is worked out in the following way: take the height of the finished article plus 3 in. for the foot-trac border plus at least 7 in. for the finishing border (this can be very much longer for some of the more complicated borders, the length given here is for the most simple one).

For the beginner, prepared wooden bases can be obtained. (Experience is needed before a woven base is attempted.) When the number of holes in the wooden base have been counted, the correct number of stakes are cut and placed into the jam jar or similar container with about 3 in. of cold or warm water in it, and left for about 10 minutes to render the cane more pliable. As mentioned before, the bleached cane is softer to start with

Woven bases are best left to the more experienced weaver.

and, therefore, requires less, or even no soaking before use. By placing only the ends of the stakes in the water it will be found that they will enter the holes in the wooden base easily, especially if the dry ends are placed in first and then the whole length pulled through to the wet part. When the cane is wet it swells and it may be necessary to enlarge the holes with the bodkin to enable it to go through the base. Put only six or eight stakes in at a time and then work the foot-trac border. If all the stakes are put in, especially on a large base, they will be dry before all the work has been completed.

The following explanations and diagrams will make clear the different methods of weaving and making the foot-trac border. Weaving can be done either from left to right by a right-handed person, or from right to left by a left-handed person. The diagrams shown here are for a right-handed person.

Foot-trac Leave about 3 in. of damp cane projecting underneath (it may be necessary to extend or reduce the amount which will vary according to the size of the base and the distance between each hole). Working from left to right, bend down each stake in turn behind one and in front of two, leaving the end on the inside (Fig. 1), all the time pressing the work well down on to the base. To work the last three stakes, thread them in order under the starting stakes, easing these up with the bodkin and at the same time making sure that the ends lie on the base. Now go round on the other side of the work and pull the stakes up straight and tight to the base.

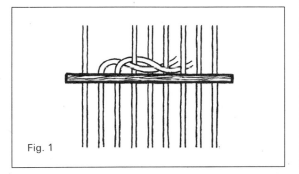

Fig. 1

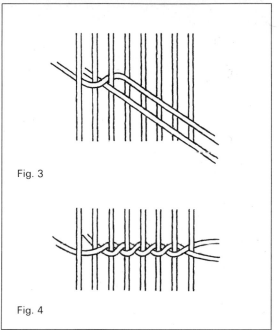

Fig. 3

Fig. 4

Randing method Using one length of weaving cane, insert it between stakes 1 and 2 with the short end pointing to the left on the inside (Fig. 2). The forefinger of the left hand is placed on the inside of the work at the back of the second stake to hold it in position and to press the stake outwards if necessary; at the same time place the thumb on the outside of the work, holding the weaving cane against the stake. Now with the tip of the thumb place the weaving cane to the back of and away from the next stake; with the thumb and forefinger of the right hand bring it to the front of the work between the next two stakes. Repeat the stroke, pulling the cane through after a few strokes.

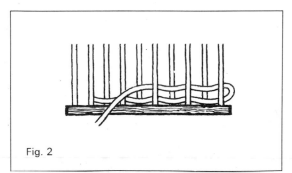

Fig. 2

Pairing method Place two weaving canes in adjacent spaces between the stakes, or take one long length of weaving cane, bend it in half and place the bend over one stake. Take the left-hand weaving cane and pass it in front of the next stake on the right, over the second weaving cane, behind the next stake and out to the front (Fig. 3). The second weaving cane is now taken and dealt with in exactly the same way. Continue working each cane alternately (Fig. 4). This is a stronger type of weaving and is the one most generally used.

Waling or upsetting method Three weaving canes are placed in adjacent spaces between the stakes (Fig. 5). Taking the left-hand weaving cane first, pass it over the other two weaving canes, in front of two stakes and behind one, bringing it out to the front (Fig. 6). Again using the left-hand weaving cane, repeat this stroke (Fig. 7). Using the left-hand weaving cane each time, continue in this way.

To join a new weaving cane Leave the old cane on the outside of the work pointing to the right. Insert the new weaving cane on the right of the work and resting against the stake (Fig. 8). The diagram shows the join in waling but the same

13

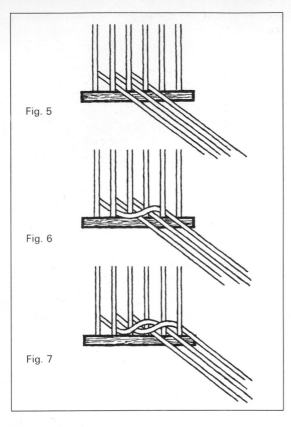

Fig. 5

Fig. 6

Fig. 7

method can be used for all the types of weaving described above. In this way there is one end finishing on the outside and one starting on the inside, and they will hold each other together when the ends are cut level with the work.

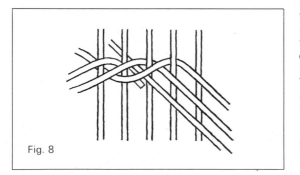

Fig. 8

It is most important to keep the weaving canes wet while working with them. They should be soaked for about 10 minutes before starting work and a

damp sponge will help to keep them pliable while working.

Having completed the basket to the required shape and size the border has to be added. There are many types of border, each suitable for different articles. However, one of the easiest and most useful is the *Three Rod Plain Border* which is worked as follows:

All the stakes should be squeezed with the round-nosed pliers level with the work (this is done to stop the cane from cracking when making a sharp bend).
The first stake is then bent behind the second and brought to the front; the second stake is bent behind the third and brought to the front; the third stake is bent behind the fourth stake and brought to the front.
The first cane bent down is now passed over the other two canes bent down, in front of the fourth stake and behind the fifth, and brought to the front again.
The fourth stake is now bent down with this one and on the right-hand side of it — making sure that they both lie flat on the top of the work and not on top of each other.
The second and third stakes which were bent down are now dealt with in exactly the same way, by which time there should be three pairs of canes on the front of the work.
Counting from the right, take the fifth one of these in front of the next upright stake and behind the next, and through to the front once again; bend the next upright stake down with it as before to make the pair.
Continue until there is only one stake left standing, then take the fifth weaving cane in front of this stake as before and from the inside thread it under the first stake bent down (this may have to be eased up a little with the aid of the bodkin). Now bend the last stake down beside this.
The right-hand weaving canes of the three pairs are now threaded through in the same way so that there is no obvious start or finish.

When the basket is dry the ends of all the border, and any joins made, can be cut off close to the work. Should there be a lot of 'whiskers' on the basket they can be removed by singeing with a spirit lamp or gas lighter, but care must be taken not to burn it!

A selection of basket-work

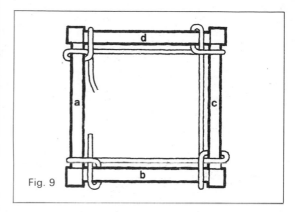

Fig. 9

Begin by fastening one end of the seagrass on to the inside of the bottom left-hand cross bar of the stool or chair 'A' (Fig. 9) with a small carpet tack; proceed by bringing the remainder of the seagrass over and under bar 'B', then over and under bar 'A'.

From here, take it over and under bar 'C', then back and over and under bar 'B'.

Do exactly the same over bar 'D'.

Continue in the same way, making sure that the work is kept tight and even and the mitre in each corner is correct and in line.

Work small pieces of brown paper between the two layers of seagrass at each corner as the work proceeds. This will help to stop overlapping and keep the mitre straight, besides making it very much firmer.

When the work is completed the four mitres should meet in the centre of an equal-sided stool. The end of the seagrass can be tied off on the underside. The steel needle will be required to make the last few rounds through the centre.

Should it be necessary to make a join during work, it should always be done on the underside.

Rushes

For many years both freshwater and saltwater rushes have been used for seating chairs and stools. Rush baskets and mats are also familiar objects. However, rushes are not popular as a craft material for use at home or in school. Firstly, they are somewhat expensive to use on one chair or stool; secondly, they are rather dirty and often difficult to handle. Good results are not easy to achieve, the plaiting being difficult for the novice to keep to an even width.

There is, however, another type of material called *seagrass* which can be bought ready for use. It is worked in the same way as rushes and similar patterns can be obtained.

Tools The only tool required is a large steel sacking needle and a quantity of brown paper for packing. (When rushes are used the odd pieces are saved and used for this purpose.)

Seating a stool The usual method of covering a stool or chair is known as the 'rush' pattern and is one of the easiest to follow, provided the work is

Raffia

Nowadays the use of natural raffia has been largely superseded by that of synthetic raffias marketed under various names and obtainable from art needlework counters and suppliers of craft materials. Synthetic raffia has many advantages over the natural product: uniform width, continuous length, repeatable and fast colours. It may be used in the same way as the natural material for making table mats, lampshades, handbags, hats and many other articles. Another advantage is its suitability for knitting, weaving, plaiting, etc. Patterns may be obtained for raffia work but, having assimilated the methods of use, it is not difficult to create original work.

Indian coiled basket-work is yet another form of this work. Indeed, there are various materials and methods which cannot be included here through lack of space. Those interested will find valuable further reading suggested in the bibliography (page 245).

Industrial Advisers to the Blind/Maurice Broomfield

Clay and Synthetic Modelling Materials

Alan Lewis

Modelling

Of recent times there has been a very considerable increase in the variety of materials available to the modeller. This is probably a reflection on the shortcomings of the traditional methods in a situation where the interest is growing more quickly than the availability of special facilities. Having made a model there is often a need to make it permanent and it is here that the real difficulties lie and the answers are to be found.

To achieve permanence has always been difficult. The requirement to change a plastic medium into something hard and durable called for the use of a kiln or some knowledge of the casting process. Neither way was easy. Papier mâché could be considered as a possible alternative, but as a modelling material it leaves much to be desired. Plasticine was never in the running, in that it never hardens. But times are changing and, although prices are rising, so are the options.

Materials The available materials can be divided into three groups. Firstly, those that remain soft; secondly, there are those that start soft but can be persuaded by some special means to go hard; lastly there are those that start soft but dry into hardness without any help or persuasion. Papier mâché is a member of this last group but its handling characteristics are so different from any other that it will be dealt with separately at the end of this section.

Plasticine The first group is typified by Plasticine. At an adult level, this is an ideal medium for working out one's thoughts in the hands, and ideal for making little abstracted shapes that will indicate whether or not the idea is worth following up. It is also ideal for little experimental models, such as a small dog or cat. Move the head and note the complete change of expression that this action will bring about. Move the legs into a running

Experimenting with textures by pressing metal oddments into clay or Plasticine.

position. See how the balance is changed if you wish to raise the front leg. Work out the mechanics of these problems and you will begin to understand a little more about the nature of four-footed movement—and be a better modeller to boot.

There are, in fact, several other materials in this group but they are the same in principle, and there is no need to dwell further on them here. Mostly everything that can be done with them was done some time ago; they are still enjoyed today. They have their obvious limitations in that size and scope are determined by the inability of the materials to withstand more than a limited amount of their own weight, and nothing made in these materials can be retained. Nevertheless, within these limitations they are useful.

The newcomers It is in this second group that we find the range has mushroomed. The qualities and techniques offered are so various that they cannot be typified by any particular one. Generally, they are sold by the pound and come in tins or neat plastic packs of some sort. All are carefully designed materials that remain workable for long periods and are either self-hardening through long exposure to the air or require some mild heat treatment in a domestic cooker. Normally, the degree of hardness will be adequate. Some can be recovered by breaking down and re-wetting, but most are irretrievable. The technique of modelling a small chunky object is much the same as with Plasticine.

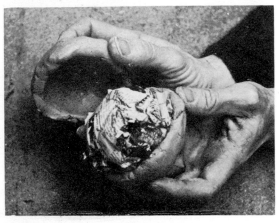

Making a ball around screwed-up paper.

'Knitting' the joint together.

It is developed from a ball but, as the mass increases, we can economise by forming the material round a lump of screwed-up paper. Alternatively, if the shape is to be long and lean, we shall have to start with a wire frame. Any techniques peculiar to a particular material are covered in the instructions provided with it — read them with care. These materials are not cheap but you will get your money's worth if you are able to use them properly and to some effect. Less common aspects of modelling, such as jewellery-making, are also described in these instructions.

Clay and Reinforced Clay This last group can be considered as an alternative to the materials just described. It includes two types — the common clays and prepared clays, and the reinforced modelling clays such as 'Newclay' — and accounts for the majority of all modelling that is done. Hundreds, possibly thousands, of tons of clay are consumed each year. A small proportion is fired and turned into pottery but much of it never sees the light of a kiln.

Something about the nature of clay (aspects that are not vital to the modeller) is discussed in the section on pottery, but there are some points — particularly those relating to its handling properties — that should be mentioned earlier.

Clays are normally purchased in a plastic state ready for use. They become hard on drying. Unfortunately, they are much too brittle to be of use in this state. The modeller who wishes to retain his efforts must either have his model fired or cast it in some casting material or other. This could be a very real problem for the beginner who may have no special facilities, but the problem has been largely overcome with the introduction of reinforced modelling clay. The fact of the reinforcing permits a hardener to be used when the work needs to be made permanent.

All the clays in this group are cheap by comparison with the materials previously mentioned and are, in consequence, sold by the hundredweight or part hundredweight. One hundredweight of any of the normal modelling materials measures about one cubic foot. One large pot or model can weigh many pounds so it can be seen that cost is still important.

Tools and Techniques The great beauty of modelling, when compared with almost any other craft, is that so few tools are necessary and very little technique. Settle for a piece of wood sharpened rather like the blade of a knife (called a spatula) which you can buy for a shilling or two if you wish, a broken hacksaw blade, an old wooden rule (or similar piece of wood) and a sponge. Rodin and Epstein will have had little more. And technique too. Look at a piece of Degas' work, it is all so obvious you would swear that you could have done it yourself. And that's a great comfort — even if a little mistaken.

To make a start As suggested earlier, squeeze your first little models out of a small ball of whatever material you have chosen. If you are teaching children, then they too should begin this way, whatever their age. There will be no special difficulties except those that arise from your own inability to create the shape that you have in mind. If this is all new to you, you will enjoy the sensation. It is, as they say, very therapeutic.

With some modelling materials, and clay in particular, you may find that there is a tendency for the surface to stiffen as it dries in the hands.

Use a sponge to replace the moisture and carry on. Don't be too serious and laboured with your first efforts, but it will probably be worth your while to finish off each item with colour, or some other finishing medium, if only to get a better understanding of the type of problem that will arise later. Then pass on to something more substantial.

Let us consider the making of a four-legged beast such as a horse — one of those splendid shire-horses — yet not because he is so splendid, but rather because he has great thick legs which can support the mass of the body. Think of a race-horse and you will see the point. Even so, the body may still be too bulky to be made from the solid so, as already suggested, you can wrap the clay around a mass of screwed-up paper.

With the body of the horse lying on the table, attach the legs. These will be rough rods of clay, quite unfashioned, *but with a good strong joint.* This is best achieved by knitting both parts together. Treat this as of first importance. It is always a sad sight to see good work develop faults in the later stages through initial carelessness.

It may well be that your model can stand on its own four feet already but, if not, put a support under its belly until the clay is drier and stronger. Now add the head and tail, with the same care for the joints mentioned in the previous paragraph. The basic shape is complete. Now, using your fingers, supplemented where necessary by the finer edge of the modelling tool, begin the shaping and modelling. No further words of advice. This is for you to develop in the way that you feel is right. This model is an expression of what, to you, is implied by the term 'shire-horse'.

The early stages of modelling.

'Old Uncle Tom Cobley and all' — a more complicated model.

This may be in terms of solidarity, or power, or even humanity. Yet there should be no need for you to be consciously aware of all this. Any serious piece of sculpture tells us as much about the artist as it does of the subject.

Most four-legged animals can be treated in the way described but at the half-way stage considerable modification could be necessary to accommodate all of the possible positions.

Coiling To achieve really large volumes in clay we must learn to coil. This is a technique used by potters and modellers alike. Here I shall instance the making of a head, but in the early stages it could just as easily have been a pot, or any abstract form.

Press out a lump of clay into a disc about three or four inches across and rather more than half an inch thick. Now take a piece and roll it backwards and forwards on the table pressing gently with both hands until it stretches out into a long rope the thickness of your thumb. One might expect this to be easy but you will find that your first efforts are rather bumpy affairs. It doesn't matter. Wind it round on to the edge of the disc so that it begins to form a cylinder. Smear over the joint inside and out as you go.

More and more coils are wound one on top of the other, enlarging the diameter as you get higher, until you estimate that the level of the top of the forehead has been reached. Now wind the coils a little on the inside to shape and close in the top. Even at this stage there need be nothing about the shape that suggests a head, and you still have a hole in the top large enough for your hand. So put it in and with your beating stick knock some intelligence into it. Press out from the inside and beat in from the outside; a crude, rough shape to begin with, refining it gradually stage by stage. Once it begins to take shape the top can be closed in. A little more beating, and then the modelling can begin, but don't be too disappointed with early attempts — portraiture is a very difficult art.

Modelling on a wire A separate problem is the long attenuated figure that has little bulk and much length. The giraffe is a walking example of this, or the stick insect, but even cats and dogs can be interpreted in this way. The wire that you use to support the clay will remain inside, for even on hardening none of the materials acquire

sufficient strength to take that much strain. *Rule out normal clay for this work.* The shrinkage will cause it to dry in a procession of cracks. Use reinforced clay or one of the specialised materials.

The thickness of the wire required for this work will depend to some extent on the model, but if you start with a coil of something a little thicker than one sixteenth of an inch (16 S.W.G.) it will cost you only a shilling or so and last ages. Figures standing on one or two legs will require a base of some sort. Having twisted your wire into shape, model a base and push the bent ends of the wire into it. Bend the ends to enable it to lock more securely. Now let the base dry a little and start working from the bottom up.

Something a little different and quite exciting can be produced using the new corrugated modelling wire that is a part of the reinforced modelling clay process. This wire was designed to permit young children to bend the wire more easily in their hands, and also to improve clay adhesion, but more interesting from many modellers point of view is the fact that the wire can be left exposed to give quite an unusual look to the models.

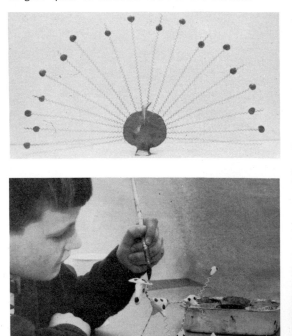

Cutting out a motor car for use in relief work. Pieces of clay can then be added and modelled.

A more permanent 'Willow Pattern' model in reinforced and hardened clay.

Modelling in Relief Another aspect of this craft is modelling in relief which differs from those already described in that there is, or can be, a tremendous amount of technique involved. The methods are fascinating and well worthy of your time, although in fact the result may be of only limited use, for anything bigger than a cameo can be difficult to place. Normally, one would relate it to the development of a tiled area for exterior use, in which case it would have to be fired.

Consider for a moment the head on a coin and realise that although the nose is, in fact, on the same level as the ear, the modeller has persuaded you that this is not so. It is indeed a highly skilled mystery which there is no space to probe here. But that is at one level. At its most basic the process can be much simpler. Sketch a rough outline of your intentions across the face of the surface to be treated. Dampen the area with a sponge and build out from the surface with small pellets of clay. Alternatively, draw on the surface of a very thin tile, cut away the superfluous clay, and then model the rest. This separate item can be welded, with others, to a clay backing using liquid clay, or, on drying, be glued to a back board. Very large relief panels can be built up in this way.

To Increase Durability The procedure by which your work will achieve durability will depend on the material that you use. Wherever the weather or water are involved, firing or casting will still be a necessity. But these methods are complicated and often costly, and for this reason manufacturers are producing useful alternatives. The different treat-

Pots and a dish which have been treated for sufficient durability.

ments as prescribed by the makers are simplicity itself and will always be sufficient for indoor use. (It is a bit of a trick, but one means of containing water in a clay vase is to incorporate a polythene beaker or bottle into the construction!)

Papier mâché

Personally, I find little joy in the making up of papier mâché pulp but it is an unfortunate and necessary prelude to working with this very useful, although not ideal, modelling material. In handling it compares rather poorly with clay, but once the technique is acquired and the form achieved, what a rugged substance it dries out to be. I use the word rugged not just to indicate toughness—a

Preparing the pulp from egg boxes.

The proportions of papier mâché pulp and clay prior to kneading.

smooth finish is really not possible with paper pulp.

We all have our pet way of making up the mash. Newsprint is normally the basic material but egg boxes break down rather more easily. Tear it up small and leave it to soak for as long as you can. For anything special use an egg whisk to finish it off, but otherwise rub it through the hands. Drain off the surplus water, first by sieving it through a cloth; then give each handful a final squeeze. Now make up a concentrated solution of one of the cellular adhesives. Wait until it is clear and then mix it into the pulp. As quantity goes, the weekly newspaper at eight ounces will need about a dessertspoonful of the glue — plus water of course.

This mixture could now be considered ready for use but, in fact, it will be much improved by the addition of a filler of some sort. It must be realised that water adds enormously to the bulk of the mixture and this will all disappear as it slowly (very slowly) dries out. Models that were made with bulk will fade away in large lumps as the drying progresses. A filler will help to diminish this effect, and the smaller shrinkage will also mean a smoother finishing surface although, as stated, the surface can never be really smooth. The greatest advantage gained by the addition of a filler will be in the handling properties. If to any given mass of paper pulp you knead in a quarter of its volume in plastic clay much will be gained. There will be an increase in weight, but that may not prove to be a disadvantage.

In assessing the value of papier mâché it should be judged on three counts: The effort required in preparation; the ease with which it can be modelled, and the resulting end-product. It must be acknowledged that it does not come out very well on the first two, but on the last count its claims are unique. The toughness/weight ratio of well-made papier mâché is probably surpassed only by metal alloys and fibre-glass. It is by taking advantage of these properties that we can expect to get the best from this material. Masks made over clay shapes for a start, puppet heads, thin spiny insects, models and structures made around wire, pendants, dishes, jewellery. Try framing broken glass. In fact try any of the normal modelling processes too. It may by chance give just the result that you were looking for.

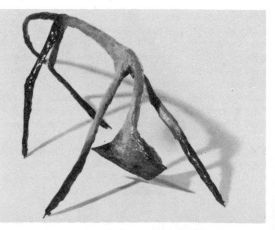

Cat made from papier mâché round a wire frame.

Papier mâché monster and tree made by Jack Williams.

Decoration

Strangely, the finishing off of your work could pose the greatest problems. You would be well advised to try out the different effects on your early pieces so that your experience in one matches your experience in the other. The surface qualities of the material as such are seldom interesting enough for present tastes.

Any water-bound paints can be used, and these can be covered later with a PVA gloss or satin finish. A little of this adhesive added to the water used for painting will prevent smearing. All of these modelling materials are inert so they can be expected to accept almost any medium. Oil paints if you wish, bronze powders in shellac, polyester resins with metal fillers, acrylics, cellulose — there are plenty to choose from and many clever techniques. But don't be hidebound by the conventional. Try a brick dust in weak glue; stone dusts are available, I believe. Glue parrot seed all over the surface. Tiles impressed with mixed seeds are a satisfying exercise for children. Weave a line of string over the surface, glue it in place, and then fill up the different areas with colour and texture. Think up new ideas and try them out. It may not be great art but it is creative, and usually enjoyable.

Pottery

The raw material A definition of pottery is fired clay — clay that has been made red-hot in a kiln. But if we are to understand the full significance of the term we must first know a little about what we mean by clay. Scientifically, clay is an aluminium silicate, but that fact need not concern us a great deal. More to the point is the fact that clay is at times a wet sticky substance, and at others a rather hard and brittle rock found in quantity in many an English garden. But whatever the condition of this garden clay it is unlikely to be of any use to us. Mostly, such clays are full of impurities and have a tendency to shrink badly and crack on drying. You can, if you wish, experiment with them and you may learn much, but I am loath to recommend it. There are too many imponderables even under ideal conditions. Starting at ground level can make a tough job even tougher.

Clay is a plastic rock, malleable in the hands yet when subjected to heat it can be transformed into a substance that only the very hardest steels can scratch. These facts have made clay uniquely useful to mankind. The qualities of clay vary from patch to patch, and much time and money is spent on categorising even the limited number of clays put at our disposal by the industry. You will do well to get yourself a hundredweight of a 'prepared' clay as opposed to a clay 'as dug'. It may cost you up to £1·50 but at this stage it will be worth it and will probably last quite a long time. A 'prepared' clay is one where the natural clay has been reduced to a liquid for the purposes of cleaning and for the addition of other ingredients calculated to provide the user with the properties required to fulfil particular needs.

One of these additives will almost certainly be 'grog', i.e. ground pottery. This reduces shrinkage, opens up the pores, and also endows the clay with a gritty-ness — a texture considered by most to be a desirable quality. After the mixing, the surplus water is filtered out and the residue packed for use. Even at this stage it still contains about twenty-five per cent water. Using this mixing method, the natural clay can be easily modified with any of a dozen or so additives which will ensure, among other things, that it matures at a specific firing temperature. This may be anything from about 800°C. up to 1300°C., or even higher; anything from earthenware to stoneware or porcelain. Here we shall concern ourselves almost entirely with earthenware fired at rather more than 1000°C. Lower than that most clays are too weak, higher and the process becomes more expensive in all sorts of ways.

So, you buy your earthenware clay, and it will cost you money. It must be cared for. Look after it. Out-of-condition clay is a sad business; in condition it is a joy. The most suitable container is a plastic bin of some sort, plus an extra bucket or two for damping down the odds and ends that have been allowed to go hard. To reconstitute dry clay, break it into small pieces and sprinkle with water periodically. Just how much water will be required, and how long it will take, you will have to find out from experience. The rate at which various clays absorb water differs, and so too does the amount of water they will hold, depending upon the size of the particles making up the clay structure. Anyway, you are bound to be surprised by the quantity required.

Wedging Clay that has been reconstituted requires to be worked into a smooth even consistency, free of lumps and, if possible, free of air bubbles. The former is achieved by cutting through the block with a brass wire like a 'cheese cutter', and then thumping the top piece hard down on to the lower. (This process is referred to as 'wedging'.) Do this a few times and then, depending on the state of the clay, do it a few more times for good measure. It is a most satisfying performance so you won't mind the extra effort.

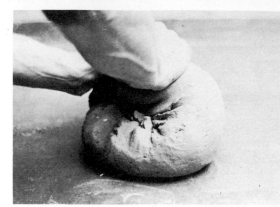
Kneading to remove air bubbles.

Kneading Air bubbles are removed by kneading. Just how this is done almost defies description. Bernard Leach in his 'A Potter's Book' does it well — but that is only one of many reasons why you should read it. It is, however, worth pointing out that when a baker kneads dough he does it to engulf as much air as possible. Therefore his technique is not to be recommended. But, contrary to all the advice given by my betters in many books, the beginner need not trouble himself too much about captive air pockets. The consequence normally predicted is that as the air expands on heating in the kiln it will burst pieces off the ware. The risk is grossly exaggerated. A little extra care in the firing will cut out most of it.

Shaping the Clay When the clay arrives on your doorstep it will be in a near-unmanageable mass. Drag it into your workshop and open the polythene wraps. There may be a certain amount of sweating over the surface of the clay, but it was probably despatched in a slightly overwet state so that it can afford to lose a little. Pull it to pieces and drop it into your bin. Even that little exercise may have taught you something — clay is unexpectedly heavy for its size. There is, however, a great deal more than that to be learnt about the clay you have chosen. Some factors could be described and categorised, others are just personal reactions — feelings not easily defined but aspects that add up to the personality of the clay. You like it or you don't like it. It suits your purpose or it does not. It will take time, but you will come to these conclusions eventually.

Wedging. Reverse the top half before banging it down on the lower.

Pull off a piece of clay and smear it through your fingers. Any gritty-ness can be accounted for as sand or grog, introduced to add texture to the clay and reduce the shrinkage (neither sand nor grog shrinks on firing). Roll a piece into a long thin coil. Do this by rolling the piece backwards and forwards under your hands on a table. Now wind it round your finger. A good clay in good condition will show no signs of cracking. Now lay it out flat and make two marks on it 10 in. apart. Measure it again once it is dry and calculate the degree of shrinkage. A probable figure will be 8 per cent to 10 per cent or thereabouts. If you don't think that is of much importance you are due for a surprise. In fact, the greater part of the whole pottery process is the attempt to come to terms with shrinkage.

A group of inter-relating, geometric shapes.

A coil wound round the finger showing a good clay in condition.

Making a Start Let us start making some shapes. Pull off another piece of clay and roll it into a ball—a smooth round ball that gives you pleasure to hold. Stand it down and make another shape to put alongside it—a tall cone or a long thin cylinder, a half hoop, anything. Position it and then re-position it and consider the effect. Note that as the gap between them increases the dominance of one over the other decreases. Bring in a third and fourth shape and play at architects. Design your contribution to Expo 2000. If you teach children, set them this as an exercise: a group of shapes on a thin tile base. By now you will have noted that your inexpertness in forming these shapes causes you to be slow, and drying cracks form on the surface. Obviously a small sponge is called for to replace the moisture as you work.

A Pinched Dish To return to the ball. Make another, but don't fuss too much with it. Now push your thumb steadily but firmly into it, right into the middle of it, but not quite so far that you penetrate the other side. If you now turn the ball with your other hand and, at the same time, rhythmically pinch the clay that rests between your thumb and finger, you will steadily enlarge the hole. The trick is to turn the original solid sphere into a hollow hemisphere. This is not easy, but as a technique it is one that will serve you well and is worth acquiring.

This hemisphere, raised to a high state of perfection, can remain as a small bowl. Just what one means by perfection must be a personal matter but in this context it must have something to do with accuracy. As the clay stiffens on drying you can begin to beat it gently on the outside with a flat slat of wood, supporting it on the inside with the fingers. With some care quite delicate shapes are possible.

Developing a Ball You could make two pinched bowls and, while they are still in the rough state, join them edge to edge. The result is a hollow sphere that is relatively light for its size. Large, solid masses of clay are usually undesirable. *Take care with the joint,* ensuring that the clay is knitted together before smearing and smoothing.

A pinched bowl made from the ball of clay.

A sphere engraved with concentric circles and later treated with copper carbonate.

Here again, time spent on the ball can result in an accurate shape that feels right and true in the hands; a shape that offers some scope for superficial development in terms of incised, overlaid or coloured decoration. A pin-hole inserted before firing will allow the compressed air to escape from any enclosed shape—a very necessary precaution.

Developing a Basic Shape By using a basic shape we can develop a great range of models. Here we will attempt to select a number of pieces, each typical of its type, and assume that the reader will work out the permutations on each line.

First there is a pebble. If you collect pebbles, pick out one that has the qualities you find interesting and then work out your own interpretation of them. Use your wooden slat to re-form the ball until it takes on the same type of pebble shape as your specimen. Perhaps not quite the same, but rather a shape that gives you the same feeling; a shape that distinguishes between the weather-worn, the sea-rolled, the stratified or the crystalline.

A group of 'pebbles', some real and some modelled.

Smooth it, roughen it, sculpt or dig holes in it, most anything goes; although, on the last point of digging holes, it is worth mentioning that all the time your shape contains compressed air it will remain fairly firm—puncture it and most of the strength hisses out with the air. As the clay stiffens the lost strength will steadily return.

The ball could be re-formed into an egg and, from this egg, not surprisingly, a great range of birds and animals can be developed. This will require the addition of more clay pieces—heads, wings, feet, arms, etc. Care with the joining is important. Try not to trap air under these additions and, wherever possible, knit the clay together. A little water or slip (a liquid mixture of clay and water, see page 40) daubed on the joint area will assist the bonding process.

A pig developed by a pupil from a clay 'egg'.

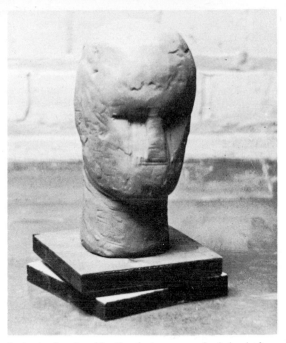

A basic head with the features roughed in before modelling.

As your skill increases so will your ability to make larger spheres. A diameter of four or five inches should not be too difficult. This is large enough to form the basis for modelling a head. Not life-sized, but large enough to be able to develop the features. Having made a rough ball, beat it into an egg-shape and then set it aside. Now press out a flat strip of clay that can be bent round into a neck, and then place the egg on top of this with the point of the egg downwards and overhanging the neck a little to make a chin. Smear in some clay to make a joint and, when all feels firm, use your beating stick to improve the shape. A few structural guide lines sketched over the surface and the real modelling begins.

No comment or advice is offered on how to model but—just to repeat—you cannot expect soft clay to bond to hard clay. Do not allow the model to dry out, dampen it with water now and again if necessary, and make sure that any addition of any size is well keyed on.

The Coil The technique of rolling coils is so necessary and so much used by the studio potter that you can be pretty certain that after a few years you will have added several yards to the many miles fabricated throughout history. The method by which these coils are achieved is described in the section on modelling (page 25). When you start you will rapidly conclude that a smooth, even coil is not within the bounds of possibility but in no time you will find it almost as difficult to roll a bad one. Probably the greatest yardage is consumed in the building of pots: pots of all shapes and sizes, some too big to be thrown on the wheel like the 'Forty Thieves' jars, but mostly the more usual sizes where the potter prefers this method or the intended shape makes the wheel irrelevant.

Small Coiled Figures Before actually trying to make a pot let us play with a few short lengths to make some coil models. With the minimum of fuss join a few bits and pieces neatly together to make little figures and animals. Not great art this, but interesting. There are, in fact, some delightful Staffordshire pieces made in this way. A little historical precedent can make any technique respectable.

The early stages in coiling a pot.

Make the base for your pot by rolling a piece of clay into a ball and then pat it flat into a disc. Now roll a coil and form it into a ring around the top edge. Join it by smearing a little of the clay from the inside of the coil downwards to the base. The outside of the coil remains exposed unjointed, as it will all the way up to the top. This presents a real challenge to the coiler for the shape of the pot must be accurately formed as the coiling progresses.

Proceed by placing ring upon ring, always smearing the inside of the coil down on to the one below. If, through your slowness or the warmth of the room, your coils get a little on the dry side, wipe them with a damp sponge. Let the moisture soak in before carrying on. Never attempt to join soft coils to a dry or even to a very firm pot. To make such a joint is not difficult, but it will crack away some time later as it shrinks. Store your unfinished work in a polythene bag to retain its condition. The shape is created as you go with little chance of changing it appreciably at a later stage. There will inevitably be some stiffening of the body as the work progresses, and this is desirable for the weight of the clay could cause some sagging, particularly in a full-bellied pot.

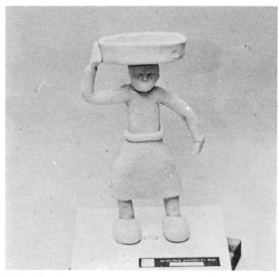

A simple coil figure.

A Coiled Pot Now try your hand at a small coiled pot. There was a time when every student of pottery occupied much of his or her time in the production of coiled pots. I was never a great enthusiast, although I have seen some fine examples on occasions. Like them or like them not, I think that as an exercise it is worthwhile.

There may be a need for some extra emphasis on the top rim of your pot: a thicker coil, a broad band, possibly tooling of some sort. It could be necessary too to break up the monotony of the coils with tool marks or finger marks that follow round certain of the coils.

A group of coiled pots. The coils forming part of the decoration.

A Pot from Coils There is no logical reason why coiled pots should have a circular section, except that the fact of leaving the coils exposed seems to insist that this should be so. However, once you change from coiled pots to pots made with coils – pots where the method of construction is obliterated by smearing the surface both inside and out – you will then feel free to break with almost all convention, free to sculpt the shape as you wish.

It could be that this is the time to sit back with pencil and paper and do a little planning. You should by now begin to know a little of what is and what is not within your capacity. Think back to those early shapes – the little, solid forms we started with. See them now as larger shapes – large pots if you wish – sketch them, modify the form and finish with a full and thoroughly designed drawing. It may not work out that way (they seldom do in my experience), it could even

This pot's coiled method of construction has been smeared over and then developed further.

be a massive failure – a 'back to the drawing board' job – but this does not invalidate the case for doing it.

A very much more robust approach is acceptable when you coil these shapes. You can build with thicker coils and, once the joint is well smeared over, reduce the thickness by pinching the rim to increase the height. Even before you have reached the top, begin to beat it into shape. Support the wall by a hand on the inside. This will enable you to strike more firmly, compacting and strengthening the walls. Having completed the shape according to your own specifications, I think there is every excuse for modification, even reconstruction, if the result does not satisfy. To insist on sticking to the original idea could show a very unadventurous attitude.

A coiled pot developed into a reclining form.

Lugs and Handles Fresh clay can be tooled on to the surface to develop an area, lugs or handles can be fixed as a useful or decorative feature. Handles that are to be used as such are difficult to make and position, but it is possible to modify a coil to give a passable imitation of an expertly pulled job. Do not be restricted by the fact that you originally decided to call what you are making a pot. If necessary cut a few holes in the side and thereby render it useless for holding water and maybe the next one will be ideal for daffodils.

Slabs It often happens that the shapes you so painstakingly coiled into a round form were eventually beaten into a square form. It will then have become obvious to you that there is an alternative method of doing this, namely from slabs. Six slabs of clay joined together at the edges and you have a box. What could be easier? These are ill-informed thoughts. This method is by no means easy, with such inherent difficulties that it has the experienced craftsman struggling at times.

Slab Construction However, it is worth trying slab construction and there are some interesting exercises from which you should learn something. Just as earlier we used the coil for simple models,

so the slab can be used for some basic constructions — the 'Meccano' of pottery in fact.

Roll out a few pieces of clay on cloth and allow them to stiffen. Now cut them into a variety of shapes — rather angular, mechanical pieces. You will need no special plan in mind. Pick up a few pieces and join them neatly together to form a structure. Add a flying buttress, a tower; add pieces that have no special point or meaning, except that you feel they look right. Treat the whole business very lightly if you wish but, if that goes against your nature, then treat it with the utmost seriousness. Structures developed in this way will help the understanding of mass space relationships, and that is what sculpture is all about.

An abstract construction in slab work by a pupil.

The stages in luting a joint in slab construction.

It is not necessary or desirable to follow everything through to the firing stage. Make them and break them, but every now and again put your work to the test by completing the process. You might find that a little copper carbonate scrubbed on to the surface and fired at about 1080°C. will be all the decoration you need. The very permanence of the fired piece will cause you to assess your own standards more critically. It will also invite criticism.

Larger Shapes Once you get on to the making of larger objects one unexpected difficulty will arise from the very speed with which the sections can be prepared. A lump of clay rolled out on cloth to about $\frac{1}{2}$ in. thickness and cut to shape (the whole process will take no more than ten minutes) and you are ready to put them all together. Try, and you will get into all sorts of trouble. The clay *must* be allowed to stiffen appreciably before you are able to handle it sensibly, and yet it must still be sufficiently soft to enable a good joint to be made. Apply a damp sponge along the edges and then press the joint firmly together. Follow this by running a thin coil along the inside corner tooling it in position to form a neat fillet. This process is called 'luting'. The lute is vital to the joint. It must be realised — indeed you will find out soon enough if you are careless — that the strain imposed by uneven shrinkage on these slabs is very considerable and, since the outside of any container will always tend to dry more quickly

than the inside, uneven shrinkage is inevitable. One of the most difficult shapes to make successfully is an open box. Even by taking the greatest care it is still next to impossible to finish with flat and not incurved sides — not to mention open seams.

Teachers be warned: the box is a tempting little exercise, but one fraught with troubles.

You might feel, as I do, that completely flat-sided objects are rather dull. So, before you close the top in, work the shape over with your wooden beater. Soften the corners maybe, dome the sides a little, slope the shoulders and, incidentally, compact the clay. All these things increase the strength factor and also provide interest. Where some degree of accuracy is needed in the final piece it will be necessary to wait until the clay has reached an advanced state of drying and then use a broken hacksaw blade to scrape the surface. The body will lose its soft clay look, but this may not be important.

The Tile For a very long time the tile was the only acceptable method of covering a flat area with a durable and impervious material. Commercial tiles, generally speaking, are dull and cold but this is not true of home-made tiles. In fact, the very reverse applies. Heavy great slabs glued (as if they could ever again rise by themselves) to a plank of plywood, straining on stiletto legs, ready to bore a hole through any carpet. Yet full of interest. The bumpy, impractical surface throws up rippling lights, each tile an allotment of colour and texture, contained by neat black or white paths, keeping them apart yet pulling the whole thing together. I love them — but they are so heavy. The position in this respect has improved of late (and this we will discuss later) but the means and method of production are much the same.

To Make a Tile Make your tiles in any of these three ways:

(1) Roll out a slab of clay, using side battens to set the thickness, and then, once the clay has stiffened, cut round a cardboard template made for the job. With most clays something over $4\frac{3}{8}$ in. square will be necessary to finish at four inches. (Your shrinkage calculations will tell you this more exactly.)
This is a short quick process and you will soon have a set of tiles.

(2) Slower in production, but more accurate, is the tile frame. This can be made out of four battens joined with halving joints to give a flat top and bottom surface. The frame is laid on a piece of cloth and lumps of clay are rammed in to fill the well. A wooden or metal scraper will take off the surplus clay and a drip or two of water will help smooth the finished surface. On drying it will shrink out of the frame.

(3) The third method is to use a manufactured tile-cutter. These work on a similar principle to the ice-cream wafer-maker. You fill up the well with clay and then force the tile up and out by causing the false floor to lift up.

Drying Clay tiles always require careful drying if they are to remain flat. Normally, the thinner the tile the greater the tendency to warp. Good stacking and slow—very slow—drying is the key to success. Build your tiles into a pyramid but with an overlap of no more than a quarter of the length, thereby leaving holes through which the air can contact the clay. But no moving air; no draughts; still, drying air.

I make no mention here of decoration and firing as they are described later. Sufficient to say that, if the first is not too difficult, the firing is always tricky. Use the same stacking method and use the middle of the kiln if possible.

Newclay Tiles The process of tile-making has been made easier by the availability of 'Newclay' — the reinforced clay referred to on page 18. This clay is excellent for tiles, although it is not normally sold as a potters' clay. The reinforcing agent may cause you a little more work in trimming the tiles before firing, and it is important to biscuit fire at a minimum temperature of 1060°C., but with this clay you can achieve a very thin and very flat tile and, if you wish, a very big tile. Most of the special drying precautions are quite unnecessary and for this type of work its handling properties are very good. This particular clay suffers from very small shrinkage and remember that any clay that shrinks a lot will also warp a lot.

Tesserae There is no lower limit to the size of a tile but once you get down to the square half inch the purpose has normally changed and the pieces will most likely be intended for use as tesserae in the making of mosaics. The subject of mosaics

A group of tile-cutters.

Tiles stacked for drying.

can be very grand and very vast, it is also very old. Regretfully, the following passage must confine itself to the making of these little pieces.

Initially one must expect to work with a very limited palette of, perhaps, half a dozen colours. The picture or pattern must be thought of in these terms. By this simplification the quantity of tesserae can be limited to manageable proportions. Even so, the total area to be made is bound to be quite a lot more than the final amount used. More than sufficient is needed to allow a modicum of selection.

Making a Picture Make your sketch in colour and from this estimate the quantity of tesserae required for each colour. Assuming that 100 sq. in. of pale blue are needed, pull off handfuls of clay and roll them out on cloth using a wooden rule on each side as a thickness gauge. One-eighth in. is about the right thickness for tesserae. You will probably need three or four of these slabs. Allow them to go leather-hard and then turn them over to score the backs to the greater part of the depth of the clay. Depending on your nature, you will do this freehand or use a set-square. The size of the pieces is optional—meticulous squares or random shapes. Take some care with the scoring for it will determine how easy it is to break the pieces after firing. If you score the top side the groove will fill with glaze and nothing will be gained.

The adhesion of tiles to a surface presents no problems these days. There are so many proprietary tile adhesives on the market that time would be wasted in describing the process. Buy the adhesive and read the directions, then grout (i.e. fill in the gaps between the tiles) with a plaster-sand-powder colour-P.V.A. mixture.

A slab of clay scored for tesserae.

Plaster Moulds When you introduce plaster of Paris into your pottery you do so at some risk. It is difficult to think of pottery without plaster (the industry would fall apart if supplies dried up) but it does hold some danger for the careless or unknowledgeable. So, before going further, let us try to understand what we are dealing with and how to use it.

Plaster is made from rock gypsum and much of this originally came from the Paris area. Gypsum is a white crystalline rock which the manufacturers reduce to a fine powder. It is then dehydrated by raising its temperature to around 300°C. By returning the moisture we allow the crystals to re-form and lock together, making a solid. This process can be speeded up by using warm water, but the crystals will be smaller and the material relatively weaker.

Mixing To give some idea of the quantity required, 1 pint of mixed plaster will result from $\frac{2}{3}$ pint of water. Break the powder into the bowl by the handful until the peaks reach the surface. Whisk it up and it is ready for use.

Now for the dangers: Number one is the little chips of plaster that can so easily stray into the clay. At some later date, a piece of your ware, fired and glazed, will shed a flake from its side—forced from the body as the plaster that was dehydrated in the kiln grows in size on taking moisture from the air.

The second danger comes from the careless disposal of waste plaster down the sink. If you finish up a mixing session with a U-bend solid with plaster, you will not be the first. *Never pour waste plaster down the sink.* Throw it into a cardboard box and pick it out later when it has set; then get rid of it into the dust bin. If you absolutely must pour it down the sink, then have both taps going flat out to wash every scrap away.

There are two distinct types of moulds: those for press moulding with firm clay and those for casting with slip. Both are described here but it is unlikely that the latter will be of any great concern to you.

Press moulding is a process where the shape is accurately modelled and then covered with plaster. Later the original clay is removed and a succession of reproductions pressed out. This can be fairly simple, as with a dish mould, or very complicated, as with a figurine. Let us talk about the simple one.

A Dish Mould Take a piece of paper the size of this book and draw on it the outline of a dish viewed from above. Keep it simple. Barrel-shaped, pear-shaped, a tear-drop, ovoid — but no incurves to begin with if you can help it. Now imagine your dish inverted on that shape, and model it in clay. Make the flat base about a quarter of the total area. The sides will curve away from the base to the edge. Care and precision is called for. The unnoticed bump will be repeated in every dish that you make.

Surround the shape with a wall standing about 1 in. higher than the dish. Make it from clay, card, roofing felt, or whatever, but do fill in all the little holes with clay, and then be ready with some more for the inevitable emergencies.

Now assess how much plaster you will need to fill up the space, but be prepared to be wildly wrong. Too much and you will just have to throw the rest away, but too little and you will straight away have to mix more. Score the surface of the first lot so that the second can key well to it.

Should you at any time not want plaster to key to a surface, give that surface a wash with liquid clay.

A few hours after the mix you should be able to pick up the mould and carefully remove the clay, but it might be as well to leave it for a couple of days to dry out before you attempt to make your first dish.

Roll out some clay to a thickness of about $\frac{1}{4}$ in. and 1 in. or so greater in area than that of the dish. Pick up the slab and gently ease it into the hollow. Try not to mark the top surface and use a wet thumb rather than a sponge which can badly score the surface. Use a wooden tool to carve away the surplus clay from around the edge.

The clay shape prepared to receive the plaster.

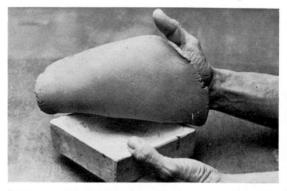

Easing the clay slab into the mould.

The dish shrinking away from the plaster mould.

The dish extracted from the mould.

Methods of decoration will be discussed later, but it can be pointed out here that if slip is to be applied to the surface it should be used at this stage. Pour it in, swill it round, and then pour it out. The water contained in this amount of slip would crack an unsupported dish.

The combined effect of the absorbent plaster and the drying air will eventually cause the clay to shrink away from the mould so that it will soon be strong enough to be tipped out.

There is no obvious alternative to this method of making these dishes. Circular dishes can be thrown on the wheel, but even this can be a lot more difficult than you might imagine.

Sprigging Nothing is ever easy in pottery but the production of these asymetrical dishes can be classed among the more basic tasks. Not so the complicated mould-making required to produce figures of humans and animals. There is, however, an associated exercise that is well worth trying. It is called 'sprigging'.

Although, as a piece of pottery, Wedgwood jasperware leaves me unexcited, it is, nevertheless, a splendid example of the technique to which I refer. Generally on a deep blue unglazed ground, near-opaque white figures, with accompanying flora, surround the ware in Greek regality. Each section is exquisitely modelled by sensitive craftsmen and then welded to precision pottery. Coldly Wedgwood, coldly Greek.

Let us suppose that you have created your pot and wish to decorate it with such applied decoration. A spray, shall we say, of lots of identically-shaped leaves. On the surface of a glazed tile or a piece of glass model just one of the leaves. When it is finished mix up half a cup of plaster and heap it over the shape. There is no need for a retaining wall as the amount of plaster is so small, but take the opportunity to practise modelling the plaster.

Once this is well set, ease it off the tile and pick out the original clay. Clean the mould carefully and let it dry for a day or so. Pull off a pellet of clay and press it into the mould; then scrape off the surplus with a wooden tool. Wait a few moments more and then, with another piece of clay, press it gently against your moulding and

A Wedgwood teapot with a traditional sprigged design.

pull it out. Look at it carefully and you will note that even a finger print has been faithfully recorded. As you make more, rest the leaves on a damp cloth until you have sufficient. You can now apply the whole lot in one session to the surface of your pot. Use a little liquid clay slip as an adhesive.

Casting Using liquid clay in a plaster mould to cast shapes is to my mind an unsatisfactory method for the studio potter. At an industrial level it is a highly specialised technique used to produce millions of cheap cups. Recognise such a casting by noting that the inside shape follows the outer. Where the foot of a cup shows no comparable depression on the inside then some other method was used. This would be the product of the 'jigger' and 'jolly'. Lovely names these, used to describe a mechanical method of producing circular shapes, where a lump of clay is dropped into a spinning mould and, under the pressure of a metal former, pressed against the sides to take up the shape of the mould. The clay dries a little and is then picked out to be put on a moving belt where on its travels it meets a handle. The two are wedded with a dab of slip, and pass on their way together.

But to return to the casting. The mould is made by covering the clay pattern with plaster to a thickness of about 2 in. This extra thickness is needed to take up a great deal of water out of the slip. Once the mould is set and dry and the original clay removed, slip of a thick consistency is poured in, topped up when necessary, and then, after about ten minutes, poured out again. A residue of firm clay will cling to the plaster walls and, once this has dried, come away as an exact reproduction of the original, except that it will be some 10% smaller. If this does not sound much then you may be surprised. You will find that you need to take this shrinkage into account where size is important. A small coffee cup reduced by 10% would double as an egg cup.

So much for casting. If the description is inadequate it is partly unavoidable and partly deliberate. I feel that casting should make up no great part of the beginner's troubles.

Throwing Because the reader will expect a section on throwing it is mentioned here. Most other books on the craft of pottery do include such a section and the notes are usually supported with copious action shots. However, this has always seemed to me to be like learning to ride a bike by pictures. Throwing can only be learnt by

doing it, and then only under instruction.

Perhaps learning to ride a bike is a poor analogy. The art of the thrower is a skill that is acquired over years, not minutes. It can be defined as the technique whereby a mass of clay is spun on a turntable and formed into a round and hollow shape in the hands. The skill is ages old and is still considered by some to be the essence of the potter's craft. If this overrates it, it is nevertheless a highly satisfying process and one that allows the performer readily to demonstrate the depth of his understanding for the material he uses.

But there is more to clay work than this. Many competent potters never, indeed cannot, throw pots, but if you want some guidance on throwing most of the books on pottery listed on page 245 will help you.

The ball of clay placed on the wheel.

'Centring' the clay. Note the position of the hands.

Hollowing out the mass.

Drawing up the pot.

Forming the rim.

Throwing the shape.

Cutting away the surplus clay.

Picking off the pot.

Decoration It has been difficult but necessary as we went along to refrain from comment on the decorative aspects associated with the various production methods. Not to have done so would have involved too much repetition. I will now attempt to describe all the normal methods of decoration, making reference to each one's suitability to a particular process.

Two methods which require nothing extra in the way of materials are incised and applied decoration, i.e. cutting back and building up. Texturing, of course, can be something of each of these.

Incised Decoration Incised work can be delicate — as in the case of the small depressions along the rim of a dish which are later filled with glaze, finally showing as dimples — to massive holes cut

through the side of a pot, or both sides to give an added eclipse effect as you pass by. Texturing can be achieved in various ways, for instance by superficial scratching from the coarse teeth of a hacksaw blade, or deep depressions hacked or beaten into the firm clay surface.

Applied Decoration The reverse of this is the delicate or heavy application of quantities of clay to the surface. More care is called for here as you will probably be adding soft clay to firm. The stress resulting from the shrinkage differential can be sufficient to lift the outer layer from the surface. Roughen the surface of the firmer clay to permit a good key; any slip or water used to assist adhesion should be applied to this roughened surface and then left for a short time to allow it to soak in a little. Clays vary so much in their rates of shrinkage that one cannot be dogmatic as to what is and what is not possible. You will learn from experience. This much is certain; it is unwise to join two different types of clay together, and it is difficult to persuade large masses of the same clay to adhere to a surface.

Colour Any addition of colour to your ware will involve the use of metal oxides. These are, I believe, the only form of pigment that will withstand the heat of the kiln. Almost all clay has in it at least a trace of iron oxide which causes the original white to fire cream or, as the percentage of iron increases, turn an increasingly deeper shade of red-brown. Iron, and many other metals, can be purchased in their oxide form, and as such can be painted directly on to the surface of the clay. To the beginner this form of colour is confusing because the final result bears so little relationship to the original powder, and the fact that the final colour varies with the firing temperature and the atmosphere prevailing in the kiln. A solution to this problem is offered by the industry who supply very predictable prepared colours called 'underglaze colours' for use on the clay. Other colours, called 'on-glaze', are for use on the raw glaze. These do provide an answer but one that I, for one, do not suggest as a good one, although such things are largely a matter of personal taste. If you want a palette of true-to-shade, obvious, rather flat but very stable colours, then these are for you. If, on the other hand, the element of chance sounds more interesting, then take to the oxides — where copper oxide, for instance, starts as a black powder, yet turns green in a glaze; but when applied too lightly might disappear altogether; or when applied too heavily forms a black metallic skin over the surface. I am sure you will be right.

Here is a list of the more common oxides and the colours (under what might be called normal conditions) you might expect from them:

Iron oxide: yellows, browns and near blacks.
Copper oxide: pale green, dark green and metallic black.
Cobalt oxide: blue.
Manganese oxide: browns.
Chrome oxide: green.
Antimoniate of lead: yellows.

You will notice that no reds are included. At this level reds are virtually non-existent. The oxides will give varying colours depending on many factors.

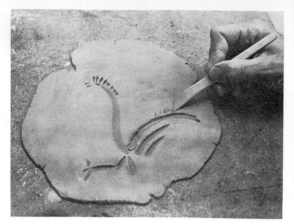
Practising an incised motif.

A thin white glaze over copper oxide was used on this coffee pot and mug.

Copper, under very special conditions, will in fact provide red — the Chinese 'sang de bœuf' — but this is not for you, nor for me either I am afraid. I have never succeeded in achieving it.

The under-glaze and on-glaze colours are purchased from a long list of exotic titles. They too have a metal base but are often the result of very sophisticated processes including firing, sintering and then grinding. All very clever and fairly expensive, but not used too much by the studio potter.

Applying the Colour Colour can be applied to the surface by any method you feel suitable. A potter brought up in the Leach tradition will tend to reach for his Chinese brush and with it demonstrate great dexterity and feeling for the value of the brush stroke. And what a joy to behold the results can be.

However, we know better than to restrain ourselves to any one method of application. When you have made up some colour into a paste, use a sponge to stipple it on to the surface. Now over-paint that with a more fluid colour using an inch-wide brush. Finally, texture the colour by scratching through the surface with a piece of stick.

Practising brush strokes.

A teapot by David Leach. Oxides were brushed on to the raw clay pot to produce the design.

Wax Resist Melt a little candle wax in a dish, add some oxide and, while it is still runny, brush a few well-chosen strokes on to the clay surface. (Try this in the hollow of a dish.) Now brush over this with a watery wash of another oxide. The wax will resist the water, although a little may rest as globules on the top, and the colours will be separate from each other.

Slip These same oxides (but *not* under-glaze colours) may be added to liquid clay to provide coloured slips. As mentioned earlier, slip can be poured over a surface completely covering it, or confined to a limited area of colour. A full round form can be dipped just a little on one side which will result in a coloured panel suitable for other decorative treatments such as *Sgraffito*. This is a process of scratching through the slip to expose the clay body underneath. Do it when the slip is still wet and a soft fluid line will result. If the slip is dry the line will be hard and sharp. Dust a little powdered oxide on to the wet slip, and brush it across the surface with bold sweeping strokes.

A very traditional form of decoration is the trailing of one liquid colour over another. A rubber bulb full of slip is used; the slip being allowed to flow out as lines or blobs. If you make a mess you shake

Pot showing where the waxed areas have resisted the glaze.

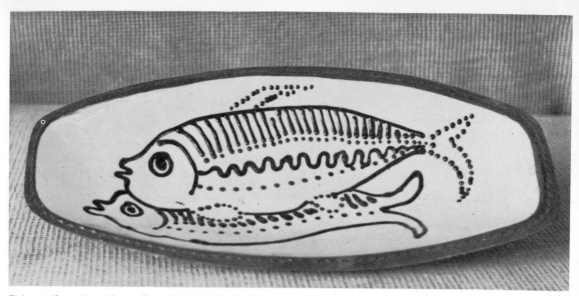

Fish motif produced by trailing slip over the surface of the dish.

the object a little and the liquids will run together to produce what is called *'marbling'*. With some control of this instrument you can draw pictures. A past master in this art was Thomas Toft (mid 17th cent.) and you could do worse than contemplate one of his dishes.

To prepare slip clay is reduced to a liquid by the addition of more water. It is necessary to pass the liquid through a sieve to get rid of the lumps, and the consistency should be that of cream. Oxides can be added in something like the proportions given below, after which it should be sieved again. Both white and red clay are necessary.

White: white clay.
Green: white clay plus 5% chrome oxide.
Blue: white clay plus 1% cobalt oxide.
Brown: red clay.
Black: red clay, 4% manganese oxide, 1% cobalt oxide.
Yellow is best obtained by the addition of a yellow 'body stain'.

Glazing Glaze is glass. When you glaze a pot you put a layer of glass over the surface usually with the object of sealing off the pores. The cup that you drink from is coated with glass, sometimes clear like window glass, but it may be opaque.

In effect it is applied as a powder, white like snow, and, like snow, it can be melted by the application of heat. And when the heat is withdrawn it freezes again into ice-like glass.

You could, if you so wished, demonstrate this point by crushing a piece of window glass in a mortar, mixing it in water and then dipping a pot into it. You would fire this at around 1000°C. — it is bound to be hit and miss if you don't know what type of glass it is — and you should get a glazed pot. Obviously, this is a clumsy and unsatisfactory way of doing things for, among other things, we need a glaze to suit our special requirements.

A Recipe Glass is a fusion of silica, but silica has an extremely high melting point at 2000°C. — higher than the clay in fact. Added fluxes lower the melting point. The higher the proportion of flux the lower the melting point. Such fluxes are lead oxide, lime of some sort, potash in the form of feldspar, borax, and many others.

Glazes are made up from recipes on this basis. You can make them up yourself. Here is a recipe for a clear glaze that will melt at around 1060°C. You will note that it has a lead content *which makes it unsuitable for use in schools*. The quantities are percentages by dry weight.

The Recipe.

Flint (silica)	18%
Lead Carbonate	42%
Whiting (lime)	5%
Feldspar (potash)	29%
China Clay	6%

Ready Made Glazes You can also buy glazes ready-made. Ready-made glazes never use raw lead oxide and for this reason, as well as that of early simplicity, I suggest that you opt for one of these.

The Catalogue A pottery catalogue can prove to be a very confusing document. Many different types of everything are offered but be cautious.

When in doubt about which glaze, write to the company from which you bought your clay and explain to them your requirements, e.g., 'An opaque white matt glaze for use on their "X" clay, and firing at about 1080°C.' They will answer by offering you a choice of two or three. If you don't know the difference, take the cheapest.

Adapting a Glaze Let us suppose that you have ordered 28 lb. of a clear glaze which has cost you about £2 plus carriage. This can be divided into four lots, each of 7 lb. with which you can experiment.

The first 7 lb. will be mixed with water to the consistency of thin cream, run through a 60-mesh sieve, and then be ready as your clear glaze.

The second 7 lb. can be made into an opaque white glaze by the addition of a glaze opacifier — between 5 to 10% usually. Tin oxide is the best of these for bringing out the colour of your oxide painting but also the most expensive. There are others, such as zircon, at more reasonable prices. The difference will be in the quality of the white — like soap powders

The third and fourth lots can be coloured, opaque or clear, whichever you wish. 6% of manganese oxide will give you a deep brown; 1% of copper oxide will give a hard green; add 1% of iron oxide to it and the green will be softened. A quarter of 1% of cobalt oxide gives a blue, and so on. After some initial experiment settle on a few basics and then try to improve on your handling and methods

of application rather than switching from one colour to another.

Application Glaze is normally applied to the biscuit-fired ware. The method will depend to some extent on the area to be covered. For the inside of a pot, pour it in, swill it around, and pour it out again. For the outside, you can dip a pot, but it is usually better to pour the glaze over it from a jug with one steady continuous action. Glaze can be sprayed on but this is not a method to be recommended except for small items. Brush it on if you like; sponge it on; put it on and rub it all off again, yet leaving small traces in the open surface sufficient to indicate its presence, to fill the pores and get rid of the dryness.

Broken Glass As an interesting experiment with future implications, make a tile with a number of depressions in the surface. Fill some of these with a different glaze, a mixture of glazes, glazes with added oxides, and so on, and in other depressions place pieces of broken coloured glass. Fire it and see the effect. The implications are for you to decide, but it might be a good idea to make notes for later reference.

Glazing, as with every other part of the pottery process, must be thought of as a part of the whole. It will take time, but start early in trying to think in terms of the finished piece even before you have started making it. A pot or model that is made for glazing should be different in many ways from one that is to remain unglazed. The very clay that you use will have a tremendous influence on the type of work that is possible. You are entitled, indeed expected, to change your mind as you go along, but that is different from just muddling through.

The Kiln There can be little alternative for the beginner to the small electric kiln. It is possible (and the occasional book will suggest that it is the correct approach) to start with your own home-made kiln in the back garden. It is possible, but the results will have little to do with the type of pottery described here. Fascinating as this primitive approach may be, it would be misleading to suggest that it is easy to follow or even much cheaper. It could well be the reverse.

You can get an oil-fired or gas-fired kiln, but here again the difficulties are very much greater than with electricity.

A kiln partly packed for glaze firing.

Earthenware pot and mugs.

The Electric Kiln An electric kiln is really just a well-insulated electric oven. The wire of its elements is thicker to withstand the higher temperatures and, of course, the walls are thicker (about 6 in.). The element is made up from a series of double springs that rest in fireclay racks. The ends pass through the back wall of the kiln to join up one with the other. Usually these connections group the elements into two banks.

When the kiln is switched to low heat both the elements are linked (in series) to give a quarter heat. When the kiln is switched to medium heat only one bank runs (but at full power) the other bank being cut off. When the dial is switched to 'high' both banks run at full power. The walls of the kiln are made from a light insulating firebrick held tightly together by a metal frame.

The beginner should look for a kiln new or second-hand with a firing chamber of 1 cub. ft., or thereabouts, using a current of 15 amp. or 3 kW. at 240 V. This will permit the kiln to be worked off the home mains supply. One or two shelves will be needed with a few fireclay supports to hold them up. The possession of a pyrometer from which you can read the temperature is a nice luxury but, if not, you will have to use temperature cones that can be seen to collapse at the specified temperature viewed through the hole in the kiln door. All these items can be seen in the catalogues.

Firing By raising the temperature of clay to something above red-heat it is changed into pottery. The process is irrevocable. Clay can be turned into brick but not brick into clay. Any heat

Stoneware bowl and pots.

over 600 °C. will alter the chemical composition of the clay. One of the effects of this temperature is that more water vapour is driven off. This is just one of the facts that must be taken into account when a kiln full of pottery is fired.

Normally, the top temperature with which you will be concerned is something over 1000 °C. Indeed, I have a fairly specific temperature in mind when writing this. All these notes apply to the making of earthenware at about 1060 °C. There are lower temperature earthenwares, and there are higher temperature stonewares, that you could make, but with these there may be greater problems, so we start with something easier.

Moisture and Shrinkage The two crucial considerations to be taken into account in the firing of earthenware are: firstly, that moisture, for obvious reasons, is driven off at 100°C. and more still at around 600°C., and, secondly, the fact of shrinkage. By going through a firing cycle we can see how these points are taken into account.

Before placing any work into the kiln it must be as dry as anything can be that is left out in the air. Any damage that occurs in the nature of a blow-out will almost certainly be due to dampness. Very seldom will it be due to air in the clay. Drying out will exercise your patience but any attempt to rush it will increase the chances of failure.

Biscuit Firing The first 100° then must be taken slowly to allow the remaining moisture to get out. In terms of an electric kiln this means 'low' with the door open a few inches. Close it after a couple of hours and in a further hour switch to 'medium'. This setting should increase the temperature up to 700°/800° in about six hours—just red-hot.

Towards the end of that period the chemically combined water will have gone. Now proceed on 'full' to the temperature that you require. This may take only an hour or so but, having reached the temperature, try to hold it there for at least half an hour. This is necessary because small kilns are notoriously bad for producing big temperature differences throughout the chamber. An extra half hour 'soak' will help the temperature to even out. One has to realise that a large pot in a small kiln could have as much as 100° difference from top to bottom and at these temperatures, when one is getting close to the vitrification point of the clay, some shrinkage will be taking place and unless it is even cracking will result.

This whole process will have taken about twelve hours and the kiln will require another twenty-four hours to cool down again. Rush the cooling and you may be in trouble.

Once the contents of the kiln have been removed, it is good policy to get on with the glazing as soon as possible afterwards. Frequent handling and a layer of dust hinder the adhesion of glaze.

Glaze Firing When the glazed pot is returned to the kiln a great deal more care will be required with its placing. Little pointed stilts are available on which the pot may be stood. Alternatively, wipe the powdered glaze from the bottom of the pot, or it will weld itself to the shelf. Glazed pieces must not touch one another for the same reason.

Start the firing slowly, to dissipate the accumulated moisture, but between 200°C. and 800°C. the increase can be much more rapid. The glaze will begin to melt now. The powder will solidify, and then eventually liquify like treacle, but not always without some convulsions. Many things happen within the glaze and it is not uncommon to see bubbles form. Allowed to soak for a while it will usually settle down again. Soaking is as important for glaze as it is for biscuit. Without it you may hear that all-too-familiar 'ping' of the 'crazing' glaze as you take the now cool pots from the kiln.

The foregoing section is intended as an introduction to pottery. In a subject so vast and complex that even the production of an apparently simple tile at factory level can involve the attentions of numerous chemists and technicians, it is obviously quite impossible to do more than just mention those matters calculated to give the reader a fair picture of the interests and problems involved.

Like all art forms pottery can be studied at any level, but it is true to say that one cannot get very deeply involved without a certain amount of technique and technical knowledge edging its way in.

Foil   Leon Metcalfe

'Foil' is a vague term, but for this work the limit is usually set at a thickness of metal which can be cut with scissors and manipulated by hand. This ranges from sweet-wrapping foils to 26 gauge sheet metal, the whole range being readily available from a variety of sources.

Materials Hardware shops and ironmongers usually stock rolls of lightweight kitchen foil and also aluminium sheeting. Art suppliers often stock Neofol, a medium-weight sheet foil, in gold and silver. Other useful materials are milk bottle tops, pie trays, sweet wrappings, and even empty tins, which can be cut down the seam and flattened into sheets for heavier work.

Tools For working on this range of foil only very limited tools are required, and these basically consist of scissors, a ball-point pen, pencil, enamel paints and a strong adhesive such as Evo-Stik.

Method Generally the work need not be confined to one gauge of foil; with a little thought it will be found that finished objects can often be enhanced by adding decoration and detail with foil of a different weight from the main structure. The aim, when using a material such as foil, is to take advantage of its ability to pick up and reflect light and, therefore, painting on completed objects should be kept to a minimum. For colour, and also image variations, rely on the reflective nature of the foil from its many facets produced by bends, curves and angles.

Perhaps the simplest work to attempt with light-weight kitchen foil is the production of figurines; no tools are required — all the modelling and manipulating can be done with the hands. A good preparation for this work is a 'play period' — a square or rectangle of the material being torn and crumpled to produce small animated figurines. In this way much valuable information is gained about the nature and limitations of working in foil. With care and thought it will be realised that a reproduction of almost any object, creature or being can be produced in this simple way, and that the finished models are quite permanent and sturdy.

Medium-weight sheets of Neofol can be 'tooled' by using a ball-point pen. First trim the sheet to the shape and size required and sketch in the main outline of the design to be tooled; a soft pencil is useful for this. When the tooling actually begins, keep an even pressure with a wad of newspaper under the foil and remember that the work is being done in reverse, the embossed lines being produced on the opposite side of the sheet. Rubbings may be taken from either side of the completed tooled design (see Brass Rubbing, page 121).

A rubbing technique can be used with kitchen foil. Lay a sheet over a church brass (first seeking the Vicar's permission!) and smooth over the foil with a soft duster. Work carefully and with an even pressure to avoid tearing. An impression of the brass form will appear on the foil, and this can later be accentuated, either by following the lines with a dry ball-point pen or by using a coloured felt-tip pen. With the rubbing completed the figure can be cut out, using scissors or a craft knife, and mounted on to a paper- or material-covered board ready for hanging. Rubbings need not be confined to church brasses and provide scope for experiment.

Any type of foil which is rigid enough to hold a form is suitable for moulding, cutting and decorating in the shape of masks or three-dimensional creatures, both real and imaginary. These can be left free-standing or used to decorate walls. Mobiles (see also page 154) can be made from

Brass rubbing using foil.

various types of foil, and the range of weights available enables the mobiles to be carefully and accurately balanced. Similar suspended work can take a more abstract form by basing the design on parts of circles or cones, or even multiples and combinations of geometric solids.

These are but some of the ways in which foil can be used creatively. You may now like to try some experiments of your own.

Glass   Peter Tysoe

Glass is a hard, non-crystalline substance which is created by fusing silica sand with solvents or fluxes. There are different types of glass depending on whether lead, soda ash, lime or boric acid are used with the sand to produce the 'metal' (glass material). Each of these will produce a material with varying characteristics. Oxides of cobalt, copper, gold, iron or selenium, etc. are used for colouring glass, which usually has a decolorising chemical added. In the molten state it can be blown, rolled, pressed, threaded and twisted. Glass making is first thought to have started at least 4,000 years ago — probably by the accidental fusing of sand and minerals on to ceramics by Egyptian or Mesopotamian potters. Its use was developed to make beads and then it was formed (precisely how is not at present known) around a core of clay or sand to make jars or other vessels. When the glass had hardened, the core was removed. Blown glass was not fully developed until the Roman era, when it spread with the trade routes throughout North Africa and into Europe. Following the decay of the Roman Empire, Venice developed as an important centre after 1200 A.D. and the eventual spread of Italian craftsmen into other countries led to a revival and the further development of glass making as far away as Britain. The full story is an interesting one and will be found in some of the books listed in the bibliography.

Types of Glass

Blown Glassware is the traditional method of making glassware by taking a hollow iron tube four or five feet long, dipping it into the molten glass and gathering a blob of glass on the end, which can then be blown and formed into a free shape, or into a mould. This will give a repeat run. Since 1962 there has been a revitalisation, started in America, in the exploitation of new, free forms in blown glass by artists/craftsmen working in the

medium. In the commercial field hand blowing has had a revival with the setting up of firms like Caithness, Dartington and King's Lynn (now Wedgwood). Automatic blowing is used for large-scale production of bottles, etc. by large companies.

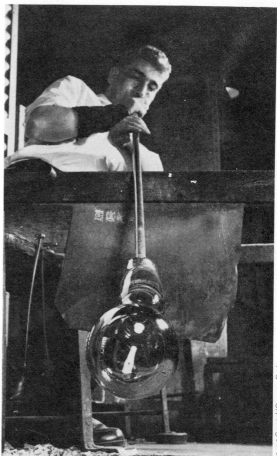

Blowing glass.

Stuart Crystal/George Perks

Pressed Glass is made by pressing a molten lump of glass into a mould. A slab of molten glass can have simple shapes pressed into it to form decorative slabs. The production of glass bricks, ashtrays, etc. is carried out on a large scale using automatic presses.

Flat Glass is now mainly mass-produced by drawing out and rolling a continuous ribbon of glass from large tank furnaces. Sheet and 'figured' (decorated) glasses are made in this way. Plate glass is polished to achieve the flat surface and there is the new invention of 'float glass' by Pilkington Brothers where a continuous sheet is drawn over a bath of molten tin. Some flat glasses are obtainable in grey and bronze tints and in colour.

Antique Glass is the hand-made sheet glass made by hand blowing a large cylinder and cutting it lengthways to allow it to fall flat into a sheet. It is irregular in pattern and thickness and can be very beautiful. Its main use has been in the making of stained glass windows and it is obtainable in clear coloured tints and in rich colours. A colour may also be 'flashed' on to the surface by dipping the glass blob on the end of the blowing tool into a glass of a different colour. When blown the surface has this colour as a thin surface layer.

Slab Glasses are cast in a mould and are approx. 1 in. in thickness, 12 in. long by 8 in. wide. They are also available in white and coloured tints and full colour.

Cutting Glass

Flat and slab glasses are cut by drawing a diamond or a wheel glass cutter across the flatter of the two faces with a firm stroke, where the break is wanted. Flat glass is tapped firmly under the cut line with the 'heel' of the cutter, as the glass is held in the left hand. The waste piece will either break off as the tapping follows under the score line, or it can be broken off with a firm breaking motion with the two hands, which hold the glass at its edge on either side of the line. A straight cut may be broken by pressing on the edge of the bench. Deep curves can be 'nipped' out with glazier's pliers. Edges can be scraped against another glass to remove sharpness.

Slabs are also scored with the wheel cutter and are usually divided by striking downwards over a sharp steel edge, well secured and pointing upward. The slab should be held firmly with one hand on each side of the cut line. They may also be chipped away or cut with a tungsten-edged hammer.

Decorative Treatments

Engraving Diamond point is executed by hand using either a small diamond set in a holder or a pencil-like tungsten carbide-tipped steel tool. The surface is scratched in dot or short delicate lines which appear light against the darker background of the untouched glass.

David Peace

Coat of arms by David Peace engraved *in situ* by a rotary carborundum tool in a hand-chuck. Details are added with a dental drill or, as in the picture, a diamond point. Manchester University of Science and Technology.

Wheel Engraving is carried out using a series of copper or stone wheels mounted on steel spindles in a lathe. The glass has to be moved to bring it into contact with the wheel. Designs can be engraved in low or high relief. John Hutton, who produced the engraved panels for the Great West Screen of Coventry Cathedral, has developed his own method of using grinding wheels, driven by a flexible drive shaft on an electric motor. Using this method he can work freely over fixed glass panels.

John Hutton using a carborundum wheel to engrave a glass panel.

Etching Glass is attacked by hydrofluoric acid, which can be used to achieve an etched design if a 'resist' wax or varnish is painted all over the surfaces to be immersed in the tank of acid. The design is cut through the protective surface to allow the acid to eat into the required glass areas. Various depths can be obtained and both a 'clear' and a 'white' etch are possible.

Sandblasting is a process where unprotected areas of a glass are exposed in a special cabin where an abrasive powder is blown at it under pressure from a compressor. Various depths are obtainable by covering previous areas which have been blasted. Subsequent exposure of remaining exposed areas will result in their being deeper. Glass can be lightly 'peppered' or deeply engraved using this method.

Enamelling Colours are available from ceramic manufacturers which will fire at a variety of temperatures on various types of glass. These can be hand painted or screen printed on to the surface and fused in a furnace. Transfers holding enamel pigment can be made or bought ready for applying and firing on to glass.

Stained Glass The traditional use of leaded coloured glass in windows is known as 'stained glass'. This developed and came to full flower in the Middle Ages in Northern Europe, an excellent example being the windows of Chartres Cathedral. Since the rather dead work of the Victorian era, stained glass has been revitalised by work done by individual artists/craftsmen and by centres like the Stained Glass Department of the Royal College of Art. Fine examples of contemporary work are to be seen at Coventry and in other, smaller, modern churches. This term should be applied to leaded antique glasses, usually with designs painted on with an iron oxide mixture, which fires on to the surface of the glass, giving a brown/black colour. Stippled and scratched, as well as brush painted, lined effects, are obtained with this pigment. Silver stain can also be fired on to give pale yellow or deep orange colour. 'Flashed' antique glasses can be etched to give light patterns against colour. After firing, the separate pieces are fixed together with leads, ready for framing into window or screen panels. Designs are drawn up into full size 'cartoons', over which the glasses are placed, during drawing and cutting to shape.

Glass Appliqué This technique is carried out by bonding glasses — mostly antique coloured glasses — to a base panel of clear plate glass. The adhesive most generally used is an epoxy, which has good bonding properties if both surfaces are absolutely clean and free from grease. Any number of variations can be achieved using the adhesives now available. Intermediate spaces left between the cut pieces of coloured glass can be filled with a dark colour to give added definition, if needed. Coloured glass decorations can also be sandwiched between two layers of plate glass in order to give complete protection. Both polyester and epoxy resin can be used on their own, without filler, to bond coloured glasses into panels which are completely clear or translucent.

Coloured Glass, extending from the stained glass technique, developed the use of 1 in. thick slabs, made first in France and now also in England, cut to shape and set into concrete panels for walling features, etc. A further development of this has been to use the new plastic resins, e.g. polyester, epoxy, which have been developed since the war, to produce thinner, lighter panels than can generally be obtained with concrete by mixing them with sand or other filler powder, which, like concrete, is poured around the glass pieces placed in a casting frame. Many recent churches, cathedrals and secular buildings have work of this type built into them, giving structural character as illuminated wallings rather than being windows in glass.

Glass Constructions

Use of the new resin-based adhesives and resins has been exploited by some contemporary sculptors and craftsmen to carry out exciting work in two and three dimensions by bonding glasses both to themselves and to other materials like metal. This, together with the additional fixings available using mechanical methods, allows for the development of complex three-dimensional forms. In architectural work this new-found freedom has resulted in a complete breakaway from the idea of 'stained glass' as such and this term should not be used to describe glass-construction sculpture or coloured glass panels.

Detail of an architectural panel by the author, in 1 in. thick, slab glass set in clear resin with aluminium tubes.

Regeneration Church Missionary Society Chapel. This window by Keith New, combines two contrasting techniques, leaded glass and glass mosaic, juxtaposed in clearly defined areas. This forms the main image which is sandwiched between plate glass on the inside and figured glass on the outside. This doubling up of layers achieves a density of colour plus great brilliance.

These materials have the great advantage for the craftsman and teacher that they are what are termed 'cold cast' materials and any heat that may be required for helping resins to set can be provided by electric radiant or fan heaters. Expensive kilns or furnaces are not required. The main cost will be found in the glass and resins themselves, together with the materials needed to make wooden formers (tray-like frames) to hold the glasses whilst the resin is poured around or over them. Sheet polythene or cellophane make good releasing agents in order to stop the panel from sticking to the former. Both antique and slab glasses can be used, with any other type that is wanted. Fibre glass mat can be used to give additional strength to panels which can be made of practically any thickness and metal strengthening bars can be incorporated into the laminates as part of the design.

Fused Glass

In their molten state glasses can be fused together. There are difficulties, however, when glasses of varying compositions are fused as their rate of contraction/expansion may vary and thus lead to cracking. When glasses of the same type have various oxides added as colouring there is also the same problem, but the Whitefriars Glass Company, after some years of experiment, is producing very interesting contemporary panels in coloured fused glass.

An interesting technique using fused silica sand and quartz is being carried out by the Thermal Syndicate Co., in Northumberland. Being the pure silica, absolutely clear quartz-like decorative panels are produced in furnaces working with temperatures up to 2,000 degrees centigrade. Opaque coloured work is also made from silica sand with oxide added. This material is thermally stable, i.e. it can be heated and cooled at will without danger of cracking. This is, technically, a very sophisticated technique requiring an elaborate technology to handle the high temperatures.

A pottery kiln can be a useful base for experiments in fusing plate glasses, etc. to make small constructions and panels. (Reading should be done on annealing before undertaking this work.)

Fused silica/quartz panel made in collaboration with Thermal Syndicate Co., Wallsend

Conclusion

Unfortunately, it is not possible in a limited space to deal in detail with the great variety of techniques mentioned above. Further reading is essential to cover full technical details (see Bibliography), but it is possible to start working in glass, with simple equipment and materials, in the school and smaller workshop.

Leather

Dorothy Wright

Many beautiful and useful things may be made of leather, and the better the leather the better the work. Nevertheless, good work may be done with inexpensive leather provided it is suitable in type and weight. Accuracy in measurement and good finish are essential and both old and young will find satisfaction in learning the skills which come with a little practice.

There are four ways to join leather: stitching, sticking, thonging and riveting. The first two are most used today. Handstitching well done is a decoration as well as part of the construction and, until the invention of the sewing-machine, all leather was sewn by hand by the methods the craftworker now uses.

Types of Leather for Craft Use

Hides from cattle are treated by the tanner in many different ways for making luggage, harness and car upholstery among other things. Skins are very large but it is possible to buy *Kip Sides* which are smaller and suitable for heavier articles. *Natural Hide* and *Calf* are used for embossing or tooling, staining and polishing, Skins run at 20–30 sq. ft. but may be bought in smaller sections.

Morocco is goatskin. The hard-grain type skins come in lovely colours in area between $3\frac{1}{2}$ and 12 sq. ft. Every sort of small article may be made from this firm fine-grained leather. There are two weights, wallet and bag weight. The soft-grain type is used for bookbinding (see Bookbinding section page 114).

Sheepskin is cheaper than morocco. In tanning the surface is often embossed in imitation of the grain or surface of another leather. *Roan, Basil* and *Persian* are all sheepskins. Natural sheep is sold in some craft shops. It is cheaper than hide and can be tooled lightly.

Pigskin is a fine leather for the more advanced worker. Weight, i.e. thickness, varies and the buyer should state his purpose. Skins are about 15 sq. ft. and come in golden and tan colours with a distinctive marking of small holes, varying in pattern. (A pig-grained sheep will have an even pattern.)

Suéde is not a separate leather but the velvety surface given to sheep or goat. It is used mostly for clothing or for bag-linings.

Skiver is very thin leather from a skin split horizontally. It is used for stuck linings or with a firm backing. All sorts of fancy surfaces are put on it, but it has no tensile strength and without reinforcement will tear like paper.

Watersnakes are long narrow skins in jewel colours. They are paper-thin but quite strong and with reinforcement many things may be made from them.

Off-Cuts Mixed pieces are sometimes sold by the pound. Very careful selection is needed because the heavy coarse-grained pieces and scraps of furniture hide are virtually useless. One should go to a good supplier for these.

Care of Leather Skins and pieces must be kept flat or rolled, *never folded*. It is almost impossible to get creases out of grained leather. The wrapping paper should be fastened with Sellotape or soft tape, *never string or elastic bands*.

Essential Tools

For cutting-out: (a) Knives, one for cutting, one for paring
(b) Oilstone
(c) Stropping board or razor strop

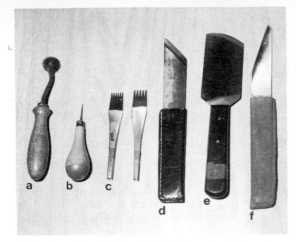

a) Spacing wheel; b) Awl; c) Hand-made stitch markers
d) English paring knife; e) French paring knife; f) Cutting
knife.

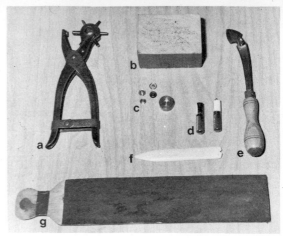

a) Circular punch; b) End-grain softwood block; c) Four
parts of press fastener; d) Tool to set press fastener;
e) Screw creaser; f) Bone folder; g) Stropping board.

	(d) Metal square
	(e) Metal ruler
For stitching:	(f) Stitch markers or pricking irons, preferably hand-made. 10 to 1 in. and 8 to 1 in.
or	(g) Stitch-spacing wheel
	(h) Awl, diamond-shaped point
	(i) Wooden mallet
	(j) Harness needles Nos. 5 and 6. (These have no points.)
	(k) Linen or button threads
	(l) Beeswax
	(m) A block of end-grain wood
	(n) Improvised clamp
Finishing:	(o) Concentrated leather stains
	(p) Creaser
	(q) Methylated spirit or gas burner
	(r) Press stud tool
General:	(s) Bone folder
	(t) 6-hole plier punch
	(u) Iron hammer (household)

The experienced worker may add other tools to his kit. In a class most tools can be used jointly. Knife, ruler, awl, and if possible stitch marker, should be personal tools. A satisfactory knife with blades that can be used for cutting and paring is the Stanley Slimknife 5900. Blade 5901 is suitable for paring but the knife is not strong enough for heavy class use.

The stropping board for heavier knives, should be made at home, emery cloth being supplied by a good ironmonger. Emery powder for the leather back may be difficult to find but Okey's Knife Polish is sometimes found among household relics. Nothing is more essential to the craft than sharp knives and they will need constant attention.

The old saddler used a wooden clamp, now unobtainable, so that both hands were free for sewing; but an improvised one of two pieces of hardboard about 12 in. by 5 in. with two spring clothes pegs will hold small articles when sewing. Larger things may be held between the knees or on the table.

Fittings Various fittings may be bought and need only simple tools and the knife, hammer and 6-hole punch to put on:

Press fasteners
Eyelets
Heavy Zip fasteners (dress ones will not do)
Rivets
Buckles
Purse fasteners
Button moulds

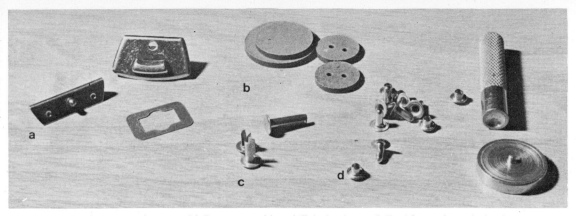

a) Three parts of a purse fastener; b) Button moulds; c) Tubular rivets; d) Tool for setting tubular rivets.

Bag-making needs domes, rings and turnlocks which may be found at special suppliers.

Adhesives The leather worker should approach the many new adhesives with caution. Those he will use constantly are:

Rubber solutions such as Flameless or Stycco, which are spirit solutions, or Bateman's or Copydex, the latex type. These are flexible and should be applied lightly to both surfaces and allowed to become tacky before joining.

Paste, the cold water type is applied with a brush in turned-over-edge work, also in reinforcing with card.

Glue, animal and fish glues are used for rigid parts. The new epoxy resin glues such as Evo-stick Resin W are useful because they are cleaner and easier to store than Seccotine or Croid. UHU is satisfactory for small things.

Reinforcements and Padding Some small leather goods are reinforced with strawboard and flexible white card bought from a stationer. Thin foam-rubber and domette make useful padding between leather and lining or reinforcement and give a rich look and feel. Thin leathers such as fancy or ecrasé skivers may be backed with Vilene (the non-woven interfacing used by dress-makers) to strengthen them. Rubberised linen is sold by the yard for belt and bag-making and is ironed on.

Types of Leatherwork for the Craftworker
In the past amateur leatherwork meant punching and thonging. It is little done now in this country though in Germany and Africa, for instance, intricate patterns are still made with soft leather. Thongs are difficult to get here and very dear and the plastic ones look horrid on real leather. Modern tools bring beautiful stitching within the range of all.

Cut-Edge Work is the simplest and the techniques are described here. Morocco, pigskin, sheep and fine hide will make wallets, purses, writing and key cases, photograph frames, folios and many other things.

Morocco leather writing case illustrating cut-edge work.

Sewing kit made from soft-grained leather lined with suede and illustrating turned-over-edge work.

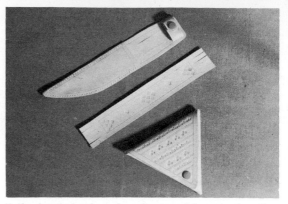

Knife sheath, book mark and purse all in natural tooling calf tooled with home-made and commercial punches.

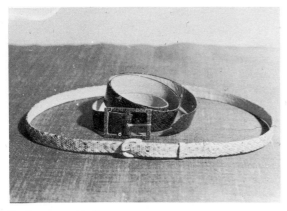

Snake covered belts.

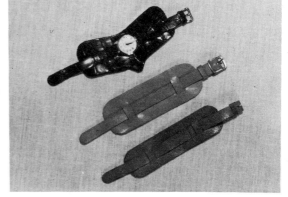

Leather watch straps.

Turned-Over-Edge Work requires good paring and assembly, sometimes with reinforcing and padding. Leathers used are as for cut-edge work and also soft goat and sheep for flexible articles.

Tooled or Embossed Work is suitable for blotters, bookmarkers and small purses in simple shapes. The technique is described here.

Built-up Work Leather is mounted over a rigid foundation such as strawboard to make folders or boxes. Sticking is used more than stitching and here grained skivers may be used to good effect.

Dress Accessories The proficient worker will be able to copy fashion goods seen in the shops. Covered belts, buttons and hair slides are made from watersnakes and skivers, belts from hide and

modern watch straps from offcuts. Suéde is suitable for sectional berets, soft bags and belts. Here stitching is done on the sewing-machine and the work turned. Hems may be stuck with rubber solution. Moccasin patterns may also be bought.

Techniques

Cutting Out Layout on moroccos, pig and sheepskins as in (Fig. 1). The back is the firmest and finest grain. Main pieces and those which show most should come from here. Sides and flanks are looser and often thinner, so these should be used for pockets, gussets, etc. As a rule, pieces for one article should run either up and down or from side to side of the skin. Leather is expensive and economy and care are needed in cutting out, but the pieces can be laid right against each other

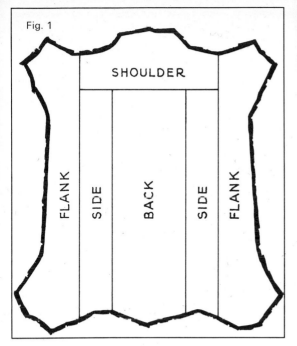

Fig. 1

SHOULDER

FLANK
SIDE
BACK
SIDE
FLANK

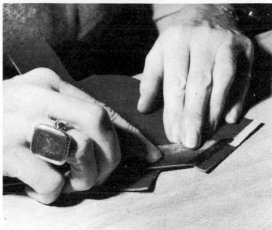

Paring with the English knife, the left hand controlling the action.

Sticking Leather cannot be tacked or pinned like materials and rubber solution is used instead. Sometimes corners and difficult spots are tied temporarily with thread.

so there need be little waste. Scraps saved will often be useful for small articles.

Patterns Always cut a really accurate cardboard pattern first. (Professionals use sheet zinc.) The time and trouble expended is well worthwhile. Such patterns are not only a valuable way to learn accuracy in cutting squares and curves but by filing them away one can always repeat the article without trouble. A pattern with a tricky shape should be cut in paper first, folding at the centre so that both sides are alike. Then it is transposed to cardboard. Cereal packets are good for pattern-cutting.

Mark the right side of the leather from the pattern and cut all straight lines with square and knife; cut curves with shears or scissors. Hardboard makes a good cutting surface.

Paring When more than two surfaces are to be joined together the edges may have to be thinned by what is called paring or skiving. The edge of the leather is held at the edge of the table and is bevelled for about $\frac{3}{8}$ in. The knife is held almost flat and must be very sharp. Paring requires practice and is an essential part of turned-over-edge work.

Using the stitch marker and mallet. The leather lies on the end-grain block.

Close-up of sewing with two needles showing the stitches, the holes and the position of the hands. Note the improvised clamp holding the work.

Stitching The most important operation in stitching is the marking of the holes. Firstly, using the cold creaser or ruler and bone folder, mark a line the width of a stitch from the edge. Holes may be made in two ways:

(a) With the hand-made stitch marker or pricking iron and the mallet. The leather is placed on a piece of end-grain wood and the marker held with the left hand vertically on the marked line. It is tapped lightly and smartly, not bashed hard. Then the first two prongs are placed in the last two holes made, the other prongs on the line, and so on. The operation is completed by going through the holes with the diamond-pointed awl, holding it vertically and at the same slant as the holes. Some workers use the awl as they sew.

(b) With the stitch-spacing wheel, which runs along the marked line making dots which are afterwards awled through. Provided the diamond

awl is used and held to make holes with an angle of about 45° to the marked line, this is quite a good method.

Sewing When both sides of the work are visible this is done with two needles, one at either end of a long length of waxed thread. The work is held with the edges just showing in the improvised clamp, the marked side facing the right hand. Starting with the hole furthest away, put the right-hand needle through and centre the thread by holding the needles together above the work. Then put the right-hand needle through the next hole forward and the left one in front of it in the same hole. Pull both through and repeat this. The threads should drop below the work, well out of the way.

When only one side of the stitch line will be visible one needle is used in a backstitch. The thread at the back of the work must be held

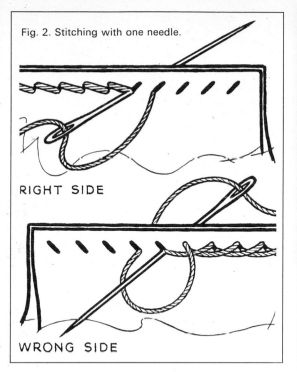

Fig. 2. Stitching with one needle.

RIGHT SIDE

WRONG SIDE

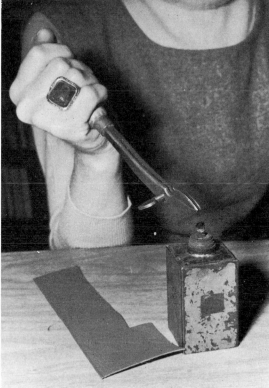

Heating the screw creaser in a methylated spirit flame before making the permanent decorating line.

forward so that the needle is always behind it, this looks like stemstitch on the back. The ends at start and finish are threaded away into the back (Fig. 2).

Finishing The edges of morocco, pig and sheep-skin articles should be finished with a colour stain let down with water and polished while damp with a soft rag. This improves the appearance and closes the edges. Polishing is done with a pinching action, using finger and thumb. The final finish is to hot-crease a line about $\frac{1}{16}$ in. to $\frac{1}{8}$ in. from the edge, heating the creaser by spirit lamp or gas burner. It should leave a clean polished line. These finishes are done to the edges of pockets, etc. before assembly.

Tooling or Embossing Natural hide, calf and sheep may be decorated with lines and patterns stamped into the damp surface. Lines are made with a tracing tool and patterned punches can be bought or made from filed brass screw-heads set in short lengths of dowel. The simplest method is to draw a design on thin paper first and lightly mark through it to the leather before hammering the punches with the mallet.

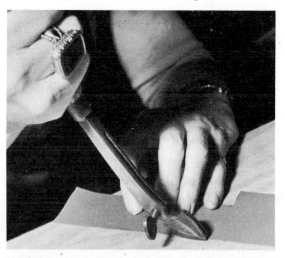

Using the screw creaser cold to mark a stitch line. The screw adjusts the distance between the blades and hence the distance of the line from the edge.

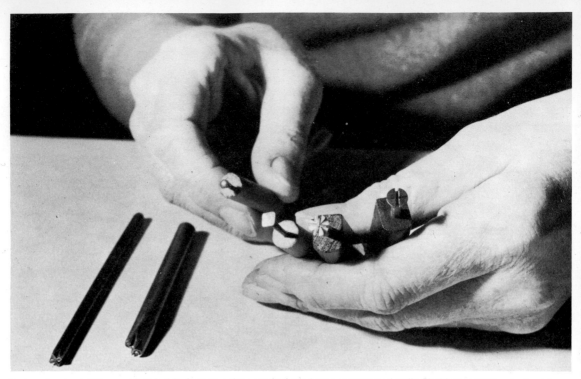

Embossing tools. The worker holds four punches made from brass screws and nails filed into patterns and set in dowel. On the table are two commercial punches.

Hide may be left plain or stained with spirit stains and polished.

These are the basic techniques of leathercraft. Now comes the business of perfecting them with practice and the student will soon be producing attractive and useful objects which will give him lasting satisfaction. There are a number of useful books on the subject which will help him to progress beyond the beginner's stage. See page 245.

Metalwork

L. A. G. Howard

The craft of the metalworker has a long history. The importance of the craft in shaping the destiny of mankind can be readily assessed by the student. If one accepts the term in the broadest sense, metalwork is a craft that can be practised at home with the simplest of tools and yet range to the complex industrial processes of mass production. What follows is a simple account of some aspects of metalwork. It is hoped that the reader will be induced to practise and study in greater depth this fascinating and rewarding subject.

Benchwork

Benchwork forms the basis of most of the metalworker's activities.

The metalworker's bench The bench should be of sound and rigid construction. Ideally, the bench top should be of hardwood at least $1\frac{1}{2}$ in. in thickness. The edges need protection and this is given by angle iron housed flush with the top and screwed in position. The bench height is a matter of personal choice, 30 in.–32 in. appears to be the norm.

The engineer's parallel vice Being solid and strong with a positive parallel action, this vice is most suitable for general benchwork. Removable jaws are fitted as standard and have either serrated faces or smooth. The body of the vice is of cast iron and the vice jaws of hardened steel. The body being of a brittle nature should never be struck with a hammer heavily.

Vice clamps are protective pieces of soft sheet metal fitted over the vice jaws. They prevent the gripped metal from being marked. They are simple to make, the most suitable metals being lead, copper, brass or zinc. Clip-on vice clamps with fibre faces can be obtained ready made.

Hand vices These are small portable vices for holding small work. They also provide the craftsman with a 'steel hand' to hold sheet metal in position for machine drilling.

The toolmaker's clamp This clamp is used to hold pieces of metal together in a firm precise manner. Marking out, drilling and cutting are some of the techniques carried out on metal thus held. Heavy treatment of the clamp must be avoided as once bent, the screws will render the clamp useless.

The hacksaw A frame saw that uses replaceable blades. A wing nut and screw enable the correct tension to be given to the blade. The shape of the handle may be D-shaped or pistol-shaped or cast in aluminium alloy or simply a wooden file-type handle. The frame is normally adjustable to allow blades of various lengths to be fitted. The depth of cut is limited to the depth of the frame. Provision is made to overcome this by allowing the blade to turn at right angles to the frame. Depth of cut is thus made unlimited; only the position of the cut from the end of the work is restricted by the frame.

Cutting technique The hacksaw cuts only in straight lines. Slight errors can be corrected by twisting the handle in the opposite direction of the error. The cutting action is continued until back on course and then the slight twisting action is released.

Junior hacksaws Small hacksaws which hold their blades by springiness in the frame. The frame and handle form an outline shape in one piece of metal. The blades have fine teeth for small work.

Hacksaw blades These are made from high-speed steel and are either 'all hard' or 'flexible'.

The flexible type, as the name suggests, will take more mis-use without breakage than the former. The teeth of the blade are 'set' to give clearance to the thickness of the blade (0·055 in.) and when fitted the teeth point away from the handle. The number of teeth per inch (T.P.I.) are obtainable at 14, 18, 24 and 32.

The following table will enable the reader to select the correct blade for the job in hand.

T.P.I.
14 Soft metals of thick sections.
18 Harder metals of thick sections.
24 Hard metals of small sections.
32 Thin walled tubes, hard metals of thin sections.

Tension files These are held in the standard hacksaw by special clips. Being round in section, the cutting file can move in any direction with ease. Correct tension in these files is important to avoid breakage.

Piercing saws These are used by decorative metal workers. The pierced work produced is the counterpart of the woodworker's fretwork. The frames are adjustable to enable broken blades of reasonable length to be used.

Slotting blades Hacksaw blades which cut slots of special widths, e.g. a screwdriver slot on the head of a screw.

Sheet saw This saw uses the standard hacksaw blade and having no frame allows unlimited positioning and depth of cut. The hacksaw blade is attached to the bottom edge of the sheet saw blade which in appearance is similar to the carpenter's hand saw.

Files These are of great importance to the metalworker. The function of the file is to remove waste metal and in the final process to impart a surface finish. Filing by hand tends to be an arduous process and, therefore, the amount left after cutting should be minimal. About $\frac{1}{16}$ in. to be removed by hand filing would be an acceptable margin.

Files are designated by length, cut and section. They are made in a variety of types and sizes. The following are in common use:

(a) Flat — tapers in width and thickness from the middle to the tip. File teeth are cut on both faces and edges and it is used for general work.
(b) Hand — tapers in thickness only, the width is parallel. Normally, one edge is smooth (safe edge) to enable accurate corners to be filed.
(c) Half round — segmental shape used for filing flat and concave surfaces. It is also most useful for filing sharp corners.
(d) Round — used for concave surfaces and the enlarging of circular holes.
(e) Three square — used for forming accurate corners. Sometimes called triangular.
(f) Square — used for filing slots and holes that are rectangular or square.

Cuts The teeth of the file can be formed by either single or double cuts. Single cuts are parallel and at an angle of 55°–60° across the blade. The double cuts criss-cross to form a surface of diamond-shaped sections. Single cut files are used on softer metals, such as aluminium, as the teeth do not clog easily. Double cut files are suitable for iron and steel.

Grades For general use the following grades are used — rough, middle, bastard, second cut, smooth and dead smooth.

For heavy work the first three grades are used. The most useful file for general work is the second cut. The smooth file is used for general finishing, and the dead smooth grade is for finishing on hard metal.

Lengths Files in general use are made in lengths from 4 in.–14 in. The blades are made from hardened and tempered cast steel, the tang being left soft to avoid breakage and perhaps injury to the user.

File handles A file must never be used without a properly fitted handle. The handle may be of wood or plastic and some of the latest type have excellent methods of securing the handle to the file tang.

The technique of filing Filing is a difficult art to acquire. The student will need practice and guidance in the workshop situation.
The correct stance is important. The feet are positioned in a natural splay, the body remains

stationary. The action comes from the shoulder, the file blade moving parallel with the floor. The movement and stance are comfortable and natural. A speed of 60 strokes per minute will produce maximum results with the minimum of fatigue.

Drawfiling This is a finishing process, imparting to the metal an accurate surface with the sheen that is characteristic of good work.

In drawfiling the file is moved over the work at right angles to its path of motion. Both hands are used to hold the file, the index fingers meeting on the top of the file immediately above the work. A smooth or dead smooth file is the grade used, with the unworn part of the blade near the handle the area of the file chosen.

Pinning During the action of filing, small pieces are apt to get lodged in the file teeth. Thus held they travel with the file stroke causing deep unwanted scratches on the surface of the metal. Chalked files have less chance of picking up pieces. The pieces once lodged can be removed with a pointed piece of soft metal such as brass or mild steel.

Wire brushes or file cards are used to clean files to prevent pinning, but over-use blunts the teeth and shortens the effective life of the file.

Drills and Drilling

Flat drills These are simple to make and, in exceptional circumstances, are most useful, e.g. when a special size hole is required and a twist drill is not available.

Twist drills These are highly efficient when ground at the correct angle. The tip ends in an edge called a web; a spiral groove called a flute allows the swarf (waste metal) to escape. Modern drills are made from high speed steel.

Centre punch A hardened and tempered punch made from tool steel and ground to a conical point. The body of the punch is knurled (diamond-shaped segments cut by a knurling tool) to make for better gripping. The purpose of the punch is to make a conical shaped indentation on the surface of metal in the precise position of the centre of the intended hole. The centre punch hole

locates the tip of the drill (web) and prevents it from wandering.

Pilot holes Where larger holes are required it is normal practice to locate the larger web in a drilled hole (pilot hole). The pilot drill is positioned by a centre punch in the usual way.

Speed of drilling The speed of the drill is an important factor both from the point of view of the life of the drill and the quality of the work produced. Tables giving the speed in feet per minute are obtainable and are calculated with regard to the material worked (soft to hard). The 'feet per minute' is converted to 'revolutions per minute', for the particular drill diameter, by reference to another table. The experienced craftsman can select the correct drill speed by what appears to be sheer instinct.

As a very rough, rule of thumb guide it can be said that the smaller the drill the more r.p.m.; the softer the material the greater the r.p.m. Therefore a small drill in soft material = very fast and, of course, conversely a large drill and hard material will produce the need for very slow r.p.m.

Drill designation Drills are generally designated in four size systems: (a) Fractions of an inch, (b) Numbers, (c) Letters, (d) Metric.

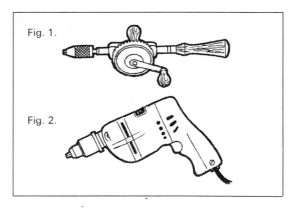

Fig. 1.

Fig. 2.

Hand drills Used for work of a light nature on the bench or in the vice. (Fig. 1.)

Electric pistol drills Used for drilling holes up to $\frac{5}{16}$ in. in situ. They are of great value to the maintenance fitter. (Fig. 2.)

Taps and tapping The hole to be drilled must always be smaller than the size of the thread intended. The correct size tapping drill is easily obtained from a table.

Taps A tap is a screw made from hardened steel. Flutes are cut along its length to provide cutting edges and to allow the swarf to escape. Taps are made in sets of three:
Taper — for entering and centralising (starting the thread)
Second — suitable for finishing a through hole
Plug — used to cut a full thread to the bottom of a blind hole.

Dies These are used with die holders to produce external threads by hand. The external thread (die thread) is always the last to be cut of a pair (nut and bolt) because of the adjustment in diameter size that is possible.

The popular die is circular and split at one radius. A tapered mouth allows the thread to be started. The split die can be adjusted by screws in the die holder, to close the split or allow the split to be fully open. This allows a small control over the exact size of the thread produced.

The die holder is used with the circular rebate uppermost. The work should be slightly chamfered to ease the start. Care should be given to start off square or a drunken thread will result.

Brazing, Hard Soldering and Soft Soldering

Brazing This is a method of joining metal by the fusion of brass (Spelter). The metal must be clean where it is to be joined. The cleaning is best done with a file or emery cloth and in some instances a small chamfered edge where the spelter is to run is an advantage.

Flux The flux used is borax or brand equivalent. This is supplied in powder form and is mixed with water to form a smooth paste the consistency of cream. The purpose of the flux is to aid the running of the spelter and to prevent oxidisation during the brazing operation.

Technique The job to be brazed is positioned on the brazing hearth with fire bricks placed to trap the heat from the torch around the job. The job is cleaned, fluxed and the joint held in position. The torch flame heats the job to cherry red and the

Upton House School

A gas brazing torch being used at the brazing hearth.

stick of brazing rod is touched on the joint line. If conditions are correct the brass melts on contact and floods the joint forming a small fillet on either side.

A clean job, the right flux, a good joint and the correct heat will result in success every time.

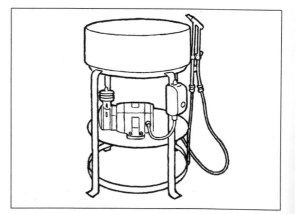

A revolving brazing hearth with brazing blowpipe.

Silver soldering Much less heat is required for this process, otherwise it has much in common with brass brazing.

Borax or brand equivalent is again the flux used. The solder is an alloy of silver, copper and zinc. For general use in the workshop, the solder is obtainable in three grades: easy; hard; enamelling; in ascending order of their fusion point.

Having three distinct melting points it is possible to make joints close to each other without melting the previous joints.

Silver soldering is easily practised at home, the equipment necessary is simple and inexpensive. A small square of asbestos, a gas or spirit blow torch (Fig. 3) and a few fire bricks is all that is required.

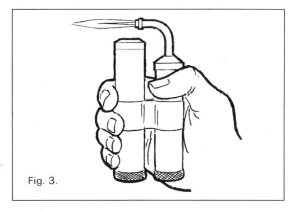

Fig. 3.

For soldering silver only the best grade solder is used. This consists of 4 parts silver to 1 part copper and zinc.

Soft soldering This is the term given to the method of joining metals together with an alloy of lead and tin. The solder is carried to the job by means of a soldering iron.

Soldering iron (tinman's) This consists of a copper bit fixed to a steel rod which in turn is fixed to the handle. The bit may be straight or hatchet-shaped and can be obtained in a variety of sizes. (Fig. 4.)

Electric soldering iron The electric soldering iron is convenient to use; reaches the correct heat and remains constant at that heat. (Fig. 5.)

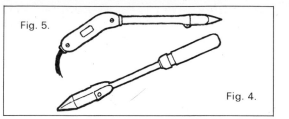

Fig. 5.

Fig. 4.

The techniques of soft soldering The following procedure notes outline the technique involved for the tinman's iron heated by gas in the tinman's stove. Exclude the references to green flames and reheating when using an electric iron.

1. The point of the iron is first coated with solder (tinned). This is done by filing the copper bit bright and clean, taking care to remove a minimal amount of copper. The iron is now heated until the gas flame turns green (correct heat) and dipped into the flux and then into solder, twisting the bit to ensure coating on all sides.

2. Once tinned the iron is reheated, dipped again into the flux and rubbed against a stick of solder.

3. Having thus picked up a liberal coating of solder, the bit is placed in position on the joint. Heat is transferred to the job. The solder flows into the joining gap. This continues as the bit is moved slowly along, the solder flooding the joint as it goes. When this ceases to happen, the process outlined in step (2) is repeated.

Important The joint must be clean (free from grease or oxides) — a finger mark will ruin the preparation.

Fluxes These are either 'active' or 'passive' or, to put it in another sense, acid or non-acid. The non-acid types are usually resin-based and can be obtained in powder, paste or grease form. Solder is used in a wire form with a core of this type of flux. Because the flux is non-acid, the residue left on the joint has no corrosive effect. All electrical work is soldered with this type of flux.

The acid fluxes are usually in a liquid form. Zinc chloride is the commonest flux and is used for tinplate, brass and copper.

Forge Work

Of all the traditional crafts none hold the magic of the past so convincingly as forge work.

There are four main sections of equipment:
The forge — for metal heating using blacksmith's breeze (small coke).
The anvil — for supporting the metal during forging.
The tools — hammers, fullers, swages, etc.
The tongs — to hold hot metal.

The forge Basically the forge consists of a brick-lined hearth, a hood to extract the 'coke' fumes, and an air pipe to carry a blast of air to the forge fire (tuyere). The air blast can come from hand bellows but it is more common today to use a mechanical blower. A water tank is fixed to the back of the forge for the purpose of cooling the tuyere. (Fig. 6.)

The anvil is of the well-known traditional shape and may weigh up to 3 cwt. The body is made of wrought iron and a hardened steel face is welded to the top. The curved tusk is used for curving metal (beak). A small ledge close to the face is the cutting table. The hardened steel face is used to support the metal and should not itself be hammered. At the opposite end to the beak are two holes, one square for holding various tools and the other (round) is used as a punch hole. (Fig. 7a.)

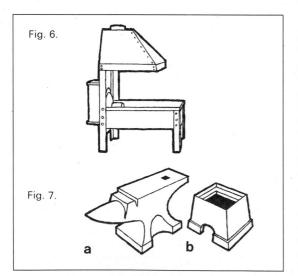

Fig. 6.

Fig. 7.

a   b

The anvil is supported at working height on a cast stand (Fig. 7b.) or, in the manner of old, on a section of tree trunk.

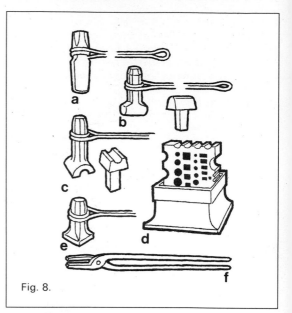

Fig. 8.

Tools

Hammers The larger weights of the engineers' hammers are often used. There is, however, a special forging hammer with a striking face slightly convex.

For heavy work a sledge hammer is used; two workers are needed, the smith and the striker. The smith holds the work and indicates to the striker with a small hammer where the blows are to be struck. The signal for the striker to stop is given by the smith ringing the anvil with his small hammer.

Chisels These may be designed for cutting hot metal or cold metal. The hot chisel is never hardened and tempered and has a cutting edge of 30°. The cold chisel is hardened and tempered and has a cutting edge of 60°.

Chisels are used in pairs, the bottom chisel's square shank fitting in the hardie hole. The top chisel is held by a long metal handle fitted at right angles to the chisel and struck by a hammer held in the smith's other hand. (Fig. 8a.)

Fullers Fullers are used for necking the work (a shoulder with curved corner). The shoulder formed is often used as a start to a continuous reduction. (Fig. 8b.)

Swages These are forming irons used to produce work of hexagonal or round section. Fullers and swages are held in a similar fashion to the chisels. (Fig. 8c.)

Swage blocks A block of cast iron with a series of grooves of various sized hexagon and round half sections around the edge (Fig. 8d). In the centre of the block are an assortment of holes of useful size and shape. The blocks are usually 20 in. square with a depth of 7 in. The block is used for a similar purpose to that of the swage and does away with the need for a huge collection of swages.

Flatters These are used for finishing off a flat surface. Only one is used, the work being supported on the anvil. (Fig. 8e.)

Tongs The blacksmith uses a variety of shapes in the mouths of his tongs. Shapes in common use are the open mouth, close mouth, hollow bit, vice mouth, square mouth and pick up tongs. (Fig. 8f.)

Techniques of Forging

Drawing down The length of the metal is increased and the cross-sectional area decreased on width and thickness.

Upsetting This is the opposite of drawing down; the cross-sectional area is increased at the expense of the length.

Setting down Thinning down of a local area in thickness.

Bending Sharp bends are made in the blacksmith's leg vice. Softer bends are formed by forging on the anvil's beak.

Welding This only applies to wrought iron and mild steel. The metal is heated to white heat, dipped in flux and hammered together. The joints used are the butt joint, scarf joint and the vee joint. The flux for wrought iron is sand and for mild steel calcinated borax.

Alen Lewis

Gas welded figure showing how textures can be built up in blobs and ridges by painting with the welding flame and texturing with a brush.

Bending features These are mechanical aids to bending and are most useful when a number of uniform curves are required. A lever causes a roller to bend the metal around a central disc.

Punching The hot metal is held over the punch hole. The metal is punched from both sides.

Drifting A final stage. The tapered drift opens up the punch hole to a particular shape or size.

Dies When a die hole is used, punching is a straight through operation — the hole in the die block being the exact diameter of the punch.

Heat Treatment of Ferrous Metals
Steel is a compound of iron and carbon (alloy). The iron and carbon change at 900°C. and when the metal is quenched (rapidly cooled) the steel is hardened.

High carbon steel (H.C.S.) is known as tool steel. The carbon content of H.C.S. is from 0·60% to 1·50%; cutting tools such as taps and dies having 0·90% to 1·00% carbon.

Hardening H.C.S. is heated to cherry red and quenched.

Annealing H.C.S. is softened by heating to cherry red and cooling very slowly. Hot ashes or the hot bricks on the brazing hearth can be used for this.

Tempering The metal is first hardened as above. A section of metal is cleaned of oxide to a bright metal finish. The metal is reheated and the colour of the bright section will change to the following:

Tempering Colour	Temperature °C.
Pale yellow	210
Straw	225
Golden yellow	240
Brown	250
Purple	270
Bright blue	275
Full blue	280
Dark blue	300

The temperature or colour at which the metal is quenched determines the amount of tempering given.

Where precise results are necessary, a muffle furnace is used and the element of human error is reduced, the exact temperature being recorded on a dial.

Tempering is given to steel to impart a degree of toughness to the metal, hardened steel being too brittle for most purposes.

Case hardening An outer skin of H.C.S. is formed on the surface of mild steel or wrought iron. The result is a tough core with a hard (anti-wear) skin. The metal is heated to a bright red and plunged into 'Kasenite' (powdered carbon compound). The metal picks up the carbon on its surface. The metal is reheated, the carbon is absorbed in the surface and produces a hard skin when quenched.

Heat Treatment of Non-Ferrous Metals
Aluminium, brass and copper tend to become hard and brittle with cold working and they need annealing (softening) from time to time during the working processes.

Aluminium is annealed by heating to 400°C. and cooling. A piece of soap rubbed on the surface will turn black at this temperature. Cooling can be rapid or slow, the result is the same.

Copper is annealed by heating to a dull red and quenching in water. The scale is removed afterwards by pickling in diluted sulphuric acid.

Brass is annealed by heating to a dull red and cooling slowly.

Foundry Work

Casting is a process whereby molten metal is poured or forced into a specially prepared mould.

The basic equipment required for a sand mould is as follows:
1. A pattern.
2. The casting boxes and sand.
3. A means of melting the metal.
4. A method and means of transporting the metal to the mould.

The pattern is used to create a cavity in the sand. The casting boxes are open-ended frames, used in pairs, one above the other, and located in position by sockets and pins. The sand used by the moulder must satisfy certain demands:
(a) It must withstand the heat involved;
(b) remain porous when compressed;
(c) be able to hold a shape when damp and compressed.

An aluminium casting being removed from the sand mould.

The sand when dampened with water is called 'green sand'. Careful preparation is needed. The moulder tests the sand by gripping a handful and then opening his hand. The shape-holding qualities are checked — the wad of sand holding the imprint of the fingers. Experience and skill are of great importance at this stage.

The metal is melted in a cupola (small blast furnace) for ferrous metals, and in a crucible furnace for non-ferrous metals.

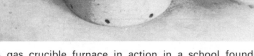

A gas crucible furnace in action in a school foundry.

Because of the danger involved and the need for expensive equipment, ferrous metal casting is best left to the expert.

For non-ferrous casting of a small nature, a steel ladle is used to transport the melt to the mould. But for normal casting the metal is poured from the lip of the crucible, the crucible being lifted from the furnace by special tongs. Lifted straight from the furnace, the crucible is placed in the ring of a two-handled lifting device. This carrier

is so designed that only one of the two operators can control the pour.

All pouring operators must wear leather aprons, safety goggles and asbestos gloves.

Molten metal must always be treated with respect. Any left over from the cast is carefully poured into pre-heated troughs.

If we inspected the sand mould before the molten metal was poured it would be in this condition:

A mass of damp sand carefully packed in moulding boxes. In the centre would be a cavity the shape and size of the pattern. Holes would lead from the surface of the sand to the cavity. One would allow entry of the melt (gate), another would allow the displaced air to escape and give visual indication that the mould is full (riser). A basin would be cut in the sand at the top of the gate to allow the dross to float to the top during the pour, and vent holes would be made through the sand with a long $\frac{1}{2}$ in. diameter pin to within $\frac{1}{2}$ in. of the cavity to help the sand disperse the locked gases.

The gates and risers were made by packing in tapered cylindrical pieces of wood with sand and

Sculptural form which has been cast.

carefully extracting later. The sand basin was made with one of the many trowels used by the moulder.

Powdered chalk was used to enable the pattern to be extracted without unduly disturbing the sand.

Facing sand near the pattern gave the cavity smooth faces when the pattern was removed.

The patterns themselves can be split, solid, flat or cored (with holes).

Centre Lathe Work

The lathe is one of man's earliest machines. All lathes are similar in basic principle, see below. The work is revolved against a fixed cutter. The cutter is fixed in the vertical plane but movable by the operator in the horizontal plane. The movement can be manual through a system of screws or automatic (from the machine's own power).

The basic turning operations can be simplified to the following:

(a) Straight turning (traversing). The movement of the cutter is parallel with the axis of the rotating work. The surface produced is cylindrical.
(b) Facing. The cutter moves at 90° to the rotating axis of the work. The surface produced is flat and situated at the end of the work exposed by the lathe chuck.

(c) Taper turning. A combination of the two above directions will produce a conical surface. In practice, only one control at a time is used — the compound slide for short tapers. For long tapers it is necessary to turn between centres with the axis of the work offset by moving the tailstock to one side of the centre line. The cutter moving along the correct path, the work's axis being offset.

Lathe Parts The four main parts of the lathe are as follows: the bed, the headstock, tailstock and the saddle.

The bed This is the foundation of the whole machine, it is machined and scraped to a high finish. The standard of accuracy must be exceptionally high; the tailstock and saddle will move along the bed. It is usual to make the bed from cast iron in one of two standard sections — the 'flat' bed and the 'inverted vee type' bed. (Fig. 9a.)

The headstock In the headstock are the gears, spindles and shafts that give power movement to the machine. The main spindle that rotates the work is bored to receive a centre and externally threaded to receive a chuck. The spindle is hollow to allow work to pass through and on some machines can revolve clockwise and anti-clockwise. (Fig. 9c.)

The tailstock The tailstock is a unit that slides along the bed and can be clamped in any position. A hollow cylinder, bored to receive a centre or

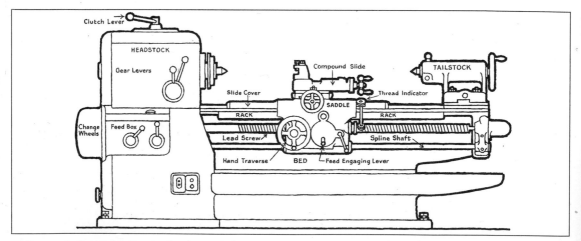

Sliding, surfacing and screw cutting centre lathe.

shank of a drill chuck, is movable longitudinally in the stock. Both the stock and cylinder have independent clamping devices.

The purposes of the tailstock are as follows:

(a) To support a non-moving centre (dead) in an accurate, solid position.
(b) To enable drilling to take place by holding a drill chuck in the non-revolving position (dead).
(c) To provide a means to offset the axis of long work held between centres for the purpose of taper turning.

Saddle This unit fits over the lathe bed and moves along the bed by a rack and pinion arrangement. The front of the saddle that is fitted with the controls is the 'apron'.

On top of the apron, fitted to a dovetail slide, is the cross-slide which, by its cross-movement, enables facing to take place. (Fig. 9b.)

Mounted on top of the cross-slide is fitted a swivel slide called the compound slide. This slide is movable to enable short tapers to be machined.

On top of the compound slide the tool post is fitted in a rigid non-moving position.

Tool posts clamp the lathe tools (cutters) in position and hold from one to four tools.

Screw-cutting By a train of gears in the head-stock the leadscrew is rotated. The heavy long screw runs the working length of the bed. When a half nut device is pressed in position by a lever in the apron, movement parallel with the axis of the work is given to the cutter. The relationship between the movement of the tool (cutter) and the rotary movement of the work is precise and constant. Thus it is possible to so arrange the train of gears in the headstock that the tool will cut a spiral groove, which is known as a thread.

Chucks Three jaw self-centre chucks hold round section metal for turning. They are quick and easy in use.

Four jaw chucks have independently operated jaws. Square and odd shaped sections can be held accurately. Some skill is needed for precise setting up which is usually a trial and error method

of centring with an accurate instrument known as a dial test indicator. (Fig. 9d.)

Magnetic chucks hold ferrous metals that have large contact areas, the best type being a permanent magnet device (the electro-magnet being dangerous in the event of a power cut).

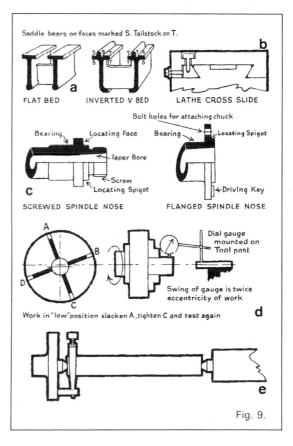

Fig. 9.

Face Plate The face plate is a large flat disc that is fitted to the headstock spindle. Irregular work is clamped to the plate by bolts passing through slots. Positioned on the face of the plate, the work can be machined.

Turning between centres Long work is drilled centrally at each end by a Slocombe drill to receive the points of the centres. The work is positioned between the points with the minimum of pressure and the centres lubricated with tallow or grease. The rotary movement is given to work via a driving

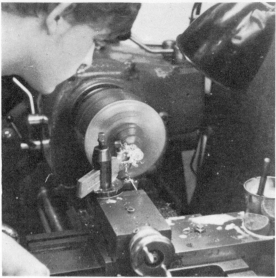

Centre lathe turning in the school machine shop.

plate and striker contacting to a lathe carrier clamped to the work. (Fig. 9e.)

Automatic feed Movement of the tool for traversing or facing comes from a feed shaft. This shaft runs underneath the lead screw on most lathes. Once set in motion the machining is completely automatic, although the operator's full attention is required to turn off at the required moment and to check the quality of the work produced.

Conclusion

Obviously, we have done little more than touch upon the fringes of the craft of metalwork. It is an extensive subject and the aspiring metalworker should make a point of reading as much as possible (some suggestions for further reading will .be found on page 245) and, if possible, join a class where he may try out the different techniques for himself.

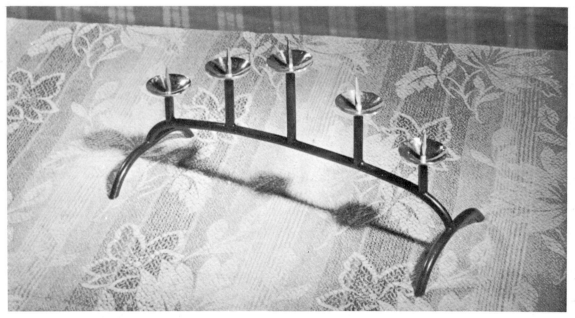

Candelabra made by the author with a steel frame, brass dishes and forged copper spikes.

Natural Materials   Derek Waters

Almost half the pleasure in this area of craft is the discovery of the materials to be used. Quite often one will come across some natural object and store it away until the need for it arises. Certain flower arrangements require material which is gathered months before use and dried. When a tree is being felled it is often possible to beg a piece from the woodman, but before you can get to work with your chisels the timber needs to be seasoned; under normal circumstances this progresses at the rate of one inch per year—from both sides, so pencil the date of felling on your green timber when you get it. Sometimes the unexpected acquisition of a piece of wood—unusual in shape, colour or size—may start the creative urge in the mind immediately; on the other hand, the material may be in store for months, or even years, before another factor stimulates some craft work.

When looking for materials, streets and roads are usually sterile places and some parks are little better when there are keepers trying to keep natural litter, as well as feet, off the grass.

Fields offer more opportunities for discovery. Since man first began to cultivate the land there have been ceremonies at harvest time which include the making of symbols and decorations. Recently there has been a revival of the rural craft of making corn dollies, see next page. The top section of the ripe straw is used for these. Wheat is best, but oats, rye, and even grass, can be used to make the various traditional designs (see bibliography).

Woodlands are worth searching, especially if they are somewhat neglected. (In the best-managed woods the forester will keep his tree-lines clear to reduce fire-risk amongst the dry debris, and the spread of fungi.) Fallen branches are one of the things to look for. Hold them up in the air; turn them this way and that to see the shape they make

Traditional corn dolly.

The woodlands and hedgerows will provide other things for displays. Spring is the time to look among the trees for flowers which bloom before the leaves grow and reduce the amount of light reaching the ground. If chemical sprays have not had too extensive an effect, there will be an abundance of flowers to collect in the summer meadow and from its edges. Come the autumn, leaves turned brown and gold, seeds and berries brightly coloured to attract the birds, make a rich harvest for the collector. Fungus, found in a surprising variety of form and colour at this time of year, can be used for brief displays; the shapes inspire drawing, and the making of moulds from which some permanent forms can be cast in plaster of Paris.

in silhouette. Look for interesting contortions, configurations and branchings as you rotate the wood.

There is an ancient right of Common of Estovers which allows one to take necessary wood from another's estate for household use and the making of the implements of industry, but the timber taken like this must be dead branchwood and few landowners would object to one taking such material. A small saw can be carried to trim branches to size.

Where wood has lain for some time, the bark may be loose or rotted away revealing the wood underneath. Sometimes bark beetles have been at work and have engraved remarkable patterns for their breeding chambers and feeding channels. Bark, with its texture, colour and shape, can also be collected and used for material arrangements.

Flower arranging is a very popular craft today. All kinds of flowers, foliage, fruit and even vegetables found on the domestic scene can be used in arrangements.

Cockerel made from dried seeds and leaves.

Alan Lewis

72

Winter is seldom regarded as the best time of year for collecting, but often berries persist on the trees and shrubs. Twigs, with variations of bud shape and formation, can be collected and arranged. It is a pity that so many people limit themselves to horse-chestnut buds when a number of others are as attractive to have indoors.

Leaves which have lain on the ground for a few months may have become skeletonised; poplar leaves are particularly good examples. These can be collected, pressed and arranged on paper. A more sophisticated display can be made under glass or perspex for table tops or finger panels for doors.

Where seeds, cones, twigs, etc. are gathered to make figures, pieces of wire can be cut and on to these the various items can be added in 'kebab' fashion. The ends of the wire can either be stapled to a piece of wood or passed through such a base to secure the figure.

But perhaps it is in those places where there is water that some of the best materials can be discovered. By riverside and sea there is usually an abundance of 'debris' which is constantly changing. Particularly after storms, both the riverbank and seashore are worth searching. The abrasive action of sand and pebbles smooths most things which spend any length of time in the water. In the case of wood, softer areas are worn away more rapidly, giving interesting texture, and edges and corners are rounded. Unusual shapes are produced which need only a little embellishment with sandpaper, files and small saws. These wooden forms can either be free standing or become parts of mobiles. Sometimes a long sinuous branch can be hung from its centre of gravity to turn slowly in the air and offer many different views to the observer below.

Among beach finds, one may come across the white oval shapes of the cuttle fish bone. These can be carved and filed to make low relief shapes. A penknife is a useful tool for this material — which is very like salt to work — without the ever-present danger with the latter of attempting features which are too thin.

The collection of pebbles is a fascinating hobby. Often the colours are less bright when away from the water, but this returns if the stones are stored

Driftwood found on the seashore is weathered into interesting shapes and textures.

in a jar of water or if clear varnish is brushed on them. Stones can be broken open with a hammer and chisel to reveal unsuspected colours and patterns for use in mosaics. A pattern can be decided upon and sketched on to a piece of blockboard. The stones are best fixed with an impact adhesive with an added hardener (e.g., Araldite). Plaster of Paris is used to fill in the intervening spaces. Alternatively, the mosaics may be planned to go on paving blocks outside, or on walls, and for such activities a mixture of sand and cement should be prepared (in the proportion of two of sand to one of cement) with enough water to make a stiff, pliable mixture; the pebbles are pressed into place and allowed to set.

Shells are plentiful on the beach and large collections can be made from which a selection for a specific work can be taken. For example, when making a small figure, a dogwhelk might be chosen for the body, a periwinkle for the head and a limpet for the hat.

Toy made from a lobster's claw — Bethnal Green Museum, London.

Ronald Chapman

Eroded driftwood makes natural 'sculpture' although it may need a little finishing off.

In utilising shells like this, problems arise when fine detail is required. There are small shells on our beaches but it may be necessary to use small beads for eyes and other features; paint can also be employed to provide such details. An impact adhesive can be used for these figures.

Certainly the natural scene has much to offer the craftsman, not only because of the cheapness,

variety and abundance of material available, but also because it offers a continual challenge in selecting and modifying each item to suit a particular purpose.

Note: Remember that some fungi is extremely poisonous, even when dried. It should be kept away from children and hands should be thoroughly washed immediately after touching it.

Paper

Michael Grater

The Material

As the basic material of a craft, paper might not appear immediately promising. It is flat. It is not strong; and while it comes in a variety of colours and types, and has many uses which we take for granted, it hardly commends itself as a material for sculpture or modelling.

If you take a sheet of paper of any sort and hold it, as a craftsman must hold his materials, you are very unlikely to get an immediate inspiration. You can demonstrate this by actually taking a piece of exercise or drawing paper — or even wrapping paper — about the size of this page.

To make anything with this piece of paper you would have to begin by understanding something of its constructive potential — what is possible with it. If you try to stand the paper, for example, upright on a flat surface it will fall down.

If, however, you fold the paper through the middle from top to bottom, it will be possible to stand the shape you have made on edge, like a greetings card.

Whether it will stand firmly or still appear to be hopelessly limp will depend on the quality of the paper you start with. If your present example is not adequately firm you will need to try again with paper of a slightly better quality. If the folded paper will stand unsupported you will see that, in a simple way, you have controlled the material. You have introduced a strength factor; and if you look closely at it, again as a craftsman must look at his work, you will see that you have also done something to its appearance.

You will now have two surfaces or planes meeting at the centre fold. If you look carefully you may be able to see that, although you have not changed the nature of the surfaces, they will now be slightly varied in tone or shade according to the way the light is falling on the paper.

What you have done is a simple example of a craftsman's technique. You could have screwed the paper up, which would have been a way of manipulating it, but the resultant ball of crushed paper would be imprecise and probably not a rewarding treatment for future use in modelling.

The simple fold is an example of a controlled technique which can be repeated and which takes into account the nature of the material. It is a technique which can be applied in many ways because it shows an appreciation of what the material can be made to do. It is the appreciation of material which forms the basis of work in any craft.

For working with paper there is no special quality requirement. Any paper can be used if the craftsman can control it and make it do what he wants. If he has ability and understanding in a few simple techniques the craftsman will appreciate whether the material is usable or not.

Creative modelling in paper is obviously best attempted in good quality material. But it is not necessary to go to a great deal of expense. There are a number of techniques which have been refined by craftsmen working with paper. These can be learned quickly and easily, and can be applied in work with all sorts of paper.

Basic Techniques

Scoring and Folding If a fold in a piece of paper will give it strength and will add visual interest, it is desirable that the act of folding can be controlled with some precision by the craftsman. Any sort of a fold in paper is assisted by *scoring* the surface along the line to be folded with a sharp knife.

To demonstrate this you should cut two long narrow strips of paper of equal size. You should now aim, by controlling the material, to make these strips stand upright. You can fold the first one freehand through the middle from top to bottom. In the second example you should lightly cut the surface of the fold, using a straight edge as a guide, and taking care not to cut right through it at any point. A knife or a scissor blade can be used.

After scoring you will find that the cut will open slightly as you fold away from it. When you have mastered the technique it should be possible to make a precise and unbuckled fold which, compared to your first example, is likely to be crisper and cleaner in effect than the unscored fold.

The Curved Score In paper modelling it is often useful to have a curved fold, for example on the surface of a leaf or a flower petal. The curved score should be made freely. It is not possible to use a straight edge, so it must be practised. For a simple exercise you could cut a number of identical leaf shapes and could try various straight or curved scores on them, comparing the effect of the folds which you are able to produce. The technique can be practised in many different ways (Fig. 1).

As a more interesting exercise, after mastering the technique, you might make some free-standing figures. These can be cut in stiff paper or card, preferably on the fold so that they are symmetrical when you open them. They can be developed as characters with drawn or painted decoration or with further cut paper shapes (Fig. 2). Coloured or patterned papers will add to the visual effect of the finished work.

Fixing For paper modelling any method of fixing can be used which gives an adequately strong fixture with the minimum of difficulty. There are three main methods, either used singly or in combination:

Glue Any of the modern impact type glues can be used. These stick on contact between surfaces, and are usually available in tube or jar. They are so efficient that the only real problem is to keep any messy excess off the front of the paper.

Fig. 1.

Fig. 2.

Staples An immediate and permanent fixture can be made between any number of papers with the use of a hand stapler which pushes and folds a small wire staple through the material. There are many different sorts currently available.

Slot and Flap When it is necessary to fix one shape to another it is sometimes useful to cut the shape with an extra flap, which can be inserted into a slot cut at the point of fixture. The location of the slot can be established by holding the shape with the flap against the background and marking its exact position before cutting. The advantage of this method is that its use will result in an invisible fixture with the flap hidden, and if necessary glued, out of sight.

Cutting The ability to cut paper neatly and accurately is obviously an essential skill for the craftsman in paper, but again there is no hard and fast rule about how it should be done. Either scissors or a sharp knife can be used. The type of craft knife which can be bought with replacement blades is likely to prove most useful for any type of scoring or cutting. It can be used in combination with a cutting surface made from a sheet of cheap cardboard, which can be replaced when the surface is too rough from constant use.

Fig. 3.

Raising Form

The basic problem of working with paper as a modelling material, since it starts by being flat, is to raise any adequate sort of form or shape. In the first application of the scoring technique a simple form was established by the two planes meeting at the fold of the paper. This particular technique, as you will have seen, can be used in many ways for modelling, either as a single fold or in multiple arrangements. There are other simple methods of raising form in flat paper.

Overlapping (cut to centre) If you take a flat piece of paper, square or disc, and make a single cut in it from the outer edge to the centre it will be possible to overlap the sides of the cut. As you make the overlap the paper will take on a new form. From a disc, for example, the form will raise as a cone. This is a technique which can be developed and applied in various ways. In Fig. 3 a disc is treated variously with the cut to centre and with scores, so that the techniques combine to make visual effects.

Curling Another method of raising form from the flat is to establish the sort of mass effect, less precise but still visually attractive, which can be achieved by curling the paper.

If you take a strip of paper and run a blade along one surface, from one end to the other, you will disturb the tension on the surface and the strip will tend to spring into a curl. This is a technique which will require a little practice.

You can cut a number of strips of varying widths and can practise by holding each of them in turn at one end and, starting at this point, running a knife or scissor blade along the underside of the length. The blade should be controlled with your thumb at the top of the strip as your hand moves along it. It is a simple scraping movement which you might have to practise, and in some of the earlier attempts you might find yourself tearing the strip. You will do this less and less as you get the feel of the technique, and will appreciate how much pressure you must apply to make the paper curl. As in all craft work the craftsman must learn to

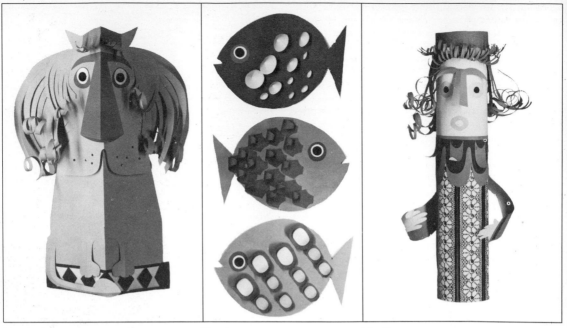

Fig. 4.   Fig. 5.   Fig. 6.

rely on his touch combined with an awareness of how much manipulation the material will stand before its usefulness is ruined.

The curling technique is one which can be used in many ways to add attractive visual effect to paper models (Fig. 4).

Surface Treatment

When you have appreciated the need in paper modelling to raise simple form, you will be able to investigate the further opportunities which may be used to make the modelling interesting. There are various surface treatments which may be used. Painting and drawing are of course methods of treating a surface, but for modelling there are other simple techniques.

Cut Texture Cuts into a paper surface can exploit the development of pattern and the play of light over the surface. If you take a piece of paper and make a number of v-shaped cuts in the surface you will be able to raise the cut shapes so that they throw small shadows. This visual effect can be developed in many ways by altering the shape or arrangement of the cuts.

Applied Texture An alternative method to cutting into a surface is to vary its visual effect by adding a pattern or texture of folded papers. If you cut a number of simple fish shapes you can experiment with some of the potential. Paper folded in various ways to produce shadows can be fixed to the surface, either in continuous strips or as a single shape repeated in patterns (Fig. 5).

Basic Forms

The various techniques which you have considered so far can be exploited in many ways in three-dimensional modelling by applying them to any of the basic forms which are possible in paper. It is unlikely to be very rewarding in this, or in any other three-dimensional craft, merely to rely on a happy accident when you are trying to make a shape. The material you are using is likely to have potential in certain basic shapes. You can establish the simplest of these in paper by rolling a flat sheet into a cylinder. This should be secured at the top and bottom — in this instance you are likely to find that stapling will be the most effective method. The cylinder you make will be a free-standing form, essentially three-dimensional, which can be exploited creatively with added papers using some of the techniques already described (Fig. 6).

Other simple free-standing forms can be made from the triangular or square prism. For the triangular prism you will need to fold the paper into three equal sides, allowing a flap at the edge for an overlapped fixture. Square and rectangular prisms can be made in the same way with four sides, and can be used as basic forms for further development (Fig. 7).

An experience of the techniques described will provide an adequate starting point for the development of a craft skill in working with paper. It is a cheap and readily available material, and anyone should be able to get pleasure and satisfaction from controlling and exploiting the paper in all sorts of interesting ways, and more important, in making the paper do exactly what is wanted from it.

The exploitation of the masks (Fig. 8) is a simple statement of the way flat paper may be used. You will perhaps have seen sometimes more ambitious examples of what the professional calls *paper sculpture* which has a wide commercial application. Any example of this which you come across might be visually impressive, but its impact is less meaningful to the young craftsman than a simple understanding of the material and what is possible with it.

In craft there is no particular merit in virtuosity or complex expertise. And in paper craft there is in fact a disadvantage in over-complication. Where the material is simple it will support simple end-products which are crisp and uncluttered and easy to look at. The potential of this craft is light-hearted. It is a fun activity which is open to anyone who can collect together some paper, something to cut it with, and some means of making a fixture — which must surely make it a craft for all of us and not just for the expert.

Fig. 7.

Fig. 8.

Plastics

John Lancaster

The range of three-dimensional materials available to artists has extended considerably during the past decade and this has provided them with a wider range of spacial expression than hitherto. It is certainly not uncommon today to find sculptures executed in metal, wire, glass, neon, plastics, or a combination of materials such as these which are relevant to a machine age in which technology, engineering and mass production play dominant roles, as well as the more traditional wood and stone which have been used from the time primitive man started to be creative.

The new, synthetically-produced materials commonly referred to as 'plastics' (a term derived from the Greek work *plastikos* meaning growing, developing and forming — Encyclopaedia Britannica) consist of formless matter which can be given moulded or modelled form by craftsmen and artists using a variety of techniques. As methods of producing the material have been improved costs have, fortunately, been reduced and this has brought a comparably cheap material within easy reach of the sculptor. It enables him to work at speed on three-dimensional works which are light in weight, and he now has the facility to produce standing structures or relief panels on a very large scale. William Mitchell, the architectural sculptor, has had considerable success in designing and making decorative reliefs for both interior and exterior walls of new apartment and office buildings, and has used materials such as polyurethane, polystyrene, cold cast bronze and cements which he has found to be so appropriate to this work.

The doors Mitchell designed for the new Roman Catholic cathedral in Liverpool are examples of modern techniques and imagery and are certainly interesting when compared with Ghiberti's Baptistry doors in Florence for the latter demonstrate earlier methods of working that were much more laborious and time-consuming.

Nicholas Servian / Woodmansterne Ltd., Watford

Detail from the main door panel of the new Liverpool Cathedral, designed by William Mitchell.

The writer is convinced that the most sensible approach to creative work is an empirical one based upon experiment and self-discovery. The artist must accept a material for what it is and go on to discover for himself just what he can do with it. At the same time, he must be willing to admit the unexpected, or what Freda Roblick, the sculptor, calls 'unplanned happenings', for these add excitement and can lead to further interesting creative work, but he must be acute enough to

80

recognise the significance of such happenings and make the best use of them. New discoveries can foster discernment as the artist sees shapes arise from the formless material, as well as stimulating the urge to make further experiments and investigations. Forms will emerge which are not pre-determined, or with their inspirations rooted in the work of earlier cultures, and the artist's own creations will be original. He must, initially, allow himself to react to materials and be prepared for a reciprocal reaction to occur. His *thought* and *design* processes will be stimulated as he comes to terms with more involved problems; his self-discovered techniques and ways of working will be extended as he gains confidence in manipulating materials, and he will gradually come to terms with technical processes which will enable him to pursue his craftsmanship further. Reading of appropriate technical literature should be augmented by visits to local workshops where plastics are used in the production of sailing dinghies, canoes, caravans, or even household utensils, for first-hand knowledge can be acquired by watching craftsmen at work, and the discussion of technical procedures with experts can be an invaluable supplement to the experience of the person who is struggling alone. Indeed, the amateur will often receive 'offcuts' and scrap materials quite cheaply from such workshops and this can considerably extend his range of personal experimentation.

One easily obtainable plastic material is foam rubber which may be purchased from local hardware stores in both thin and thick coloured sheets.

It is soft, extremely pliable and has not as yet been fully explored as a sculptural material. This means that the field is open for sculptors who are prepared to experiment with three-dimensional foam rubber forms. It can be cut, squeezed, pulled, burnt and twisted into the most incredible shapes, and it is possible to fix it in a semi-permanent position with thread, glues and wire. The additional use of wood, wire, plaster or cement will give added permanency to an otherwise flexible, temporary kind of plastic, and, as a further development, the resultant shapes may be cast in other suitable materials.

Expanded polystyrene, which may be bought from local builders' merchants in large and small sheets (12 in. by 12 in. ceiling tiles, up to 8 ft. by 4 ft. panels, as well as other shapes and sizes) is excellent for quickly conceived structures. It may be so manipulated that its nature is changed, but once again the experimental approach should be emphasised. The artist may try squeezing, sawing, tearing, routing and hitting with a sharp or blunt instrument; he may burn it with a hot wire or soldering iron, which will cut through it cleanly, in producing the forms he has in mind; its surface may be textured by the application of certain adhesives which dissolve where they touch and leave interesting pattern qualities on the surface; and it may be further enhanced with paint, stains and dry colour. When making large constructions it is possible to attach sheets of this material together by means of glues and fixing wires (U-shapes made from soft florists' wire) pushed through the expanded polystyrene like nails into

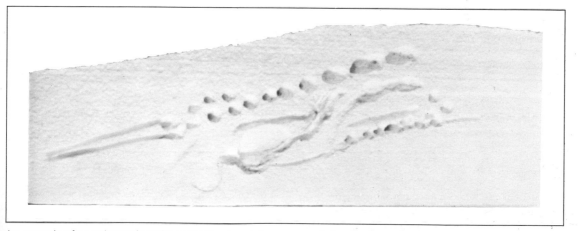

An example of experimental routings and burnings into an expanded polystyrene sheet.

wood. The addition of thin coats of plaster will add a fairly substantial outer skin and, indeed, such coverings strengthen sculptures which remain light and easy to handle.

Coating a polystyrene structure with plaster.

Yet another interesting way of working is to rout or burn shapes out of the expanded polystyrene sheet and then to use this as a mould into which cement or metals are poured. The moulded forms take on the sculptured shapes, and their accidentally-produced surface textures—which can often be most pleasant—become part of the finished structure. Styrofoam (the Registered Trademark of a material made by the D.O.W. Chemical Group of America) is a light plastic which is produced industrially by expanding polystyrene with methyl chloride gas. It is good for mould making because the molten metal will cause it to vaporize in the casting process, but it must be pointed out that there is a slight danger to health in using Styrofoam the cells of which sometimes trap a quantity of methyl chloride gas and care should be taken when trying this method (see Precautionary Notes issued by the manufacturers).

In his book *Sculpture in Plastics,* Nicholas Roukes deals at length with the two basic types of plastics which the sculptor is likely to use, and it is suggested that the reader requiring further information should read this and other similar books, some of which are listed in the bibliography (page 245) since there is not space for detail here. Roukes mentions thermoplastic resins which are softened by heat and harden when cold, and thermosetting plastics which are formed by the application of pressure and heat, and these

Two Yellows a completed sculpture in laminated Fibreglass made by a third year student, St. Mary's College, Cheltenham.

are most useful for structural work. He also propounds a number of techniques invaluable to sculptors working in resins, acrylic sheets and other forms of plastics. For those who are interested in using laminations, glass fibre reinforced polyester resins (better known by the more usual trade name of 'Fibreglass', which is strong, durable and yet light in weight) or who would like to learn how to cast in ciment fondu, Percy's authoritative *New Materials in Sculpture* should prove of value.

In conclusion, it must be stressed that the most interesting and often the most exciting 'plastic' imagery results from an uninhibited way of working which is not bound by the restrictions of traditional craft techniques. The artist should not be over-cautious. He must be prepared to make mistakes and to learn from these when producing three-dimensional work in a field that is relatively

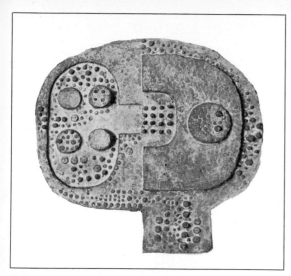

Relief sculpture cast in ciment fondu made by a student at Leicester College of Art and Design.

new and still open to individual developments. There are few restrictions or barriers to be surmounted, and this in itself should give the greatest encouragement to beginners.

Note: Some further remarks on the use of plastics in sculpture will be found in the chapter 'Sculpture in Various Media', page 220.

Expanded polystyrene relief panel in which the letter shapes were cut with a hot wire, made by the author.

Wood

Michael Laxton

Wood as a Material

Characteristics and Properties Though we know full well that trees serve as the natural source of wood it is easy to forget, when buying a wardrobe or making a simple stool, that what we are looking at once grew, was once alive! That wood is an organic material is probably the most significant factor in its subsequent use by man. For the disciplines which wood dictates stem from its own structural organisation. It has determined the shape of woodworking tools and even the manner in which we can manipulate and form wood.

The characteristics of wood are unique and individual even to itself, for no two specimens are identical. In visual terms alone, wood surpasses any other material in its beauty of colour and endless array of grain and figure marking. The combination of colour and figure – determined by species, locality and rate of growth – has stimulated craftsmen and artists alike to create some of the finest furniture and sculpture that man can

claim. In Fig. 1 some of the visual qualities of the more commonly used woods are recorded.

Wood has served man as a structural material for thousands of years, for in wood he found a strong material yet relatively light and fairly easy to work. The strength of wood is related to its cellular composition. If we liken a tree to a closely packed column of drinking straws, with little mechanical cohesion between the longitudinal straws, we can appreciate that the strength of a piece of wood is related to the direction of grain. Wood, then, is strong across the grain and weak along or parallel to its grain as the photographs below show.

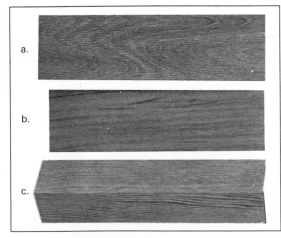

Fig. 1. a) Oak; b) Teak; c) Columbian Pine.

The relative strength of different species of wood is too complex to consider here, except to state that generally, the heavier the sample of wood then the stronger the sample will probably prove. In example, the weights of oak and pine offer us an indication as to their respective strength. The durability of wood – its resistance to decay from atmosphere and insect – broadly matches its weight/strength ratio, i.e. the stronger, the heavier, then the more likely the sample will resist decay. For example, oak will resist attack from moisture and insects for longer than common pine. Particular species do have particular qualities of resistance, e.g. teak – whose oily texture will resist water well and is commonly used in boat construction and as draining boards, etc. It is therefore possible to select a particular wood for your specific use. By carefully considering the qualities required and relating these to durability and future situation, wood can be seen as an extremely versatile material.

The last property that must be considered is the tendency of wood to take up moisture – to swell and to shrink. When a tree is felled, a large percentage of its weight is made up of water. Gradually, by being open to the air, or being artificially dried in a kiln, the original amount of water is reduced. By this process, wood becomes more stable and permits its successful use in a domestic situation. However, the tendency of wood to absorb moisture still remains, even after many years. If you move a piece of wood from your workshop indoors to a centrally heated environment, then that piece of wood will shrink, and maybe develop cracks. Basically, any sample piece of wood will eventually assume the level of moisture that is evident in the immediate atmosphere. Thus, an outside door will shrink and swell according to the time of the year.

Availability The conversion of the tree into usable and convenient planks and bulks of timber follows a fairly standard practice. The tree is sawn as in either of the two diagrams, Fig. 2, and then allowed to season, i.e. to dry out. In the case of some special hardwoods or when a particular usage of wood requires a low moisture content, the wood is kiln dried. In any event the sawn sizes are set as actual measurements, i.e. 1 in. 1½ in., 2 in., etc. After drying, the timber may be planed before reaching its destination. In the case of a 1 in. sawn plank, this will be reduced to

nearer ¾ in., but will still be classed and sold as 1 in. This is one of several points to remember when buying prepared timber and when you are designing.

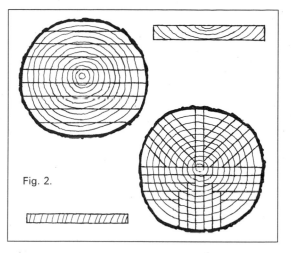

Fig. 2.

Man-Made Boards One of the most significant developments of recent years has been the employment of 'man-made boards'. These are all based on wood and all in some way increase the value or potential of wood. We can usefully group these 'boards' into two. Firstly that group in which we find plywood, blockboard and laminboard. Here, thin layers of wood are glued together, with each successive layer having its direction of grain at right angles to the previous one (Fig. 3). By this process not only can large sheets of varying thickness be produced, but by making use of the directional strength of timber, 'boards' of great strength can be achieved. Another advantage of building up a 'board' is that, as a result of the construction, these boards will resist to a large extent any movement through shrinkage and,

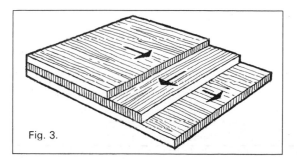

Fig. 3.

This kitchen interior by Heal and Son Ltd., shows how wood in a domestic setting gains interest through colour, texture and pattern.

lastly, can be faced with a high class veneer or even a plastic laminate, so increasing considerably their visual or surface value.

The appropriate use of these 'boards' will largely depend on the expected location and permitted expense. However, plywood is primarily used in thicknesses from $\frac{1}{8}$ in. to $\frac{1}{2}$ in. as door panels, backs of cabinets and drawer bottoms, etc.— though its potential as a three-dimensional constructional material in chair forms, etc. will be seen later. Blockboard and laminboard, coming usually in thicknesses from $\frac{1}{2}$ in. to 1 in., are used more as a constructional material in cabinets, as shelving and table tops, etc. The disadvantage here, as with all 'boards', is the rather unsatisfactory edge that is exposed on cutting—some provision, therefore, must be made to apply an edging or facing. The normal sheet sizes of ply-

woods, etc. range up to 8 ft. by 4 ft. and are available as interior, exterior or special marine qualities.

The second group of wood-based materials which we recognise as 'man-made boards' is seen in the form of hardboard and chipboard or particle board. Here the wood is shredded or chipped into small pieces which are then resin-glued under pressure to form sheets, the usual size being 8 ft. by 4 ft. and $\frac{1}{8}$ in. thick for hardboard and from $\frac{3}{8}$ in. to 1 in. for chipboard. These boards offer some of the same advantages as plywood and blockboard, except that they are unsuitable for outside use, do not have the same attractive appearance and need more care in their use as a constructional material. They do, however, serve as a cheaper base and can, as such, be used to great advantage.

Wood in Construction

Tools It is wrong to suppose that it is impossible to produce fine pieces of woodwork without an extensive kit of tools. There are, however, a number of essential tools which we must account for. A basic kit might therefore comprise:

Cross cut handsaw – used for cutting across boards and general purpose work (12–16 teeth per inch).

Tenon or Dovetail saw – used for general benchwork, cutting of joints, etc.

Coping saw – for various curved work and particular joint cutting. Saw blade can be set at any angle.

Chisels – bevelled edge 1 in., $\frac{3}{4}$ in., $\frac{1}{2}$ in., $\frac{1}{4}$ in. for joint work and general removal of waste wood.

Wooden Mallet – for use in conjunction with most chisel work.

Smoothing plane – used for achieving a fine, flat finish on basic woods. For larger work a jack plane may be needed.
Other basic tools would include a hammer, ruler, try square, hand drill and a screwdriver, rasp and file, several cramps, oilstone.

What is more essential than an exhaustive kit of tools is that those you have are used correctly and kept in good order. All makers' instructions and advice should be carefully observed.

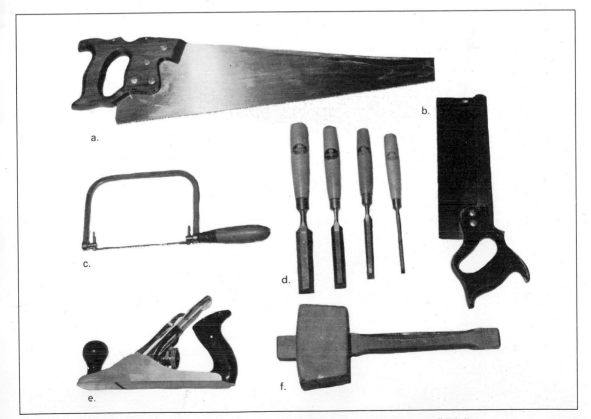

a) Cross cut handsaw; b) Tenon saw; c) Coping saw; d) Chisels; e) Smoothing plane; f) Mallet.

The basic drill with attachments for a) drilling; b) sanding; c) turning; and d) sawing.

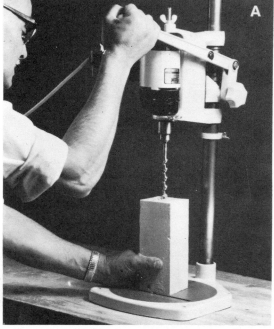

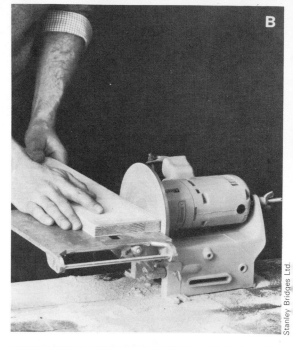

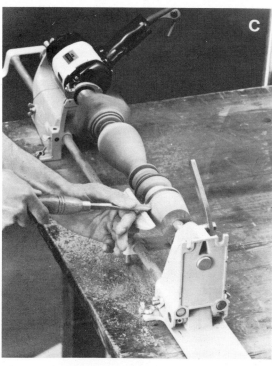

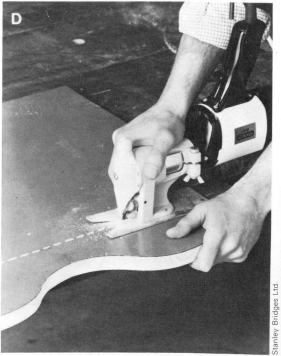

With a basic kit of tools available, the next essential requirement is a bench or sound surface on which to work, a surface which can take a standard woodworker's vice or one of the various 'devices' that are available and can be used in place of a vice.

Stanley vice No. 5702 which can be fitted to the bench or any flat working surface.

The position with regard to 'power tools' has changed dramatically in recent years and there is now available a wide selection to choose from, offering a range of attachments for particular uses. By far the most useful is the basic power drill which can in turn, with attachments, be used for drilling, sanding, sawing, etc. Here again one cannot emphasise enough the necessity to read fully the manufacturer's instructions and act accordingly. Never try to overload or overwork power tools. This is the time when accidents can occur. Well used, however, power tools can be a great asset to the woodworker, both in terms of speed of production and in the quality of work that can be achieved.

Adhesives The advent of plastics and their introduction into the glue industry has produced many new adhesives, many of remarkable strength and ease of use. Two of these glues stand out and are worthy of note.

1. P.V.A. This is sold as a thick liquid ready for use, white in colour, becomes colourless on evaporation and being 'set'. Easy to use, strong, clean and no waste. Usually requires about 4 hours to achieve full strength.
2. Synthetic resin glues — available as
   (a) A thick, clear liquid and a liquid hardener.
   (b) A powder that is mixed with water.

Here, again, these glues are remarkably strong, can be used for exterior or marine use, and are fairly easy to work with.

The traditional animal glue, sold as beads which have in turn to be dissolved and heated, still remains a powerful and versatile glue, but cannot compete with the new adhesives in terms of convenience and ease of use.

The process of 'gluing up' a job is one of the most important phases of making an item in woodwork. Always assemble and cramp up the structure 'dry', that is without glue, and ensure that the joints go together without undue pressure. Have cramping blocks ready, cramps available and set to correct length and also a piece of clean damp rag to wipe off excess glue. Go through the whole procedure first as a 'run through' and make sure you are organised and really ready to start gluing.

Methods of Joining Since his first interest in the the use of wood, man has been confronted with the necessity of having to join separate pieces of wood together in order to produce the desired item or structure. The development of 'joints', as we call them, has been a slow and deliberate process based on a sound and intelligent understanding of the very nature of wood itself. The basic requirement of any joint is to provide a *strong and durable fixing*, and from our knowledge of wood as a material we can also say that:

1. Any joint or construction must take account of the direction of grain of the pieces of wood. In order to do this the pieces are 'mated' together. That is, a section from one piece of wood is removed so that the second piece can fit or mate into it. The resulting joint is then glued or fixed in some way such as screwing or nailing.
2. The proportion of any particular half of a joint should not be such as to weaken its counterpart. Each 'mate' of the joint should therefore be approximately equal in the amount of wood

to be removed and should present equal surface for gluing. (Fig. 4.)

3. Where possible a joint should add to its own strength and bearing capacity, by the introduction of shoulders. (Fig. 5.)

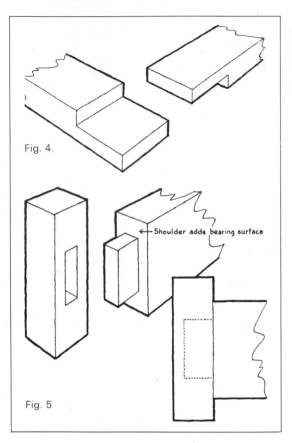

Fig. 4.

←Shoulder adds bearing surface

Fig. 5

If we look at the basic construction forms, we usually group these as follows:

(a) Flat frame construction – doors, picture frames, etc.
(b) Open frame construction – tables, chairs, etc.
(c) Carcass or cabinet constructions.

Flat Frame Construction The procedure for the jointing of frame structure is the simplest and quickest of all joint making. The common joints used are the Lap joint, Cross halving, the Bridle joint, and possibly the Mitre joint. Most of these joints can be achieved with the use of the tenon saw alone. If a chisel has to be used, as you might in a bridle joint, be sure to work from

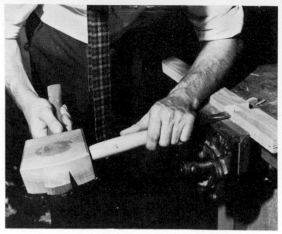

Cutting a bridle joint.

both sides, and take a little out at a time. All framing joints mentioned will need some form of fixing, by gluing, nailing or screwing, or even dowelling – a simple process of drilling through the assembled joint and inserting a locking peg or dowel.

A very important factor to consider in respect of frame construction, is to ensure you have assembled them 'square', that is that all corners register as a right angle. A very quick and efficient way to ensure this is to measure the diagonals and, if different, adjust until they read the same.

Open Frame Construction The most common and widely used joint in open frame construction is the mortise and tenon. There are many variations on this versatile joint, some of which are shown. (Fig. 6.) The making of this joint is distinct from those previously mentioned in that a mortise or hole has to be made in order to accept the tenon. The easiest way to do this is first to remove as much wood as possible with a series of drilled holes – then clean out with a bevelled edged chisel.

A problem that often arises in open construction is the necessity, for instance, of having to join two rails to one leg in order to achieve a three-dimensional corner. The problem being to make a strong joint without taking too much wood away from the leg. By far the most satisfactory solution is to offset or stagger the rails. Two convenient ways of doing this are shown in Fig. 7.

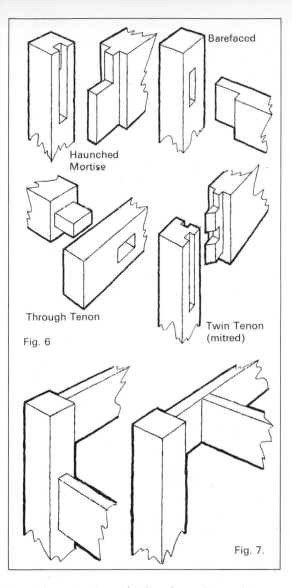

Barefaced

Haunched
Mortise

Through Tenon

Twin Tenon
(mitred)

Fig. 6

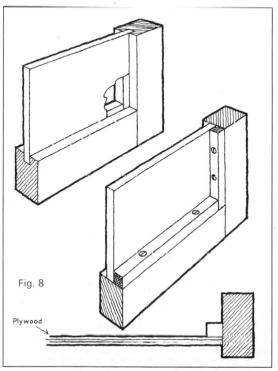

Carcass or Cabinet Construction Probably the most difficult woodwork construction is that of building a cabinet. Here, the very real problem of shrinkage and warping of timber can cause considerable frustration. Provided, however, one recognises what might happen and takes evading action, cabinets can be built quite satisfactorily. The obvious way to build a cabinet might appear to be simply to join together four planks of sufficient width. However, the shrinkage across the width of a board will give trouble and, unless you have considerable experience, to build a cabinet using solid boards wider than 9 in. is inadvisable.

There are, however, two methods which can be employed to build cabinets of some depth. The first is, in effect, to build up a skeleton frame using either flat frame or open frame construction and then to in-fill the open sides with plywood or hardboard. The best way to insert the panel is to form a groove around the frame. If you have not the facilities to do this, it is quite adequate to lay the panel on fillets as shown (Fig. 8).

A second method of building a carcass of some depth is to use man-made boards, i.e. plywood or

Fig. 7.

Fig. 8

Plywood

Apart from the large family of mortise and tenon joints, a very useful joint for open frames is the already mentioned dowelled joint. This time the dowels or pegs act in lieu of a tenon. Two dowels are necessary to achieve sufficient gluing area and to stop any tendency to twist. Although at first sight this joint would appear an easy one, the problem of accurate drilling to ensure that the dowels and holes are correctly placed, requires careful marking out. Here a very useful addition to your tool kit might well be a dowel jig.

blockboard, or even chipboard. Here the process of jointing can be fairly simple. By using a corner piece, suitably shaped to take the appropriate size of board, a pleasant looking and very effective cabinet can be made quite quickly (Fig. 9).

The other way of using man-made boards would be to use K/D fittings (Knock down). These are easily fitted and do have in their favour the facility that allows the carcass to be taken apart at any time and reassembled, maybe in a different form.

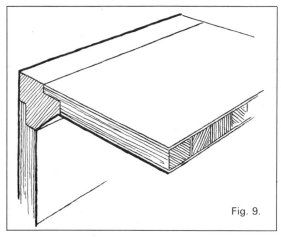

Fig. 9.

Joining by Fixing Nails and screws are widely used in constructional woodwork and, correctly applied, can be a most useful asset to the woodworker. In the use of either nails or screws their placing in relation to the edge of the wood is very important — too near and splitting will occur. In the instance of screwing, always drill a clearance hole through the top piece of wood. This allows the screw to pull the pieces together and be effective as a fixing method (Fig. 10).

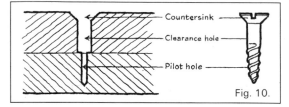

Countersink

Clearance hole

Pilot hole

Fig. 10.

Methods of Forming The fact that wood is flexible to a certain degree, and that under certain conditions can be bent, allows the use of wood to extend into curved work. Normally, to cut a curved member out of the solid plank, implies weakness, because at some point 'short grain' must be evident, whereas by steam bending or lamination (the two methods of forming) the direction of grain still follows the actual form. (See illustrations below.)

Steam Bending By subjecting wood to a source of steam, the fibres of the timber become supple and able to flex. At this point the specimen is removed from the steam and quickly bent and held in position by a jig until the sample has dried out. After drying the wooden rail or chair back will remain as in the bent form.

Lamination As well as giving a curved form, lamination, by virtue of the 'glue lines', ensures an extremely strong member. The process here is to cut thin strips of wood, usually $\frac{1}{8}$ in. thick, which by themselves are flexible enough to take up the required bend. These strips are then glued and pressed together in a mould of the desired shape. When the glue is set the lamination can be removed and the mould used again.

Steam bending wood around mould. Note steel strip being used to pull wood on to mould.

Laminated wood being removed from mould after glueing.

Finishing Although modern technology has given us many excellent finishes such as polyurethane varnish and cellulose, which in themselves have removed much of the tedious work usually associated with finishing and polishing, it is the preparation of the wood surface prior to applying the finish that is the all important factor in achieving a good final surface.

Once the job has been assembled and glued up, the first step is to remove any surplus glue and to level off any jointing that needs attention. Next, a firm rub with a fine glass-paper, making sure to rub along the direction of the grain. Finally, remove surplus dust with a soft brush or rag.

Cellulose Lacquer Cellulose is a quick drying, clear lacquer which can be applied by brush. Several thin coats being better than one thick one, rubbing down lightly with steel wool or a very fine glass-paper in between each coat. After the final coat cut down with steel wool again and rub in a thin coat of wax.

Polyurethane Recent advances in plastics and their introduction into the paint industry has produced some first-class finishes that are easy to apply, clear and have a final hard surface, resistant to scratches and staining. Polyurethane is one of these which is applied by brush and allowed to dry for about four hours. Always rub down in between coats and apply wax on final coat if desired. Polyurethane is available not only in gloss but in a matt and satin finish.

Painting Any item of woodwork can also be painted if desired, and in fact much contemporary furniture is painted in bright pure colours. Here, as with clear finishes, the preparation is all important and a good coat of primer and undercoat are essential before applying the top coat. The virtue of the matt and satin finishes which are currently available is that they do not show up the blemishes or dust as the gloss finishes do, as well as giving a softer and less clinical surface.

Wood in Use

The extraordinary variety of use to which man has employed wood is clear evidence both of the versatile nature of wood and of man's own innate ingenuity. Man's use of wood is a study in itself; here we can only outline some of the considerations and possibilities which are relevant today and confine our comments to the domestic use of wood – furniture, with a brief mention of the use of wood in the construction of children's toys.

Design Considerations The importance of thoughtful organisation and careful planning in design work cannot be overstressed. An ill-considered step or a lack of thought in design can not only cause frustration and annoyance, but can cost a considerable amount of money and waste of material. We can usefully group the essential design considerations as:

1. *Utilitarian application* – the use to which the item is intended.
2. *Intended situation* – the actual position or environment into which the piece of furniture will be placed.
3. *Available resources* – tools and work facilities that can be expected; level of experience and skill available.
4. *Cost* – level of expenditure that can be allotted to project; purchase of materials, etc.

Utilitarian Application At first sight it may seem obvious that a chair is to be sat on and that a china cupboard will have to house cups and saucers. However, the stated use of the project must be examined further. How will it be used? Who will use it? For how long will it be used? How often? etc. Once you begin to question in some detail the very nature and *implications* of the project, it will be seen that a number of important factors emerge which may at first seem unimportant or, maybe, are not even considered. From these questions will come a series of essential requirements, a specification in terms of measurements, basic form and they may even suggest materials to be used. For instance, a necessity to withstand the effects of heat and spilt alcohol will indicate a special surface.

Intended Situation As any piece of furniture will ultimately reside within a domestic environment, due consideration of the structure and organisation of that situation seems advisable. What relationship will the new piece have to form with the existing furniture? Does it have to 'fit in', or can it serve as a contrast? What sort of room and how big is it? What is the decor?, etc. Once again, our questions when answered will give us additional information and conditions which will help to formulate our design.

Available Resources As the ideas begin to grow it is as well to consider early on to what extent your design must be disciplined in order to match up to your workshop facilities, your own experience and the time you have available. Always plan within your capacity and be sure of success. This in turn will increase your experience and confidence, so allowing you to be more ambitious with the next project. Better to be simple and succeed, than complicated and fail.

Cost The estimation of the cost must also be an early consideration, as well as the local availability of the required material. The contemporary fashionable use of Teak as a furniture timber may present problems of availability, as well as being high in price. However, the use of Afromosia or even Iroko will give a like appearance at a much reduced price and be more readily obtainable. There is also a current trend to use the lighter woods such as Ash, Beech and Oak, all of which are good timbers to work with and are reasonable in price. Some of the softwoods, such as Columbian Pine and even a good quality White or Red Deal, given a suitable hard finish such as polyurethane, can also become very effective as a timber for furniture making. Whatever the wood, think well about your cutting list. Is there another way to prevent too much waste? This is a particularly relevant point in the use of plywood or blockboard. Lastly, do not forget to add a percentage for finishing materials.

Modular furniture such as these storage units designed by Heal and Son Ltd. are practical, rearrangeable and can be added to to suit the requirements of modern living.

Occasional table made entirely from one standard section of wood.

Current Trends In order to appreciate the developing trends in furniture it is necessary to at least recognise the basic factors which influence and are instrumental for change. One of these, architecture, has always had a very marked influence on furniture and rightly so, for furniture ultimately serves within the environment of architecture. Architecture in turn serves society, its needs and its patterns of behaviour. From this we recognise that the 'manner' in which we live will to a large extent determine that which we need and use in our daily life. Today, we lead a less formal life where relaxation and comfort are important considerations. Our demands on furniture are different from yesterday and therefore new forms are developed as a natural process. Emphasis is shifted and even our expectations of furniture change. Today we expect our furniture to be compact, light and versatile, even capable of re-arrangement.

While we see the influence of architecture on the style and configuration of contemporary furniture, we must also recognise the significance of the progress in its industrial production. The economic need to produce furniture in quantity has assisted the rationalisation of construction. The simplicity in form and lack of ostentatious decoration which we uphold today as virtues of good design, are largely compatible with large scale commercial production where handwork must be kept to a minimum.

Some of the most interesting developments in contemporary furniture are the growing use of colour, the interplay of textures and wide use of new materials.

An obvious post-war development in domestic architecture has been the building of smaller and more compact houses. This has in turn produced the need for furniture which is not only compact but versatile. Modular/unit furniture is an expression of this need and today a growing percentage of furniture is produced using some element of modular construction. Here, the exercise is to produce furniture that can inter-relate or build up by using a common unit, measurement or proportion. One of the most important assets of this system is that furniture can be extended or added to, such as storage units, as and when required.

While the introduction of new materials continues to grow in the furniture industry, wood will still continue to be its basic material. It is interesting to observe how the challenge of new materials has in turn brought about not only a new interest in certain woods, but also the enterprising use of plywood in chair forms – a development very worthy of further examination.

Toys in Wood The use of wood as a suitable material from which to build toys goes back to the early civilisations when small, hand-carved, wooden figures, animals, etc. were used not only in play by children, but also served as symbols in various ritual and religious activities. Through the ages a select number of wooden toys have remained favourites, such as the rocking horse, Noah's ark and the dolls' house, as well as the traditional wooden dolls of Austria and Scandinavia. More recently, the garage, the wheelbarrow, and an endless array of vehicles of transport have been introduced.

This wooden duck on castors could easily be adapted to make at home.

The making of wooden toys is a comparatively easy procedure needing few joints or sophisticated construction. The intelligent use of nails, screws and glue, in relation to plywood and small scraps of wood, can result in toys that give immense pleasure to children. Painted in bright colours (non-toxic paints!) and free from needless detail, toys are best when simple, strong and stable.

Building bricks are simple and attractive toys to make.

Wood in Sculpture

While the utilitarian use of wood has dominated man's application of this versatile material, he appreciated very early on the suitability of wood as a material through which he could express himself and his ideas. From the moment tools were available men have whittled, carved and formed images, impressions and expressions of their way of life. The natural warmth and beauty of wood are enough in themselves to inspire many men which, when coupled with its relative ease of working, makes wood one of the most stimulating and suitable materials for sculpture.

Undoubtedly the success of artists to use wood in sculptural form can be attributed to their ability to understand and appreciate the very nature of wood, its disciplines and its character. Once this recognition is made, a *rapport* and sympathy grows between artist and his material. From this point his sculpture, whether symbolic or realistic, will retain that relationship — the quality of wood.

The newcomer must learn quickly to accept and develop the suggestions made to him by his wood. He must learn to develop its grain and use its variations in texture and colour. Before, therefore, attempting to carve a definite image, far better to spend your first attempts at carving by getting to know the character of wood. One such introduction to wood is through a 'touch form'. Here the resultant form is suggested by the wood while you, the tool of its execution, react to the grain, texture and colour. The simple objective is to create a form sympathetic to handling, exposing as far as

possible the natural interest and inherent qualities of the wood. Confine your first attempts to convex form, in other words *shape*, rather than carve. Avoid sharp edges and too many changes of direction and keep it simple.

One of the first problems that arise, even in the simple exercise of the touch form, is the difficulty of shaping or carving 'in the round'. Because we can only work on one side or facet of our sculpture at a time, it is all too easy to forget the hidden surfaces. But because our form is three dimensional we should always be aware of the unseen relationships if we hope to form a sculpture that has a unity, rather than four independent sides. To overcome this problem in the initial stages, keep moving the wood around to avoid overworking any one part.

Though the professional wood carver may possess an impressive array of gouges and carving chisels, much excellent work can be achieved using a very modest collection of tools. Select only two or three gouges to start with: $1\frac{1}{2}$ in., 1 in. and a shallow $\frac{1}{2}$ in., these will be the most useful, and it is surprising how versatile you will find them. One or two good rasps and files are also a first essential as is the popular 'Surform', an excellent tool for wood-carving, being both rasp and plane in one.

Non-figurative If by non-figurative we mean abstract, namely not representational, we have only to examine samples of driftwood, old trees in decay or even large root formations, to appreciate that nature itself can be an effective sculptor. Through the natural process of erosion or decay wood is often 'wasted' or 'shaped' leaving forms which, though we may hesitate to refer to them as sculpture, do have a sculptural meaning and are worth our observation. Nature illustrates how the weaker wood is wasted or worn away, how small and inappropriate forms are broken off or integrated into the basic shape; she appreciates the character of timber.

If abstract wood carving is to have a meaning then the quality of the wood you expose by the chosen sculptural form is a prime consideration: for why else carve in wood? The wood is your inspiration; it gives you an idea, which you take up and develop or, just as valid, the wood seems 'suitable' for your idea.

Touch forms.

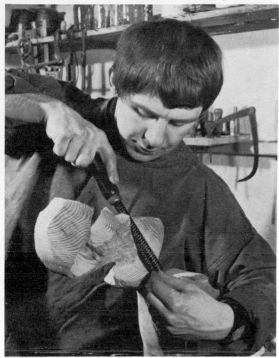

The Surform tool in use.

Natural form is natural sculpture.

subject and material. Forms will have to adjust and accommodate the material, as the image has to be compromised to fit the character and nature of the wood. Never 'force' an image on to the wood for it will surely reject it or wear it very unhappily.

Figurative Representational or figurative wood carving differs considerably from that of abstract work. In abstract work a compromise and balance is achieved between idea and material. In representational carving, however, there exists a third and very powerful consideration – the image. The strength of the image, whether it be of a bird, a fish, or human form, can, because it is so familiar, overcome and dominate our attention. Thus, wood can become incidental and often even inappropriate as a sculptural material.

Subject matter should be chosen with utmost care and due understanding of the selected wood. Avoid figures, whether animal or human, that have exaggerated, flamboyant or extended form. For example, while a seated squirrel or rabbit might be an appropriate subject, it is doubtful whether a giraffe or standing stork would make a satisfactory wood carving. Even with a suitably chosen subject the danger of dominance by the image can remain if a reconciliation is not made between

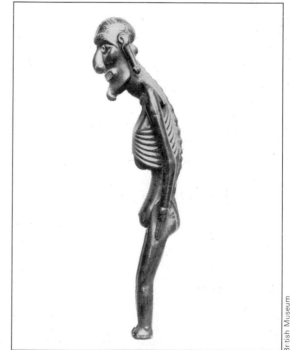

Early 19th century wood figure representing an Ancestor from Easter Island.

'Sculpture' assembled from a number of identically shaped units.

Sculpture by Assembly The concept of sculpture by assembly revolves around the idea of 'building up' or 'putting together' of a number of independent units in order to concentrate attention on to the relationship of those forms, whether joined or separate. The opportunities for an imaginative and individual expression in wood grows, as now woods can be interchanged, colours and textures used to counterbalance or complement; quite apart from the almost unlimited range of form which can be employed.

Just as with the newcomer to carving, where the touch form provides a useful initial project, so an appropriate introduction to sculpture by construction or assembly is to examine the potential of a number of identical units. To observe the wide variety of form and spatial interest that can be achieved by the use of a simple repetitive unit is a rewarding experience. This can gradually be extended until a whole range of forms can be used with confidence.

The excitement and satisfaction of using wood in sculpture can only in the final analysis be appreciated by the artist himself: when he grasps that simple and rewarding understanding of the quality of wood.

Hollow Form with White. Elegy III by Barbara Hepworth.

98

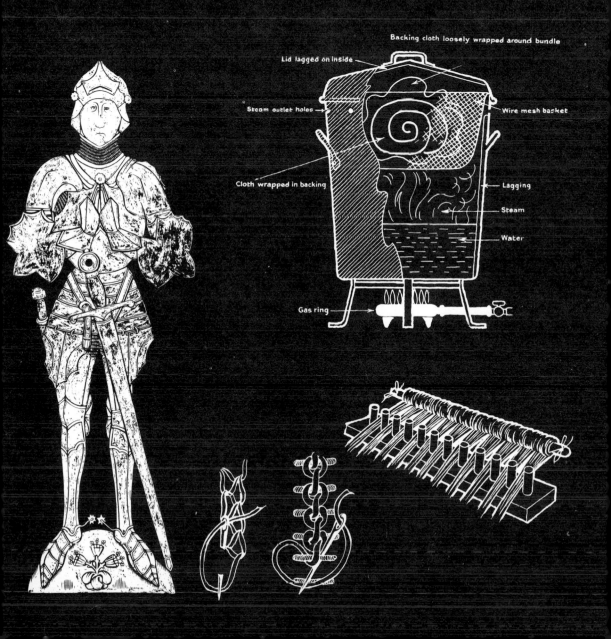

Backing cloth loosely wrapped around bundle

Lid lagged on inside

Steam outlet holes

Wire mesh basket

Cloth wrapped in backing

Lagging

Steam

Water

Gas ring

Basic Sewing

Irene Barker

Three virtues are required to produce good needlework: perseverance, patience and practice. All these are scarce in the rush and bustle of modern life, both at home and in schools; therefore they must be applied by the newcomer to the craft to projects which are quickly completed and give a feeling of success and satisfaction.

Tools and Equipment The old adage 'a bad workman blames his tools' contains great truth. A good needlewoman requires good tools, and they must be readily available and in 'apple-pie' order. Nothing is more irritating than finding, when you are ready to make a new dress, create a fabric picture or a piece of embroidery or, at a mundane level, to replace a button or mend a torn sheet, that the scissors are blunt or missing, or the only available needle is a 'crowbar' or has an eye

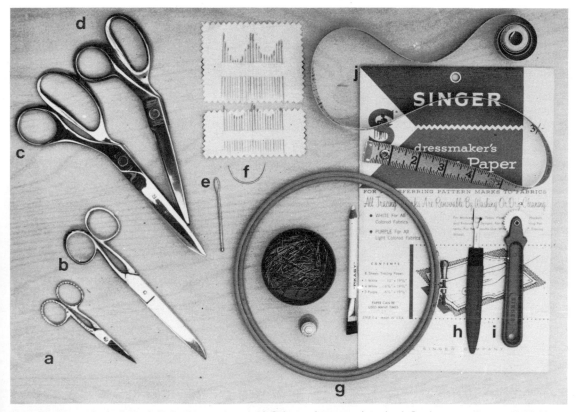

Basic equipment including: a) Embroidery scissors; b) Scissors for general work; c) Cutting out scissors; d) Pinking shears; e) Spring bodkin; f) Upholsterer's needle; g) Embroidery hoop; h) Unpicker; i) Tracing wheel; j) Tracing paper.

so fine that a magnifying glass is necessary to thread it. A well-equipped work-box (even if it is only a cardboard shoe-box) is essential. See that it contains sharp scissors — not just one pair, but a large pair for cutting out, a medium-sized pair for general work, a small pair for snipping ends and, if possible, a pair of buttonhole scissors. Make sure that you own a bodkin and a selection of needles — sharps, betweens and darners. A box of pins, sharp and rust-free, are also needed. Most important of all, buy a thimble. Half-an-hour spent in the local haberdashery store will teach a great deal about the tools of the trade.

In addition, the good needlewoman needs some of the tools associated with the artist: sharp pencils (HB and B), a ruler, a supply of plain paper, graph paper, tracing and carbon paper, newspaper and a sketchbook for jotting down ideas and sketches as and when they occur. A set square and a protractor are also useful.

Fig. 1.

Having assembled the tools, make sure that they remain sacred. Do not let anyone borrow the scissors for jobs in the garage or garden, and prevent them rummaging in your work-box for an elastic band, the Sellotape, or a safety-pin, etc.

Plain Sewing Today, the sewing machine has reduced the necessity for plain sewing. No longer are women compelled to spend long hours making every garment and household article by hand with minute and even stitches. In spite of this, a knowledge of plain sewing is still of value as articles made by machine frequently need hand-finishing. Hand-sewing, though, still brings to mind pricked fingers and slow hard labour. This need not be so if the fabric and needle are correctly positioned and a thimble used. Thimbles are made in metal and plastic. The metal ones are preferred as they are safer and more durable. The thimble is worn on the 2nd finger of the sewing hand, and must fit comfortably. Position the hands as shown in Fig. 1, and use the top of the thimble to push against the eye of the needle so that the entire needle is inserted into and through the fabric. All that is now required to complete the stitch is for the thumb and forefinger to pick up the needle and pull through the thread — all the expected effort and sore fingers are prevented by the correct use of a thimble. With practice, it is possible to sew to an even rhythm.

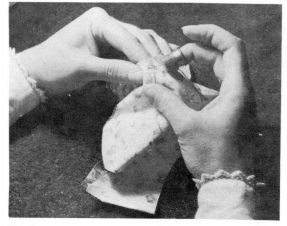

Fig. 2.

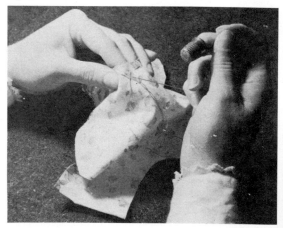

Avoid a too long or short thread; too long wastes

Fig. 3.

time in pulling through and is liable to knot, too short means frequent casting on and off and re-threading. A comfortable chair and good lighting, preferably daylight, are also aids to plain sewing. Obviously, it is impossible to arrange all sewing in daylight hours and it is worth purchasing or making a special table lamp which can throw light on to the work below eye level to prevent eyestrain.

Plain Sewing Stitches

Tacking or basting This is a quickly-worked temporary stitch which holds the fabric in place and prevents slipping while the permanent stitching (hand or machine) is worked. A line of tacking may also form a guide to mark the exact line of the permanent stitches. Tacking holds a garment together for the initial fittings. Never commence with an unsightly knot, two firm stitches on the spot are better. Adapt the size of the stitches to the fabric and to the strength you require. Where possible avoid machining over the cotton as this makes removal difficult.

Running stitch This stitch has three main uses. It can be used to join two pieces of fabric, it can

be worked and then pulled to form gathers, and it can be used as a decoration, in which case it becomes an embroidery stitch. It is worked from right to left, the stitches should be small, and even and the space between the stitches equal to the stitches themselves. One stitch at a time is wise in spite of the temptation to pick up half a dozen on the needle at once. Commence with two stitches on the spot.

Back stitch This is another stitch which will join two pieces of fabric. It is slow to work but very strong. When worked perfectly it has the appearance of a line of machining and, indeed, is the hand-sewing stitch which machining replaced. Many bitter tears have been shed by Victorian misses slaving over back stitch. Then lines of it were used to ornament the cuffs and collars of hand-made shirts! Begin with two stitches on the spot and work from right to left. First take one running stitch forward, with the next stitch go *back* (hence the name) with the needle point into the end of the first running stitch, preferably down exactly the same hole in the fabric, now take a stitch *forward* equal to twice the length of the stitch. Repeat.

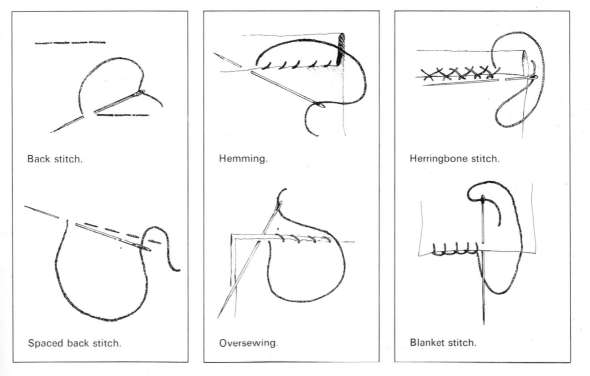

Back stitch.

Hemming.

Herringbone stitch.

Spaced back stitch.

Oversewing.

Blanket stitch.

Spaced back stitch As its name implies this is worked in precisely the same manner except that the needle does not go back into the previous stitch. It is not quite so strong as back stitch but is more unobtrusive. It is used to insert zips by hand when an almost invisible effect is desired.

Hemming This stitch is used to fix a folded edge. It may be the folded edge of an actual hem, or the folded edge of a crossway strip facing or binding, or the folded edge of a cuff, a pocket or a mundane necessary patch. Commence at the right-hand end by running the thread inside the fold and taking two small stitches on the spot on the fold itself. Hemming is a V-shaped stitch. One side of the V is formed by the thread and the other side by the inserted sloping needle. The stitches must be small and even.

Slip hemming This type of hemming is the one usually used on dress hems, as when it is well worked it is almost invisible. It gets its name from the fact that the needle slips along inside the folded edge, only emerging to make a minute V-shaped stitch visible just below the fold.

Herringbone stitch This stitch is worked on a once-folded edge to neaten and hold in place the raw edge. This stitch too may be used for decorative effects. Work from left to right. Commence by running the end of the thread under the folded edge and work two very small back stitches on the spot.

Oversewing and overcasting These two are the same. Their names vary according to where and how the stitches are worked. Oversewing joins two folded edges together and can be worked on the right or wrong side. Overcasting is worked on a raw edge to prevent fraying.

Loop stitch or blanket stitch Loop stitch is often called blanket stitch and is worked from left to right. It can be worked over a raw edge, a once-folded edge, or a twice-folded edge (a hem) or it may be worked as a decorative stitch. The edge of the fabric is held with the thumb on top and the stitch taken with the needle pointing to the worker. In this way gravity forms a loop and all that is needed is to pull the needle through the loop thus formed. These days few people blanket stitch their own blankets but many other applications will be found for this useful stitch.

Buttonhole stitch This stitch is frequently confused with blanket or loop stitch but a buttonhole so worked would not be as satisfactory as if the correct stitch was chosen. Buttonhole stitch has a *knot* instead of a simple loop. It is worked from left to right usually on a raw edge which should be uppermost in the hand, and the row of knots which are formed, side by side, protect the raw edge from fraying and wear. Insert the needle the required depth and taking the double thread from the eye of the needle go around and under the point, anti-clockwise. When the needle is pulled through this twisted loop, a figure of eight can be observed in the cotton. When this 'eight' is pulled tight a knot is formed.

Buttonholes Buttonholes are most conveniently cut using special buttonhole scissors. These have a special blade with a hollowed edge which allows the hole to be cut without damaging the edge of the garment.

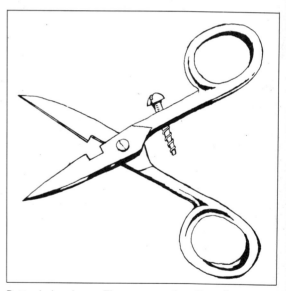

Buttonhole scissors. The screw can be adjusted according to the length of cut required.

Another method is to fold the fabric in half, snip the centre, open out and extend the snip to a slit the required length. A buttonhole may also be cut with a sharp pointed pair of scissors by swivelling the point of the blade until a small round hole forms and then extend this to a slit. The size of the buttonhole should equal the diameter of the button plus one eighth of an inch. Buttonholes may be worked horizontally or vertically on garments. Sometimes on a checked or striped fabric it may be necessary to work them diagonally to blend with the pattern on the fabric.

Buttonholes are almost always worked on double fabric. They usually have a round end which takes the pull of the button and a square end which is ornamental and keeps the buttonhole in shape. Feminine garments button right side over left side and garments for men and boys button the reverse way (probably a hangover from the day when pistols were kept in the inside left breast pocket — hazardous I should think, but convenient for a fast right-hand draw!)

Buttonhole stitch is also used to attach press fasteners and hooks and eyes, three or four stitches in each hole.

Basic Processes

Seams A seam joins two pieces of fabric. There are four seams in general use, and it is important to be able to choose the most suitable for a particular purpose.

Plain or open seam Place the two pieces of fabric together, right sides touching, make sure the raw edges are level. Pin, tack and stitch (hand or machine) parallel with the raw edge. The commercial pattern companies make the seam allowance $\frac{5}{8}$ in. wide (16 mm.).

Using the point of the iron, open the seam flat on the wrong side. The raw edges must be neatened by overcasting, loop stitch, edge-machining, zig-zag stitch using a swing needle machine, or — the friend of those in a hurry — pinking shears.

French seam This seam completely encloses the raw edges, is strong but leaves a ridge on the wrong side. This limits its use to thin fabrics.

Place the two pieces of fabric together wrong sides touching, right sides on the outside. Pin, tack and stitch. This now appears as if a mistake has been made as the raw edges are of course showing on the right side of work. Don't panic but trim the raw edges as narrow as you dare or the fabric dictates. Press open this trimmed seam. Turn the fabric so that the wrong side faces the

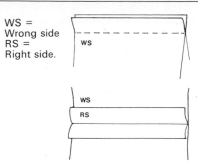

WS = Wrong side
RS = Right side.

Plain seam.

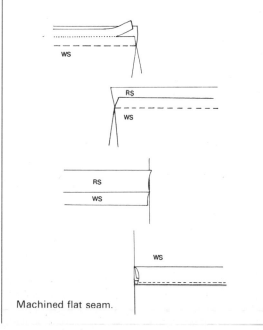

French seam.

Machined flat seam.

worker. Fold back the seam along the stitching thus enclosing the raw edges. Pin, tack and machine just below where the raw edges can be felt, or seen if held up to the light.

Machined flat seam This seam is well named; it is strong as it has two rows of machining and all the raw edges are enclosed. It is used on garments which take hard wear and washing, for instance shirts and blouses, pyjamas, jeans, boiler suits, overalls and some children's garments. Like the lapped seam which follows it is all worked on the right side.

Place the two pieces of fabric together wrong sides touching, right sides outside. Take the full seam allowance and seam. Trim the turning which is the back of the garment. Press the seam open. Turn the wider seam allowance from the front, into a hem over the back. Machine the edge of the hem. The finished seam is quite flat on right and wrong sides.

Lapped or overlaid seam This is used to join yokes and to set frills. The stitching of the seam may be close to the folded edge, or sometimes well away from it so that a mock tuck is formed to outline the stitching.
Basically, one piece of fabric having a folded edge and called the 'overlay' is placed flat on the second piece called the 'underlay'. They are then stitched together on the right side. On the wrong side neaten the raw edges by one of the methods described for plain seams.

Disposal of fullness All dressmaking from simple garments for beginners to the grandest creation has one main problem — to convert flat fabric to fit and flatter round people, to change two dimensions to three. This problem solved, the garment also has to be comfortable and to allow movement. Obviously, sports wear needs more movement space than formal wear. There are four processes which dispose of fullness: darts, pleats, tucks and gathers.

Darts A dart is a fold of fabric which is stitched down tapering to a point towards the fuller part of the figure. The point of the dart must be as fine as possible so that the finished dart when pressed is smooth and inconspicuous. The last few stitches at the point are parallel to the fold, and the very last one is off the edge.

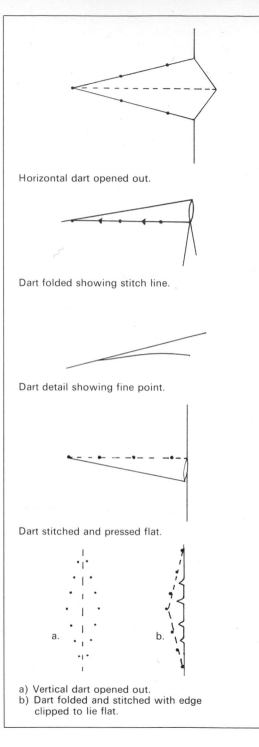

Horizontal dart opened out.

Dart folded showing stitch line.

Dart detail showing fine point.

Dart stitched and pressed flat.

a) Vertical dart opened out.
b) Dart folded and stitched with edge clipped to lie flat.

Horizontal darts are pressed downwards and vertical darts towards the centre. In a thick fabric cut the dart open and press it flat. Sometimes a dart is pointed at both ends then it must be snipped at the centre to allow it to be pressed flat.

Pleats A pleat is a fold of fabric of any width held in place by another piece of fabric at right-angles to it. This may be a bodice, yoke, cuff or band. Pleats can be left unpressed to hang in loose folds, or pressed to give sharp edges. There are three main types of pleating: knife pleats which have their folded edges pointing in one direction; inverted pleats which are in fact two knife pleats pointing towards each other; and box pleats which are two knife pleats pointing away from each other. A quick way to solve a pleat problem is to take a length of paper and fold and crease to obtain the desired effect. When the paper is opened out it is easy to measure how much fabric to allow.

Gathers To gather literally means to draw together or collect in a mass, like a bunch of flowers, all the fine stems held vertically. Gathers are really minute pleats and may be worked by hand using running stitches. Cast on very strongly, a knot and several stitches on the spot. Use thread that will not snap when pulled. Work if possible across the weft threads. Two or three rows $\frac{1}{4}$ in. apart are better than one. Hold all three threads and pull gently but firmly easing the gathers along with your thumb-nail.

Machine gathering is less irksome. Set the machine to a long stitch, 6 or 8 stitches to the inch. Work two rows on the right side, the first on the seam line and the second a quarter of an inch away from it nearer the raw edge. Pull the threads on the wrong side. These gathers are easy to arrange and do not slip as much as hand-worked gathers. The amount of fullness is dictated by personal preference, fashion or the amount of fabric available — 'cutting your coat according to your cloth'. Half as much fabric again as the finished width gives slight fullness, twice as much is an average and three times as much is generous.

Smocking is rows of gathers worked by hand with great precision which are then held in place by versions of stem stitch.

Tucks A tuck is a fold of fabric of any width which is held in place by a line of stitching (hand or

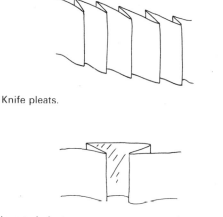

Knife pleats.

Inverted pleat.

Box pleat.

Dress using a combination of box and knife pleats.

Dress using knife pleats and an inverted pleat.

machine) along its length. Tucks hold fullness in place, act as a decoration, or serve both purposes at once. Tucks may be evenly spaced or arranged in groups, and tucks of different widths may be used together. Tucks can be separated by rows of applied lace or narrow fancy ribbon, or rows of embroidery by hand or automatic machine. The finest tucks are called pin tucks and appear on baby garments and on blouses and lingerie in fine fabrics.

Work the tucks before making up the garment. Measure and mark very accurately for even a slight discrepancy repeated on every tuck will greatly alter the size of the finished garment. Released tucks must be securely finished at the release point.

Fabric Woven fabrics are constructed from two sets of threads. Those which are set longitudinally on to the loom are called the *warp* and those which are woven horizontally across the warp are known as the *weft*. The two firm edges formed where the *weft* threads turn at the end of each row of weaving are called the *selvedge.*

By folding the warp threads until they are parallel with the weft threads a fold is obtained which is referred to as 'on the cross' or a 'crossway' fold. Strips of fabric cut parallel to this fold are called crossway strips. They are most useful as they will stretch slightly and can be eased around curves without puckering or distortion. They are used to bind or face curved edges, for instance, necks and armholes. Crossway binding is sold ready cut and folded, in a great range of colours; it is then called bias binding.

Fabrics Today's fabric departments are an Aladdin's Cave and a continual temptation to the needlewoman. They are, too, a reminder of the old parlour game 'animal, vegetable or mineral'. Until the beginning of this century, choice was limited to the four natural fibres: wool (sheep, goat's and other quadrupeds with spinnable coats), silk from obliging tame or wild silkworms, cotton and linen of the plant kingdom. Now scientists produce from wood-pulp, coal, cellulose and other chemicals with unpronounceable names, a bewildering array of synthetic fibres. Some resemble the traditional fabrics in handle and appearance.

Sometimes the synthetic fibres are blended with

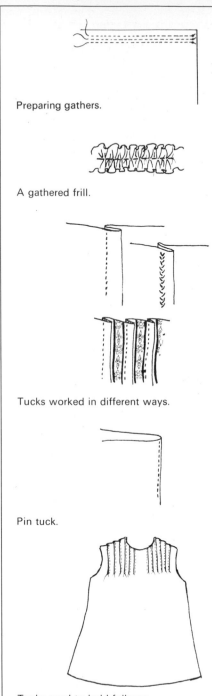

Preparing gathers.

A gathered frill.

Tucks worked in different ways.

Pin tuck.

Tucks used to hold fullness.

natural ones to give a special property; for instance, resistance to creasing and shrinkage, easy washing, durability. Rayon, Nylon, Terylene, Courtelle, Tricel, are some of these man-made fibres. Further confusion can be caused by one fibre having a different name in other countries. For example, Terylene is marketed as Dacron in America, and Terital in Italy, Tergal in France, and Trevira in Germany.

Frequent visits to well-stocked fabric retailers are of value. Study the swing tickets on the end of the rolls; they will state, besides the price per yard or metre, the fibre content of the fabric, often expressed in percentages, sometimes with hints on laundering, or a definite order 'Dry Clean Only'. It is worth keeping a notebook for fabrics. Pin or stick in snippets and relevant information — price, where purchased, purpose, how much was used and date, fibre content and any special treatment that it may require.

Having established the 'animal, vegetable or mineral' of a fabric there are two methods of construction, by weaving or by knitting; the knitted fabrics are usually called jersey. Patterns can be woven or knitted into the fabric to produce an unlimited number of surface textures, or the fabric may be printed with patterns. Some of these are perennial — spots, checks, stripes and flower designs; others, the annuals, follow the vagaries of fashion, being *avant garde* one moment and out-of-date the next. This is a trap for the hoarder. To buy fabric because it is irresistible, 'such a bargain' or 'will come in useful' and then to store it too long is dangerous.

Most fabric departments have a section for remnants at bargain prices. They are reduced because they are at the end of a roll, a discontinued line, or have some small flaw in weave or print. These counters are a treasure trove, but don't always expect your sewing to be economical. Obviously, a more expensive fabric will have advantages over a cheap one in appearance and wear, apart from that self-confident glow that comes with indulgence in luxury. Some extravagances are an economy in the long run.

In the shops furnishing fabrics and dress fabrics are usually sold in different departments. This segregation must not inhibit choice. Many a successful dress (remember Scarlett O'Hara in 'Gone with the Wind'?) was intended for curtains,

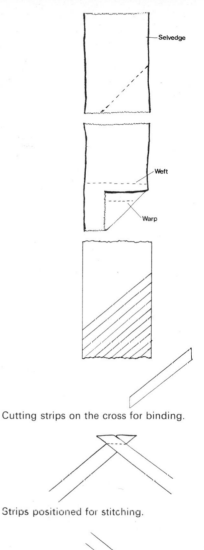

Cutting strips on the cross for binding.

Strips positioned for stitching.

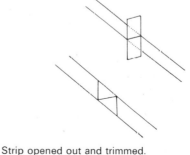

Strip opened out and trimmed.

Variations on a simple child's dress:

a) Dress using contrasting stripes and bound with ric-rac.

b) Embroidered bib and sleeves edged in lace.

c) Motif embroidered on pocket.

d) and e) Ideas for pockets.

f) Pin tucks used to decorate the yoke.

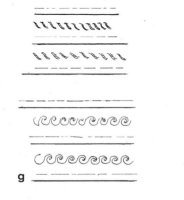

g) Simple embroidery stitches for use as edgings.

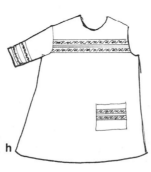

h) Decorative bindings can enhance a simple dress.

and some dress fabrics may well be used for home furnishing ideas, particularly table cloths, mats, cushion covers. Ticking, when its feather proofing is washed away, is very useful for this. The humble unbleached calico when dyed or printed may be put to uses for which it was not originally intended. Remember curtain fabrics often shrink. Check with the retailer and, if uncertain, pre-shrink fabric before making up.

Sewing Machines

'The sewing machine is man's greatest contribution to life.' (Gandhi)

Choose with care. A machine correctly used and maintained will last more than a lifetime. Many Victorian pieces are still performing Trojan service. Send to several leading manufacturers for brochures; visit, if possible, a sewing machine retailer where you may watch demonstrations and try machines for yourself. Adopt the same attitude to this purchase as to a car; after all, it will last much longer. Some retailers will allow trial periods at home. Visit friends and relations and try out their machines. Don't underestimate your own ability to improve in sewing technique. Many beginners rush to purchase a hand machine and then realise too late the advantages of speed and two free hands which are obtained with an electric model. Make enquiries about servicing and availability of spare parts. Buy the best you can afford. The choice is between the methods of propulsion, hand (turning), feet (treadling), electricity (foot-press control or knee-operated).

Hand machines Hand machines are used on a table. Make sure that it is a strong one. Treadle machines are always mounted on a stand. Electric machines may be used on a table or on a stand. Many machines are sold as 'portable' — just try it, some require a very strong arm indeed. Remember electric voltages and plugs and sockets vary around the world, so if you are a traveller be prepared with a transformer — or settle for a hand model. The second decision is between a straight stitch machine or a swing needle machine. The former will stitch forward and reverse and will efficiently perform all 'bread and butter' work.

The swing needle machine will do straight stitching but, when adjusted, the needle will work from side to side producing the zig-zag stitch which is invaluable for neatening raw edges, buttonholes, and a host of other time-savers. An automatic swing needle machine will also produce patterns. The machine must be set for patterns by dials, levers, or by inserting cams.

Care for your machine. Do not allow it to become too hot, too cold, too dusty, too dry or too damp. It will repay you in trouble-free stitching if you oil it lightly and regularly, brush away dust and fluff, particularly around the bobbin and the needle. Replace bent or blunt needles. Do not strain the machine by attempting to work materials such as leather or carpets which are too heavy for a domestic model. Study the book of instructions which will be provided with your machine. Don't let the attachments and gadgets remain in their box. Get to know them; they save time and effort.

The first Singer sewing machine, manufactured in 1851.

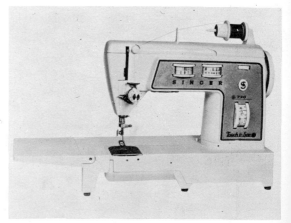

The latest model.

Having assembled your tools, acquired a sewing machine, mastered the basic processes – what to make? The choice is infinite, but walk before you can run. A simple project completed quickly is better than great things planned but never achieved. The novice dressmaker is wise if she first attempts small, simple garments for a child. Shift dresses for little girls are the simplest of all. Put your faith in a pattern from one of the major pattern companies. Their instructions are detailed and careful. They want your effort to be a success as they aim to sell more patterns. However, a basic shift pattern gives scope for experiment, and by varying the choice of fabric and trimmings many variations of one theme are possible. The sketches on pages 110 and 111 show a few.

Confidence gained in this manner allows progress to adult garments. The pattern companies grade many patterns as 'Easy to make' or 'Quick to Sew' or 'Only three main pattern pieces'. Clothes and home furnishings made by the enthusiastic needle-woman are almost always cheaper than those ready made. Frequently they are more carefully constructed and finished too and, of course, 'made to measure'; but the compliment that gladdens the heart of the amateur is 'Oh, it doesn't look home-made', and this is not difficult to achieve.

A selection of the many kinds of trimmings that are available.

Bookbinding   H. A. de Coverly

Bookbinding by hand, in common with other crafts, calls for an ability to plan ahead and to think and act quickly. It can be appreciated in every home and all walks of life. Whilst libraries can cater for the avid reader and the student, many people wish to possess books bound to their liking. Work which can be undertaken falls neatly into broad categories as follows:

Periodical issues of works intended for binding when complete with issued titles and indexes, and the regular publications of societies;

Magazines such as 'Woodworker' or 'The Connoisseur' may be preserved by being bound;

Paperbacks of the higher class need to be protected in stiff covers and hard-bound editions may be rebound in a more advanced style;

Music needs to be bound constantly — particularly manuscripts.

There is a demand for photograph albums and scrapbooks (children love them), and visitors' or guest books will provide exercise *par excellence* in choosing paper and binding methods for ideal bookbinding. Portfolios (for artist friends), bookboxes and slip cases for the preservation of valuable bindings and papers will add to your repertoire.

Do not take on, or even practise with, Victorian or any other poetry books or novels which are tattered, valueless or dull, or worn devotional books. Be kind to the owners of the latter and encourage them to buy new ones. Repairing valuable books and sheet preservation should be tackled only when confidence has been attained by practice on straightforward work.

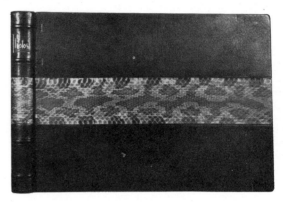

Photograph album made by the author and constructed to open flat, bound in black Oasis morocco with a wide decorative centre band of snakeskin vellum from a natural untreated python skin.

Equipment and Tools

Catalogues present a bewildering list, but very simple bookbinding at home or in schools may be undertaken with a comparatively small amount of equipment. The essentials are:

Lying Press fitted with runners on one side; it should have with it a metal bar lever termed a Press Pin, essential for obtaining correct pressure. It will have to be on a stand known usually as a 'tub' and the cutting device known as a plough with, preferably, two knives to fit. Also required are:

Backing Boards and Cutting Boards. These are both wedge-shaped, preferably made from well seasoned beech wood and the former are required to have their top edge bevelled to an angle of about 10° and, if they are faced with metal, they will withstand constant hammering and give long and accurate service.

A Knocking Down Iron, when fixed at one end of the lying press, serves as an anvil for hammering down surfaces level. All bookbinding construction i.e. forwarding centres round the use of the lying press.

A Sewing Frame to hold sections firm and level during the hand sewing process is used with **Sewing Keys** for hemp and tape.

Nipping Press or some form of clamp to give all-over pressure; an iron **Letterpress,** portable or fixed to bench, used for temporary or prolonged pressing during any binding process. These can be acquired on the second-hand market.

Pressing Boards will be needed which can be made from plywood or blockboard and faced with formica for refinement.

Small Bench Knife or strong card cutter suitable for cutting medium thickness strawboard and other card or paper (single sheets only).

Finishing Stove, Gas, Electric, or Butane gas fitted with an outer ring for holding finishing tools in a heated area.

Finishing Tools, handle letters mounted in wood consisting of complete alphabets with numerals. Other tools to obtain will be a few **Line Pallets** for tooling straight lines across spines and some modern styled **Centre Tools** of simple shapes.

Gold Cushion — a prepared, level 'cushion' covered with rough side or 'suede' calf or other leather, used for laying out gold leaf.

Gold Knife — long thin bladed edge for removing and cutting up the gold leaf.

However, if work of a higher standard is to be achieved, then it will be necessary to add the following equipment and tools at a later date.

Standing Press — large iron construction fixed to the floor.

French Press as above but made of wood.

Linen Press as above, made of wood and much lighter, sometimes sold as an 'antique'.

Large Bench knife or **Board shears** for cutting large sheets of board or card.

Guillotine Bench type or free standing, used for cutting quantities of paper, books and board.

Type Founts of brass type in definite point sizes made to special specification to withstand heat and in 'type high' dimensions.

Type Holder — used to hold type in lines for tooling.

Blocking Press — electrically heated bench model. For blocking titles, designs and brasses on to book covers.

Ornamental Pallets for tooling across spines.

Fillets Wheel form of finishing tool for making straight lines.

Rolls Wheel form of tool giving a continuous pattern of a line of design.

Gouges Single tools from $\frac{1}{8}$ in. to about 1 in. across the curve to tool continuous lines of curving formations.

Spokeshave Record or Stanley No. 151, supplementary to the paring knife; needs to have the throat slightly enlarged.

Bodkin and Awl Pointed tools for piercing boards and teasing out hemps.

G Clamps for holding down leather when using spokeshave.

Paring Stone Smooth surface provided by (a) discarded litho. stone (b) sheets of plate glass (c) sheets of marble such as a discarded marble-topped washstand.

Band Nippers for forming the bands in flexible raised banded work. Copper-plated sometimes available.

Hand Tools to Buy and Make

Bone Folders, used at every stage to supplement hand pressure. Soak in thin machine oil, shape one end with a coarse file and sandpaper smooth. They can be fashioned from wood, discarded paper-knives or old bone toothbrush handles.

Knives — many will be required. General purpose wooden handled cobbler's cutting knife with broad or long point of reliable Sheffield make; leather paring knife — English Barnsley or Swedish

Berg blade; both will need handles, easily made from thin card covered with morocco leather. Discarded power hacksaw blades can be utilised. Avoid razor blades or gadget knives. A penknife is useful on odd occasions, but it should not be regarded as a regular craft tool.

Sharpening devices of all kinds are essential to keep edges clean and sharp. Oilstones, combination India, natural 'Washita' or 'Arkansas' if kept in boxes will last many years. Strops can be made from plywood strips using brown twill aluminous oxide cloth medium to fine with strips of machine belting 'dressed' with Okey's Plate Powder ironed in with 'vaseline' on one side.

Shears and Scissors of various sizes should be of best quality, those sold as 'Binders shears' are not advised.

A Straight Edge is a luxury; most binders are content to use the usual metal ruler which should carry metric divisions.

Carpenter's Try Square, small and large and **spring dividers** in two sizes will complete the requirements for marking up and measuring.

Binder Hammer – You can make do with a Warrington but it is better to invest in a No. 3 Bookbinder's Hammer which is really a 'snob's' or cobbler's hammer.

Saw – a tenon and a dovetail will be needed for making grooves across the backs of sections prior to sewing.

Join a woodwork class and, with professional advice, you will be able to make very superior equipment such as a lying press and tub, sewing frame, plough, etc. Have professional turning where needed but metal bench screws can be obtained for the lying press. The metal fitting for the plough may present difficulties; seek professional advice in this and in the purchase of any second-hand equipment or tools. Simple basic finishing tools can be made from muntz metal blanks (professional finishers make their own). Power tools make life easier. Brass sewing keys are very satisfactory to make by hand.

Adhesives to use Adhesives are the most important commodity of all and the success of the work depends on their correct use.

Glue needs heating in a water-jacketed vessel. Scotch glue in pellet form requires soaking until soft. Flexible glues sold in a glutinous state 'ready for the pot' retain their elasticity and should always be used on the spine. Brush maintenance and a well-stirred, correct dilution make for even viscosity and enable the novice to attain confidence in gluing (*many never do*).

Hot glue is being replaced by the introduction of cold *Polyvinyl Acetate Emulsions* (*PVA*) which were developed for the mass production of paperbacks.

Paste, originally wheat flour and water, still has its place for permanence without damage to material and for the best work in paper and leather.

Cold glues such as Seccotine are useful when a quick permanent tack is needed on small areas. *Avoid 'office' glues and mountants.*

Brushes Buy a good quality and look after them. Brush maintenance means overnight soaking and thorough beating out before use. PVA on brushes is best removed with washing-up fluid. The best brushes and the most expensive are made from hogshair.

Materials Leather should be used only for advanced binding and quarter bound library style. The following is a selection only.

'Oasis' morocco, which is the retanned, re-dressed and dyed Niger goatskin, imported from Nigeria, has for many years proved the most satisfactory for craft binding. Also the Native tanned, natural and dyed are available at times and much sought after for their natural markings and texture.

The South African goatskin known as Cape goat makes a beautiful leather but is expensive and difficult for the non-trade craftsman until some skill has been acquired.

Calf, sumach tanned dyed and 'law' – natural undyed – are fairly easy to work with and readily obtainable. Skiver, which is the upper split of the sheep, is best avoided except for thin limp music

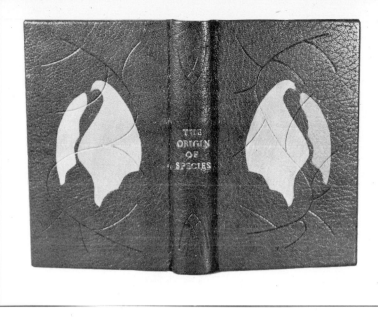

Book bound in emerald green goatskin, inlaid in gold, and blind tooled with a semi-representational design based on fossil shapes.

Made by John Britton, evening student at Morley College, London.

or other light work and it requires great care in use. Vellum of all kinds requires careful study before a novice attempts to handle it and experts do not agree on methods. Points to remember are that vellum is a stiff, dressed, slightly transparent skin requiring a backing of white or creamy-white paper which may or may not be attached to the underside of the vellum. The vellum will quickly re-act to moisture and to atmospheric changes so that complete control of the adhesive used during the drying must be maintained; even then movement will take place many days later.

Cloths and Fabrics Again, only a selection is given:
Reliance, Sundour and Art Vellum are bookcloths;
Sundour Art Buckram, Legal Buckram and Cotton Buckram are heavier cloths;
Art Canvas is like a buckram with a different finish;
Felted fabrics, Linson, etc. are about half the price of cloth.
See page 246 for list of suppliers.

Boards Distinguish between straw (straw colour), chip or Thames (light grey) and millboard (dark grey with hard or milled surface). Discarded packaging can often be utilised.

Lining Materials These are used as reinforcements for spines and mounting:
Mull—an open weave cotton mesh fabric.
Cambric—similar, but more closely woven.
Linen—lighter and more expensive than the above.
Calico—coarser and heavier, containing dressing.
Holland—natural and dyed dark-coloured 'blind' material—known to be used for binding before bookcloth and manufactured exclusively for bookbinding.

Paper Only good quality cartridge should be considered for endpapers; also hand-made and mould-made, which include the Ingres countermark now made in France, Italy and Sweden. Montgolfier and Canson are two other reliable makes.

Hand-made, marbled papers are expensive, but cheaper Continental makes are available, and also a range of fancy printed papers which may be used as endpapers, siding, or for covering boxes. (See list of suppliers).

Brown paper for lining backs should be obtained as brown kraft or from odd wrappings.

Thin, good quality typing Bank paper can be used for guarding.

117

Uncut, 16 page (8 leaves) section of a book with partly cut head to avoid creasing. The Collating back mark is also shown.

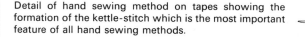

Hand sewing method showing continuity of thread from head to tail.

Detail of hand sewing method on tapes showing the formation of the kettle-stitch which is the most important feature of all hand sewing methods.

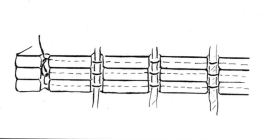

Method of hand sewing as used for leather binding and also for thick section work (magazines etc.). The hemp or cord used is recessed into the spine and on best work the cords are laced into the boards of the binding.

Principles of construction The minimum sequence of binding operations for all styles:

1. Preparation of section or sheets and pressing.
2. Preparation of endpapers.
3. Sewing or stitching or overcasting with sewing.
4. Forwarding, i.e. first gluing, cutting edges and decorating them, shaping spine, forming shoulders, preparing and attaching boards, pressing and cleaning off.
5. Headbanding.
6. Lining the spine.
7. Preparing the covering leather or other material.
8. Covering or making the case.
9. Finishing.
10. Casing in or siding and pasting down open, pressing.
11. Opening up, completion.

When recovering paperbacks, items 2, and part of 4, 6, 8 and 10 only will take place. The 'finishing' consists normally of pasting on the original paper wrapper to the new cover.

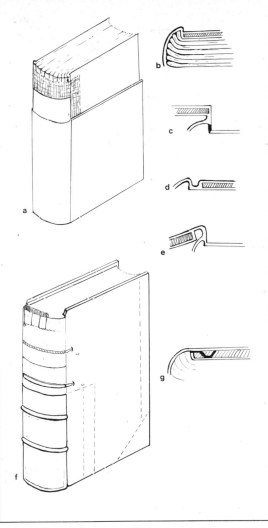

a) Construction of a cloth cased binding. The sewn book is seen to have shoulders, a reinforcing mull extending over the side, a paper lining on top of this and the case fitting overall. Note the extension or 'squares' on the long (fore-) edge.

b) The fit of the case over the shoulder giving a ridge.

c) The opening of (b) at the first endpaper showing the bend of the cloth above the shoulder.

d) The French or American groove method of casing. Note that the board is set away from the shoulder.

e) The free opening of (d).

f) Construction of a leather binding sewn on recessed hemps two of which are shown laced into the boards. A sewn-on headband is featured, also raised bands across the spine. The dotted lines on the board show the proportions for quarter, half and fore-edge strips covering in leather together with one corner.

g) Shoulder formation of (f) with detail of the position of the laced-in cords. Note that the shoulder is level with the boards, without a ridge or a groove as in other forms of construction.

Finishing, including gold leaf finishing The lettering and decoration of the covers require great concentration and attention to detail; practice is the only way to attain efficiency. Very briefly, the processes are:

1. Planning the lettering (upper case capitals), symmetrical optical centre, top centre or lower centre or assymetrical right or left. Variation in size of letters or use of lower case is not advised. Longitudinal lettering should read down.
2. Marking up or 'blinding in' on the actual material.
3. Preparation with dilute vinegar, paste water or distilled water.
4. Applying glaire – the medium for making the gold stick.
5. Greasing the area to be tooled and applying the gold leaf.
6. Heating, cleaning the surface of tool and making impression.
7. Cleaning off the surplus gold and examining for defects.
8. Completing removal of gold and grease with a solvent (benzine).

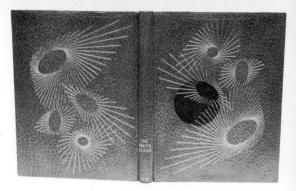

Book bound in natural Kano goatskin with onlay of natural calfskin carrying tooled and coloured coats of arms. It is constructed to give a flat opening using the 'meeting guard' principle.

Made by Hilda Fayers, evening student Morley College, London.

Book bound in purple levant morocco leather, inlaid and tooled in gold. The free flowing linear gold tooling is after the modern style of Paul Bonet of France.

Made by Brian Maggs, evening student, Guildford School of Art.

Items 2 and 3 can be omitted when tooling cloth, after practice. Items 2, 3, 4 and 5 are omitted when using foils which contain the adhesive element. The marking up of foil is difficult and is made on the carrier side, the impression made through the foil. The fine detail of very small letters may well be lost by this 'spread' of the impression.

'Oasis' morocco will always give good results if treated correctly but cheaper, cellulose-finished skins should be avoided. Some foils are not suitable for tooling on leather. Good quality cloths and buckrams also give good results but art canvas and most of the paper-felted fabrics are difficult.

When paper is being considered for the substance of a book of plain sheets for use as an album or as a guest book etc., or when assembling materials for the endpapers, it is vital that the grain or machine direction of the stock be studied so that this will *run parallel with the binding edge i.e. from head to tail.*

The movement caused by the hygroscopic nature of the paper is minimised and under control thus avoiding the pitfalls of cockling and creasing when using adhesives which can be followed on drying by warping and twisting. It also makes for easier folding and free opening of the book.

Bookbinding is, of course, a craft which demands great patience and skill. Here you have the simplest methods and from these you can progress to more complicated work. Do not lose any opportunity of examining beautiful bindings from which you can learn much. A wonderful sense of satisfaction and achievement can be gained from binding your own books.

Brass Rubbing   Mark Haeffner

Monumental brasses are a type of memorial dating from the early 13th century. They take the form of metal plates engraved with the figure of the deceased person they commemorate and correspond to sculptured effigies. They were set in slabs of stone placed over tombs and are to be found in many of the parish churches of England, large and small.

Nowhere is the costume and armour of the medieval period better displayed than in the fine, clear engraving of these monuments. The figures of knights and ladies, merchants, priests, and even shrouded skeletons, have all withstood the ravages of time, though huge numbers were destroyed at the Reformation when monasteries and other church property were plundered.

Monumental brasses have an additional interest. Excellent copies can be made which are fascinating to collect and provide superb decorations. These brass rubbings are relatively cheap and easy to do.

Materials 'Heel ball' or cobbler's wax (a black substance rather like crayon).
Large sheets of paper—detail paper is most suitable but good quality shelf paper is a satisfactory substitute should detail paper be unobtainable.

Making a Rubbing Before taking a rubbing the brass must be dusted with a soft cloth to remove all particles of grit and dust. Begin at the centre of the brass and dust *outwards*. Now spread the paper over the brass and fix it with weights at the corners (or with Sellotape). Rub over with 'heel ball' so that the engraved lines show through as white on a black background (see illustration). (This, of course, is like the popular children's game of rubbing the image of a penny on to paper with a pencil.) Indeed, for those who like to experiment, the principle of rubbing might be

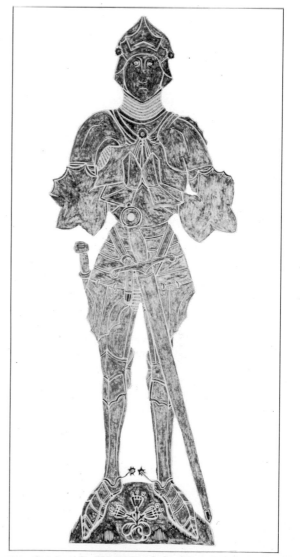

Brass rubbing from Cirencester done by the author.

121

applied to other media such as the ornamental coal hole covers still exisiting in odd corners of London and elsewhere, or to anything which has an interesting texture such as bark or fabrics (see also Foil, page 44) using wax crayons.

After a comparatively small amount of practice, it is possible to produce a good, clear rubbing; but there are usually imperfections. It is difficult to avoid going over the edge of the metal on to the stone and this gives an untidy effect, so it is often desirable to cut out the rubbing and re-mount it on paper or cloth. This is not always easy because most types of paste cause the edges of the paper to contract and wrinkle. Double-sided Sellotape can be used sometimes but is difficult to work with. Another method of improving the rubbing is to draw along the lines with a black felt-tipped pen. All too often, hasty rubbing leaves outlines blurred and unclear, and this process can make a great improvement. The black areas between the lines may be darkened with coloured pencil or crayon to make the definition even clearer. It is worth experimenting with methods such as these; they can often transform a rather shabby and uneven rubbing.

More detailed instructions and useful hints may be found in various handbooks and pamphlets (see bibliography page 245) and brass rubbing should not be attempted without consulting one or other of these. Brasses are ancient and valuable and may be damaged by using the wrong materials. Hard crayon, for instance, tends to rip the paper and damage the brass.

It is essential to obtain permission *by letter* from the vicar or rector of a church before embarking on a rubbing. Where there are exceptionally fine or ancient brasses there is usually a substantial fee for rubbing to deter the casual amateur or help finance the upkeep of the church.

Victoria and Albert Museum

Rubbing of Sir John de Creke's wife, about 1325, taken from Westley-Waterless Church, Cambridgeshire.

Collages

Eugenie Alexander

Collage, which is the name given to the method of making pictures or decorative panels by sticking materials on to a background, has become one of the most popular media of the 20th century. There are three main types: fabric collages, paper collages and three-dimensional collages. It is possible to combine all three methods in one picture as long as the whole composition does not become overcrowded, and a firm enough background is chosen.

Fabric Collages

Materials A firm background such as rayon, with a one-inch border left for mounting, is needed. Thin materials should be stuck on to a non-woven interfacing such as Vilene.
Plenty of scraps — lace, net, dress samples, sequins, etc.
Copydex, UHU or Polycell are three adhesives frequently used.

Paintings, advertisements and postcard reproductions can serve as a stimulus for designs. Sometimes, for instance, a piece of striped velvet will 'spark off' an idea — a tiger in a jungle, a mask-faced fish. The design should be drawn first and traced on to the material before cutting out. Alternatively, paper patterns can be cut from newspaper. Remember that too many colours can cause confusion and often lead to a lack of colour impact in the final work. A few colours in varying tones give a better unity.

Materials can be folded over, frayed and treated in various ways. Vilene may be used as a backing if required. Embroidery stitches can be added for extra richness in fabric collage, e.g. blanket stitch for roof-tops, or feather stitch for a bird's tail. Machine-stitching with various colours, different lengths of stitch, or the automatic embroidery

Alan Lewis

Fabric collage using felt and net on a textured background. The stitches used are extremely simple, relying on the different kinds of thread and wool for effect.

stitches incorporated in some sewing machines, can also be used.

When rayon or material which is not Vilene-backed is used as a background, a white cardboard mount one inch smaller than the allowed border is required. The picture is then stretched by using stout linen threads laced up and down and side to side across the board at the back, ready for the final framing.

Insect. A tissue paper collage.

'Jungle' by Janet Thorndike. Much of 'Pop' Art uses the technique of collage.

Paper Collages

Materials White or coloured mounting board. A selection of cellophane, various coloured tissue papers, wallpapers, gummed glossy papers, newspaper, coloured reproductions from magazines and gardening catalogues, etc. The glues used for fabrics can also be used for paper.

The illustration 'Jungle' shows that magazine reproductions make a splendid starting-off point for a composition. Photographs of one's family or friends, pets, houses, etc. can be combined to make an interesting and intimate picture.

Three-dimensional Collages

Materials Hardboard, nails, glass, plaster of Paris, wire, wood off-cuts, shells, lentils, pasta, string, whalebone, safety pins, broken crockery, milk bottle tops, etc. Bostik, UHU, Evo-stick, or one of the wood-sticking glues.

Hardboard is the background used for this type of work which can become practically sculptural.

'Cat and Bird' by Margaret Martin. Imaginative use of plaster and string.

Usually the designs, by nature of the materials employed, take on a more abstract flavour, though a semi-realistic sea scene fits nicely into this category.

Exhibitions of collages may be advertised in the daily newspapers. Examples can be seen locally in Art Schools, Colleges of Education or displays of work organised by Women's Institutes and other bodies. Museums also contain a fund of ideas for pictures through the various crafts to be found there.

Copper Enamelling   Elizabeth Carpreau

The ancient craft of enamelling has recently undergone a revival. Artists are using enamel on steel on a large scale to decorate the outside of buildings. Enamelling is equally ideal as a home craft because the basic techniques are simple and, when executed on a small scale, it is not expensive. Students often find that their very first experiments can be used to make simple items of jewellery. Later, more advanced techniques can be tried and the results combined with other media.

Enamel is glass combined with metal oxides for colour. This is ground to a fine powder and used dry or mixed with a liquid and used as paste or slush. Enamel lumps, shot, chips and strands may be used in addition to the powder for more interesting effects. Enamel may be transparent, opaque or opalescent. It also varies in hardness.

Copper, silver, brass, gilding metal, aluminium and steel are all used for enamelling. Of these, copper is the most suitable for the beginner as it is relatively inexpensive when used on a small scale and easy to handle.

Materials It is possible to buy enamelling kits which include a small kiln, phials of ground enamel, copper shapes, jewellery attachments and tools. In addition, it would be useful to have some 20-gauge copper sheet, copper wire, copper foil, snips, tweezers, small pliers, lump and strand enamel, gum arabic, paint brush, asbestos sheets and a solution of vinegar and salt.

Method When using prepared copper blanks the only preparation needed is cleaning. Sheet metal must be cut to shape and then the edges filed. If the surface of the copper is very smooth it may be given a little 'bite' by using emery paper, abrasive pads or even Vim. It is essential that the copper is absolutely clean before applying the enamel. A solution of vinegar and salt will do this.

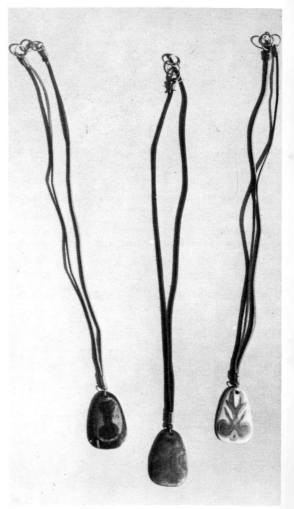

Copper enamelled pendants, using the masking method. Note how the method of fastening and attaching the pendants to the leather thongs adds interest.

The copper should be removed from the vinegar after a few minutes, rinsed in clean water and dried with a tissue. Lay the blank on a piece of clean paper. Do not touch it with the fingers. Apply a thin coat of gum arabic over the surface of the copper and the piece is ready to receive the enamel. Shake the enamel evenly on to the copper working from the edges inwards. When the piece has dried completely it is ready to be placed in the preheated kiln, using a spatula or a broad knife. After a few minutes the copper will glow red and the enamel will appear shiny. Remove from the kiln and place on a sheet of asbestos until it has cooled. It is possible to fire small pieces of enamel holding them with tongs and firing from below using the flame of a domestic cooker. A plumber's propane gas torch will fire small pieces very efficiently while larger pieces can be fired using more than one burner at a time.

When the copper has received a base coat of enamel it may be enriched in many ways. The following methods may be used singly or in combination:

Lines or shapes poured out of the shaker tube freely.

Pieces of paper cut to mask certain areas when the colour is applied.

Lines or shapes may be drawn in gum. Enamel shaken on and the surplus gently tapped off.

Copper wire which has been preshaped and cleaned can be placed on the pre-fired base coat and pressed in when the piece is hot. This wire may be left as a linear design or serve as an outline to be filled in with various colours.

Copper foil used in a similar manner can create flat shapes which could serve as a base for a transparent enamel, or be left plain.

Interesting results can be achieved by firing two soft coats of enamel with a hard layer in between. This causes a 'bubbling' effect. White, transparent brown, followed by black produces this effect.

Strands or lumps of enamel can be placed on the

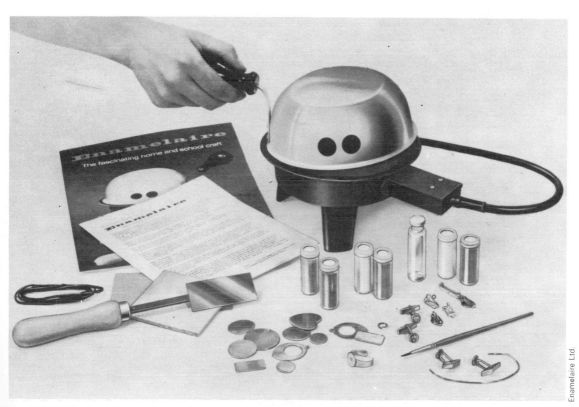

Enamelling kiln, tools, tubes of enamels, copper shapes and jewellery attachments.

Enamelaire Ltd

base coat and when the lumps are soft, swirled or drawn across the work.

A layer of unfired enamel sprinkled on the fired base coat may be scratched with a pen for decoration.

The back of the copper will have become blackened with fire scale. This copper oxide can be removed with Vim and a scouring pad. Alternatively, a 'suede' self-adhesive contact makes a very pleasant backing for pendants. The edges should be gently filed, working with strokes away from the finished surface. Emery paper will give a final, smoother finish.

Jewellery findings are easy to solder to the reverse side of the work provided the surface of the copper is absolutely clean. Cut a small length of soft solder (wire) and flatten it. Rub a little flux paste on to the back of the copper. Place solder and finding in position. Place the piece on the cover of the kiln until the solder melts. Simple fittings are made from strips of copper and copper wire and soldered in place.

Small enamelled pieces make unusual, decorative clock faces, box and table tops. Combined with other materials in a mosaic, enamel can give brilliance and add to the variety of the surface.

Fire scale formed by heating copper is sometimes used to advantage by leaving it under clear and opaque enamels. If the flame of the torch is played over the piece, reduction causes the fire scale to turn pink. If the flame touches the molten enamel a lustre will result.

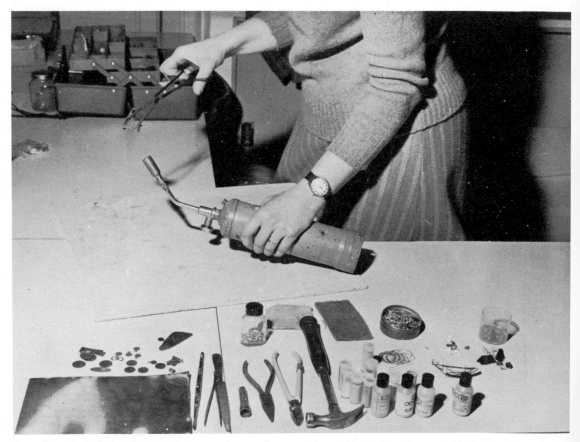

Open firing technique using a propane gas burner. A group of enamels, tools and copper blanks are shown in the foreground.

Sweat soldered findings on back of work using sheet copper and copper wire.

Paper clip used to hold solder and wire in place while applying heat.

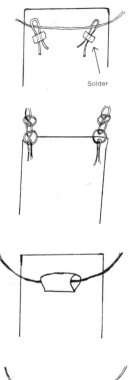

Solder

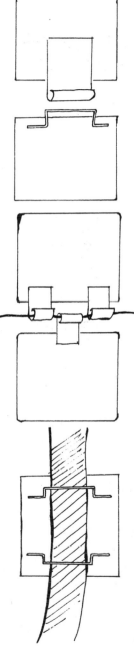

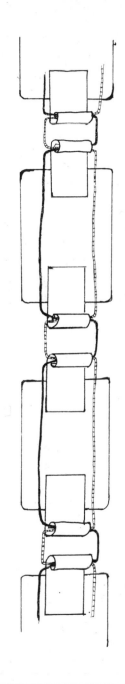

strap

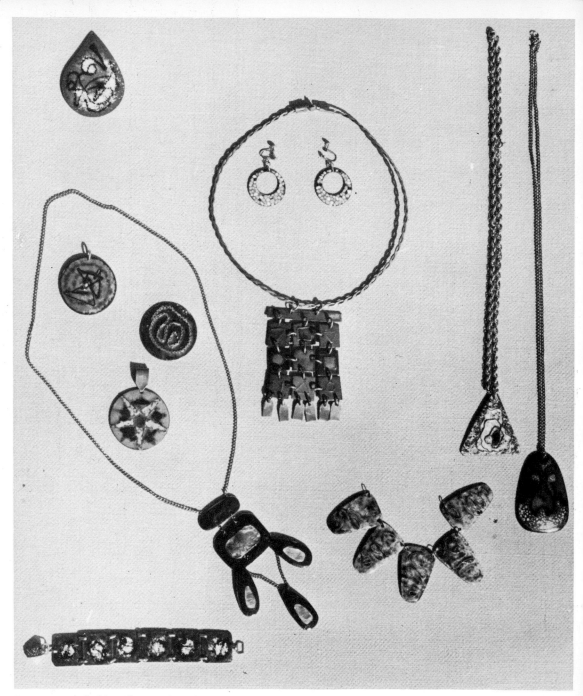

Copper enamelled jewellery made at the Sunbury Adult Education Institute.

Various examples of copper enamelled bowls. Wet paper stencils were used to mask areas of the design.

It is possible to melt pieces of glass from bottles or jars on to the enamelled surface. Not all glass will combine with enamel but the smaller the pieces the greater the possibility of success. One method of breaking up the glass is to heat it in a flame and then drop it into cold water.

Simple enamelling can serve as an introduction to the art of enamelling and jewellery-making proper. On the other hand, many students have developed an interest in metalwork, ceramic glazes, glass, and modern methods of mosaic, as a result of these simple beginnings.

Fabric Printing   Mary Oliver

Block Printing

The technique of hand printing from blocks produces a quality of mark that cannot be easily reproduced by other hand methods. A very slight unevenness of cover gives an all-over softness and variety to the print; the method of block cutting dictates the style of design, and this should be carefully considered at the outset.

Blocks can be made from a variety of materials:
Potatoes, swedes, turnips, carrots.
Thin cardboard or heavy cartridge paper, mounted on card and waterproofed with varnish.
Linoleum of good quality, at least $\frac{1}{8}$ in. thick. (Preferably brown cork lino containing no colouring matter.)
Wood, end or side grain, cut or printed on the grain.
Nails or other small objects capable of creating a slightly raised surface.
Strips of metal knocked into a block of wood.
Expanded polystyrene or foam rubber, cut or chipped.
Corrugated cardboard, mounted on ply and waterproofed with varnish.
Woven rush or cane, embossed or moulded materials, natural objects such as heavily veined leaves or tree bark.

Lino Cutting The best tools are V- or U-shaped blades about $3\frac{1}{2}$ in. long fitted into graver handles, capable of being sharpened on a stone; they are preferable to the inexpensive nib tools found in most art shops. When cutting, the tool should be held with the handle in the palm of the hand and the index finger along the blade. The lino should be held firmly with the other hand, and the cutting action made away from the body or other hand. An exercise in free lino cutting which exploits the material, at the same time achieving a variety of effects is as follows:

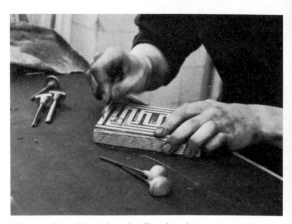

Lino cutting. Note that the lino has been mounted on a block to facilitate printing.

Take 1 in. square of lino, cut into it, freely, areas of tone, half-tone and white. Print, using finger pressure, in different ways, but maintaining in individual printing sheets the same arrangement, achieving numerous, all-over, repeating patterns which vary according to the direction in which the block has been placed.

This can be followed by a similar use of larger blocks, avoiding pencil drawing on the block, the tool only should be used.

Printing on Cloth The block, of whatever material, is backed with plywood to give it stability, using water- and turpentine-proof adhesives.

Fabric Printing Inks These oil-bound inks are mixed to the required shade in a container and a small quantity rolled on to a palette with a rubber roller, transferred on to the block and subsequently to the cloth which is stuck or pinned firmly to the printing surface. A special mallet or

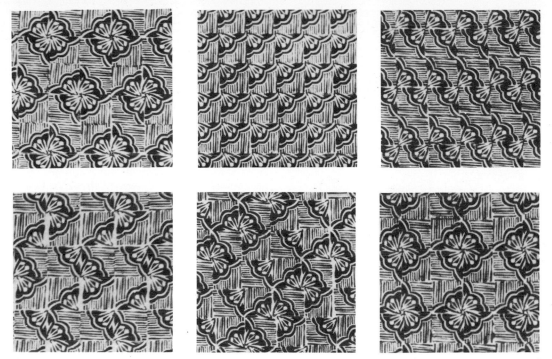

Group of patterns made from a single block.

Block printing using a special hand-held printing mallet.

foot pressure can be used for printing larger blocks requiring greater pressure to print evenly.

Registration is achieved by drawing, across the cloth, a line at right angles to the selvage. Registering the block against this line and the selvage, print, as convenient, across the cloth.

If a second colour is required, take a block identical in size to the first, trace on it in the same relationship the second colour, and register it similarly to the first line on the cloth.

Hang cloth to dry. Clean utensils and block with turpentine substitute immediately after use.

Pigment Dyes or Direct Dyes The block should be flocked for this method. The flocking mordant is rolled out on to a palette and thence to the block, it is then covered lightly and generously with flocking powder and left to dry for 24 hours. If necessary a second coat is applied after brushing off all excess powder. The dye pad, made from sponge rubber covered firmly with a layer of

Block covered in flocking powder after being coated with flocking mordant using a roller.

absorbent cloth on a wooden base, is evenly coated with colour using a 2 in. brush; the block is pressed on to it at random until the surface is fully charged with dye. Print as before. Overloading with colour fills the interstices of the block, which should be cut deeply.

Hang cloth to dry; follow relevant finishing instructions. Wash out utensils in cold water.

Potato Cuts

The cut can be made with a knife or lino tool. The block is pressed on to the colour from a palette or pad.

The printing of all types of unconventional blocks can be related to the above.

Using the dye pad which has been coated with colour.

Screen Printing

This technique is commonly used in commercial production, and derives from stencils imported from China at the beginning of this century; of great delicacy, the motifs were held together with human hairs. The work inspired a new approach to printing, at first very flat and simple, but developing rapidly into a highly sophisticated technique capable of producing a wide variety of effects.

The Frame This can be made from 2 in. by 2 in. deal, completely flat with firm corners, or any convenient size, but at least 12 in. by 16 in. inside measurement. If large areas are required, a screen covering 6 in. over the cloth width at each selvage and containing more than one repeat is advisable.

Silk, cotton organdie or Terylene lawn is stretched along one side of the frame, on the straight of the weave, and stapled at $\frac{3}{4}$ in. intervals; the opposite side is similarly treated, pulling firmly against the first side, and subsequently the remaining sides, ensuring a drum-like surface. Sheer Terylene curtaining obtainable at a drapers will be suitable for this purpose.

Placement of Design on Screen The motif should be placed to allow 2 in. on either side and 5 in. at top and bottom of the screen. After the design has been applied by one of the following methods, the screen should be masked with adhesive tape to prevent unwanted escape of colour.

Simple Gelatine Method The outside of the screen is given three coats of gelatine (50 gm — 1 pint water, dissolved in a double boiler), being

Stretching and stapling organdie to screen.

allowed to dry between coats. The area to be printed is painted in thick lacquer on top of the gelatine, dried and painted with Potassium Bichromate solution (10 per cent in water) and exposed to strong light until the gelatine hardens. Wash out from inside screen with warm water which dissolves the gelatine beneath the lacquer allowing the latter to peel off. Previously designed patterns can be traced on to the inside of the screen and lacquered on the outside.

Gelatine-Potassium Method The screen is coated with the following:
Dissolve $10\frac{1}{2}$ oz. gelatine in 35 oz. water (A) in double boiler.
Dissolve $\frac{1}{2}$ oz. Potassium Bichromate in 4 oz. water (B).
Mix, hot, 3 parts A to 1 part B, in dark room. Coat screen with mixture whilst hot, do not 'work in'. Leave in dark room to dry.

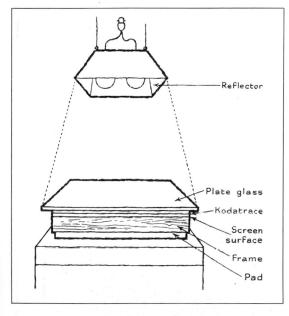

A positive of the motif has previously been prepared on tracing film using a photo-opaque paint. The screen is placed, outside uppermost, on to a flat resilient pad, the tracing — paint side against the emulsion — is placed on top, all covered with a piece of plate glass, weighted to ensure perfect contact of all surfaces. This is exposed to light, 150 watt bulbs or daylight, until the emulsion hardens, and washed out in a bath of warm running water, being gently agitated or hosed to

Clearing the screen of varnish.

clear the mesh where the emulsion has been protected by the photo opaque paint. To strengthen the screen and fill pin holes, it can be coated completely with varnish on the inside, the printing areas being rubbed clear from the outside with a clean rag.

This mixture can be used for producing free textural effects by painting the areas required to be white directly on to the screen. The mixture should be kept warm in a double boiler, and all excess should be thrown away.

With Terylene mesh, the hardened emulsion can be removed after use in a bath of weak caustic soda. Shellac, varnish or any waterproof substance can be used to block out the screen.

Simple Stencils Paper stencils can be used to print short runs; masking tape for stripes; scatter patterns can be obtained by torn paper scattered on to printing surface, on one sweep of the squeegee these will stick to the screen and form a stencil.

Profilm Stencils Profilm is a resin-coated paper. The printing shapes are cut out of the resin layer and removed without cutting the paper which holds the remaining shapes in place. The outside of the screen is placed on to the profilm, resin side uppermost, and ironed with a hot iron from the inside, which dissolves the resin into the screen mesh. The paper is peeled off and the screen varnished as described.

Textures A sheet of coarse sandpaper is pressed to the inside of a gelatined screen and the outside surface rubbed with a black wax chalk making a resist to the Potassium mixture; candle-wax on tracing film resisting photo-opaque paint; photo-opaque paint stippled on to sandblasted glass sheet.

Printing The table should be 6 in. wider than the cloth to be printed, and a convenient length. The top of $\frac{1}{2}$ in. plywood is layered evenly with news-paper or felt and covered with a rubber of plastic-coated, waterproof skin, all firmly fixed to give a perfect surface, mounted on a stable base. The cloth is ironed on to the table, previously coated with a thin layer of gum arabic or tragacanth. If the cloth is fine it should be pinned on to a back-cloth, the selvage parallel to the table edge.

Registering the screen.

Registration A metal registration bar is placed along one side of the table; the screen is positioned to fall correctly on the cloth, and screws, fitting firmly against the bar are fixed in the side of the screen at each corner; an angle is fixed on the screen to register against the repeat stop on the bar, the stops being previously fixed at the required intervals. A small screen containing one repeat is registered against lines marked accurately and faintly on the cloth and the screen frame.

In printing, the dye is put in the end of the screen nearest the operator, the squeegee placed behind it to sweep the colour firmly to the opposite end and repeated sufficient times to charge the cloth with colour. The colour should not be exhausted during printing.

Using the squeegee to sweep the colour evenly over the screen.

Other Effects

Spray painting using a hand spray or pressurised gun containing thin colour in gum over a firm stencil.

Hand painting can be done with dye or pigment colour, mixed as for printing.

Cylinders of varying diameter can be placed firmly on the cloth, filled with dye and dragged across the cloth to make trail patterns.

Colours Pigments, of which there are a number of good proprietary brands, are easy to use.

'Jerusalem'.

'Jericho'.

'Sidon'.

'Palmyra'. All the fabrics designed by the author.

Recipes

Block Printing with Helizarin Pigments
60 parts Helizarin Colour.
890 parts Helizarin Binder F.D.
30 parts Methyl Cellulose DKL (7 per cent solution).
20 parts Condensol A (1–1 in water).

Methyl Cellulose Solution
Dissolve 7 grammes of Methyl Cellulose DKL in 100 c.c. of water. Allow to thicken for 24 hours, until a gel is obtained. Print and fix as before.

Screen Printing with Helizarin Pigments
10–80 parts Helizarin Colour.

350 parts Helizarin Binder D.
580 parts Helizarin Reduction Binder.
20 parts Urea.
20 parts Condensol A (1–1 with water).
Print, dry, bake or iron with hot iron. (140°C, 3–5 min.)
During baking these colours give off toxic fumes. In most cases ironing is sufficient, and recommended, to fix the colour.

Cleaning the Screen
Remove excess pigment. Rub screen with rag soaked in Colasyl A50, a dry rag on the reverse side to absorb pigment. Repeat on other side; finally wash off with water.

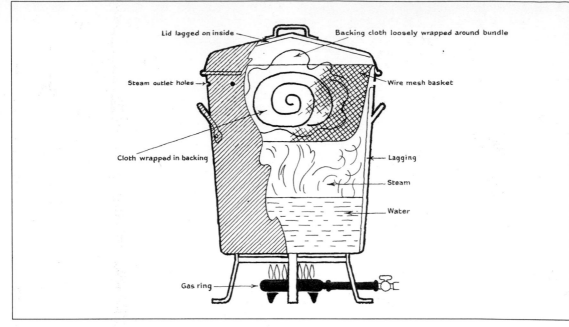

Labels on diagram:
- Lid lagged on inside
- Backing cloth loosely wrapped around bundle
- Steam outlet holes →
- Wire mesh basket
- Cloth wrapped in backing
- Lagging
- Steam
- Water
- Gas ring →

Section of a steamer showing position of cloth.

Aniline Dye for Block or Screen

Direct dyestuffs suitable for cotton or viscose rayon.

10–20 grammes of dyestuff are mixed with
50 grammes of Urea and
350 c.c. of hot water. The mixture may be boiled to ensure solution and added to
565 grammes of thickening and when cool
15 grammes of Disodium Hydrogen Phosphate are added.

Print, dry, steam 30–45 mins. and wash out in cold running water.

Thickening Gum tragacanth is most useful. 70 grammes gum tragacanth flakes or powder are mixed with 1 litre of cold water and allowed to stand for 2–3 days. Stir occasionally. Boil in double boiler for 8–12 hours. If too thick add water. A few drops of oil of cloves or phenol keeps the thickening for 2–3 weeks.

Steamer This can be made from a metal dustbin or boiler. A metal basket is fitted into the top half of the boiler, the outside of which is lagged to prevent condensation. The lid is also lagged inside and fits well. The bottom quarter of the container is filled with water and brought to the boil. The cloth is folded into a clean backcloth, rolled into a package and placed in the basket, lightly covered with a cloth to prevent dampness from condensation. Cover and steam for required time, keeping water boiling, open package immediately on removal from steamer.

All utensils, blocks, screens, etc. should be washed in cold water immediately after use with pigment or aniline dyes.

Gem-Cutting and Polishing

By courtesy of Gemrocks Ltd.

Through the ages man has been fascinated by the countless beautiful rocks and minerals found on earth. Ancient civilisations, the Chinese, Egyptians and Aztecs, learned to cut and polish many of the harder stones, using them to make jewellery and ornaments. In the following centuries, better tools and improvements upon the old and rather crude methods of cutting were gradually developed. Now modern engineering has made it possible for even the amateur of average intelligence and ability to buy reasonably inexpensive machines and cut stones, even those with complicated shapes.

Stones vary in many respects but the one factor affecting virtually all forms of cutting is the relative hardness of the material chosen. Stones to be cut must be hard enough to take a durable polish and the tools used must be made of, or faced with, harder material or abrasive. The one exception to this latter rule is, of course, the diamond, which is the hardest material known to man. As the amateur is unlikely to be able to obtain rough diamonds of a quality suitable for cutting, this chapter can be confined to the softer stones, such as the quartz family — amethysts, agates, jaspers, opals, citrines, etc., which are easily obtainable.

The one essential common to all forms of cutting is the need for absolute cleanliness during all stages of the work. Machines, stones and hands should be kept free of grit and particles as progress is made from one stage to another. Coarse grit left on at the polishing stage can ruin otherwise perfect work with scratches.

Method

Other than the simple sawing or grinding a flat surface on a slab and subsequently polishing it, there are basically three forms of lapidary work:

Tumbling or Barreling The pebbles on shingle beaches are tumbled by the action of the tides but machines can speed the process to a high degree of polish in 20 to 30 days instead of the centuries taken by nature. Tumble polishing machines provide the easiest form of 'cutting', i.e., grinding with the help of abrasive grits or powders. The machine is basically a drum or barrel which is made to rotate quite slowly. The supporting chassis, rollers and electric motor are necessary only to support and rotate the drum. A drum speed of 35 r.p.m. is quite sufficient.

Into the drum should be mixed fragments of stone of equal hardness, but preferably differing sizes, up to about 1 in. across. Water is added to cover and give a load of about 60% of the volume of the drum. The work is divided into 3 or 4 stages, commencing with the addition of coarse silicon carbide grit, going on to a medium grit and then a final grit of a very fine grade. The last stage is carried out with one of many polishing powders. Each stage takes from 4 to 6 days (and nights) of continuous rotation of the drum.

The resultant beautifully polished stones of unusual shapes are very suitable for use in modern and inexpensive items of jewellery.

Combination or Cabochon Units are small grinding and polishing machines used to fashion dome-shaped stones — known as cabochons. The machine can be fitted with a diamond-impregnated saw blade for initial shaping, and one or more silicon carbide grinding wheels in differing grades for reducing the stone to its final shape. Lastly, a hard felt or leather wheel is used to polish the stone. These processes all require a water drip feed and fairly high speeds, varying from 500 to 3,000 r.p.m., obtained through multi-speed pulleys with a small electric motor. The stone is fixed to a small 'dop' or stick to facilitate working it on the various wheels. Cabochon

a) Tumble polisher with cylindrical barrel; b) Facetting machine; c) Trim saw.

stones are used for rings, earrings and all forms of jewellery. This unit can also be used for making small stone articles such as ash trays.

Facetting machines The third and most sophisticated method of cutting is *facetting*. The facetters available for the amateur are precision machines designed to produce varying shapes of stones (such as rounds, squares, oblongs, pear shapes and other forms) which are totally covered by small facets, or flat surfaces, cut on at regular angles. These facets refract and reflect light inside and out of the stones, giving them sparkle.

Basically the machine consists of two parts plus an electric motor. A horizontally rotating table (known as the lap), dressed with diamond powder or some form of abrasive or polish, is made to revolve at a medium speed. The stone to be cut is mounted on a small stick or rod (the dop stick) which is fixed into a movable arm. The arm can be moved to varying angles and can also be rotated to set positions. The former adjustment produces the angles of the facets and the latter gives the

Combination unit.

140

Some cut and uncut stones. a) Snowflake uncut; b) Quartz uncut; c) Citrine uncut and cut; d) Agate cabochons; e) Tiger's eye cabochon and uncut stones.

stone its outline shape. Modern machines have fairly simple instructions and after a little practice it is possible to cut a stone in a matter of 3 or 4 hours.

Generally, stones which are used for facetting are of a higher quality than those used for the other two methods of cutting; the finished stones are therefore more suitable for use in better types of jewellery.

Apart from their use in jewellery-making, stones can, of course, be cut for the pure joy or interest of the pastime and in the formation of a comprehensive collection. There are several good books available and some Education Authorities run evening classes on the subject. There are also quite a number of Lapidary clubs throughout the country which welcome new members. These clubs often have machines available for use by their members.

Glovemaking

Dorothy Wright

The making of gloves is a lovely craft for the needlewoman. It requires no tools or space and can be followed at home. Though gloving leather is not cheap the saving in making one's own gloves is great and there are the added advantages of more exact sizing and fit, and a choice of styles, together with the fact that hand-made gloves are always more elegant than machine-made ones.

It used to be said that all beginners should start with natural chamois. It is much easier to learn on a firm grained leather such as *imitation peccary* '*poskin*' which will make an everyday glove which does not demand the finest stitching. From this one can advance to dress gloves made of Pittard's *suède* and *grain glovings, chamois, doeskins* and *hogskins*.

Other leathers and their uses are:
Cape, Nappa and *extra heavy chamois* for men's gloves.
Wool lamb and *Sheepskin* for winter gloves and mittens.
Coney skins for fur-backed gloves and linings (silk and fleece linings may be bought by the yard). There are also *crochet-backed* gloves with *leather* palms, and *nylon fabric* gloving which is sometimes sold in kits.

Patterns The patterns most used are the F.A. Staite Slip-on patterns: these are normal length, in quarter sizes from 6 to $7\frac{1}{2}$ women's, and from $7\frac{1}{2}$ to 9 men's. They are cut for long hands and tend to be slightly larger than commercial sizes, a 7 Staite being the equivalent of a $7\frac{1}{2}$ commercial. They are supplied with two sets of forchettes. The double forchette with a quirk is found on most bought gloves and is difficult to set in; the single forchette is perfectly easy to set in and has no disadvantages.

Streatly-Russell patterns are for broad hands and do not really make dress gloves.

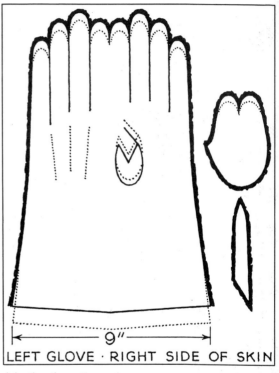

LEFT GLOVE · RIGHT SIDE OF SKIN

Adapting the pattern.

Adapting the Pattern After some experience patterns can be adapted for the shorter and broader hand. The size of pattern is the measurement in inches round the knuckles. A sizing tape measure can be bought and is a good rough guide. Where a short broad hand differs from a long narrow one is in the finger length and in the distance between the base of the thumb and the base of the first finger. This can be gauged by slipping the pattern over the thumb. If the distance is too long the thumb hole should be moved up when marking out the pattern on the skin. If the fingers are too long they may be cut and re-shaped after cutting out.

Never attempt to alter the width of the fingers of the pattern. For thinner or thicker fingers narrow or widen the forchettes. The width and length of the top of the thumb may be altered. The choice of pattern size also depends on the skin. A thin and stretchy one indicates a smaller size.

The pattern is easily lengthened at the hem but the maximum width of the new edge should not be more than 9 inches. The sides should be slanted off in a straight line from opposite the thumb hole.

Continental Glovemaking This is an entirely different method of cutting dress gloves. Only the finest leathers are used and the method is based on ratios of stretch in length and width with damp leather. There is no literature available in this country and it is taught privately by experts.

Equipment
Sharp cutting-out scissors.
Small scissors (optional).
Needles. No. 7 sharps or betweens. (3-edged 'glover's needles' are rarely used and only on the toughest leather.)
Threads. Buttonhole twist for most skins. D.M.C. No. 12 can be used for some sports gloves. Thicker D.M.C. for men's.
Tape measure, glover's (optional).
Wire paper fasteners.

Cutting-out Most gloving skins are sold to make two pairs, the area being about 5 square feet. The skin is best divided across and not down. Unless otherwise indicated by the makers, skins have the main stretch from side to side, therefore all pieces of the pattern are laid pointing up and down the skin since the stretch goes round the hand. The best-looking area is the back, though there may be a rather hard passage at the very centre which should be avoided. In general, forchettes should be cut from the flanks which are thinner and more stretchy. Areas B in the diagram may have the stretch going slightly sideways and in this case the forchettes should be slightly tilted to follow the stretch.

The skin is laid right-side-up on the table and the pattern pieces are carefully drawn round either with the thumb nail or with a pencil, *never biro or pen*. Pieces are reversed for right and left hand. Great care should be taken with marking and cutting. (Wool lamb is cut with a razor blade,

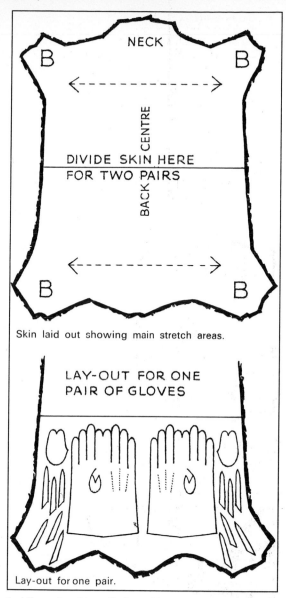

Skin laid out showing main stretch areas.

LAY-OUT FOR ONE PAIR OF GLOVES

Lay-out for one pair.

holding the skin off the table so that the wool is not cut but only parted.)

Assembly
Staite patterns describe this. Pins and tacking are never used. Wire paper fasteners do instead. The usual order is:
  (i) Hems.
  (ii) Points, if used.

(iii) Side seams.

(iv) Thumbs.

(v) Forchettes joined in pairs.

(vi) Forchettes sewn to the backs of the fingers.

(vii) Forchettes sewn to the front of the fingers.

Stitching Use a short thread and begin and end with a knot.

Prix or Stab Stitch should not be too small and is pulled fairly tight.

Single Oversew may be done with contrasting thread.

Double Oversew is the best seam for dress gloves. It should be as near the edge as possible.

Decoration may be done with points, hems, vents and buttons. The wear of most gloves is improved by some treatment of the hems. The *turned-up hem* should be sewn very lightly and with Sylko.

Facings may be done on the inside or outside. The narrow inside facing should be cut across the leather, damped and stretched fully before sewing.

Bindings should also be well stretched.

Pressing The finished gloves should be *carefully* arranged in tissue paper as shown in the diagram, then folded together and put between the pages of a stiff magazine, and finally sat on for some hours. Nothing presses gloves better than this!

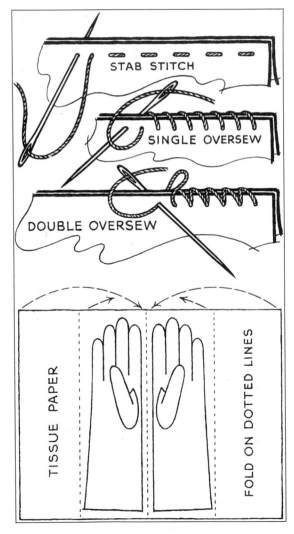

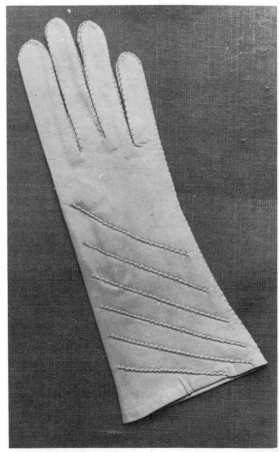

Glove made by the author.

Improvising Dolls   Mabs Tyler

Of all the thousands of toys invented and manufactured over the years, dolls (which are among the earliest ones) have retained the interest and affection of children above all others. Many families can still produce a battered, well-beloved doll or teddy, passed down from mother to child, and sometimes home-made. Children, particularly, will contrive to make just the doll they need for their immediate purpose from all kinds of apparently useless, highly improbable materials. The wise teacher or parent will exploit this imaginative, exploratory, inventive young thought by providing the kinds of materials which will enable the child to try out his ideas. Sometimes, indeed, the material itself will suggest an idea. Nothing bought or manufactured can provide the satisfaction of something developed and made successfully from an original idea.

Quite obviously the young child's rough-and-ready first efforts at doll and toy-making can be related to the early dolls of bone, wood or clay, carved and fashioned with primitive tools, and, like them, bearing no likeness to the sophisticated products of recent times. For the child its own efforts have great value in that they give tremendous scope and opportunity to his ingenuity and imagination.

In many homes and most primary schools the junk box has for many years proved its value with enthusiastic children suggesting, selecting, trying, discarding and finally producing something with which they are satisfied; something which can be easily changed or adapted when the idea grows and develops; something which to an adult— particularly one with a passion for neatness, tidiness and good finish — still remains 'junk'! In all free, doll-making activities the most important item is a piece-box of bottomless depth and variety where child or adult can sort through and experiment with every possible kind of fabric and trimming: velvet, silk, cotton, woollens, tweed, hessian, fur and fur fabric, ribbons, lace, braid, cord, sequins, beads, feathers, and so on. It helps if the different 'kinds' are sorted into bags.

The young child needs quick results — something for immediate use — so that early efforts are often sketchy, imagination playing a greater part in 'using' rather than in 'making'. As experience grows 'making' becomes of greater interest and enthusiasm, each finished doll becoming a stepping-off place, or practising of skill, for the next one, so that each stage shows signs of increasing skill in all the techniques used. Older children and grown-ups will make use of more advanced materials which their improved dexterity allows them to handle. These dolls, particularly costume or period dolls, will necessitate research from books, libraries and museums if costumes are to be authentic and true to the period or the country they represent.

145

Different in style and concept are the simple, soft, cuddly dolls made for pleasure from stockinette, socks, felt, rag and knitting. Easy for the beginner, they are also capable of development into more elaborate dolls. Other soft toys, such as balls and animals can be included here.

As the child progresses he will need other skills. He will need to calculate and measure, to deal with shapes, to use fractions, to incorporate other craft materials and use new tools, involving him in new skills and new techniques leading to wider fields of experiment and a broadening of his interests.

Paper-bag doll

Materials: A plain paper bag; wadding or newspaper; ribbon; string; wool.

The youngest children will enjoy making this from a plain paper bag; a coloured pattern can be painted or crayoned all round the open end (skirt) and features marked on the closed end. A ball of wadding or newspaper stuffs the head, tied tightly round the neck with a ribbon bow.

Wool hair can be sewn or stuck on. The doll will stand if the paper bag is a thick one, or it can be used as a puppet if a hole is pushed in the head stuffing.

Plastic bottle doll

Materials: Plastic bottle; dowel rod or stick slightly longer than the bottle; a piece of soft wire or 3 pipe cleaners twisted together to measure 16 in.; wadding; an old nylon stocking; wool; string.

Pad one end of the dowel rod with wadding, cover with a light-coloured nylon stocking and tie tightly. Insert rod into neck of bottle, wedge firmly round neck and Sellotape in position. Cover head and whole of bottle with nylon stocking so that toe fits over head. Pull tightly and twist under bottle; sew securely keeping seam as flat as possible so that bottle will stand. (Bottle can be weighted with sand or Plasticine before inserting rod.) Find middle of wire and twist round neck; bring the two ends back to neck and twist firmly. Twist the two loops of wire to form arms, leaving small loops for hands. Bind with nylon; paint or embroider features; sew or stick on wool for hair. Dress as required.

Paper-bag doll.

Plastic bottle doll.

Carton or small bottle doll

Materials: Various cartons and bottles; a piece of thin wire about 20 in. long; wadding or newspaper; old nylon stocking or any stretch material; wool.

Families of dolls can be made by using different sizes of cartons or bottles. The open end of the carton becomes the base of the doll and also forms the skirt. Make a hole in the bottom of the carton. Fold wire to find centre, insert finger in loop and twist round two or three times to make loop for head. For arms bend ends back about 3 in. from neck and twist together about ½ in. from neck. Bring two remaining ends together in triangle and twist leaving two ends. Push these through hole in carton and twist and knot firmly inside. If carton is a deep one, then make two holes opposite each other in carton, thread wire through each hole and knot separately. Wedge neck tightly and Sellotape firmly. Pad head loop with ball of wadding or newspaper and cover smoothly with nylon stocking or any stretch material. Bandage arms and hands with similar material. Paint or sew features, stick or sew on wool for hair and then dress.

Wire doll

Materials: A piece of wire about 30 in. long makes a figure about 6 in. high; wadding or newspaper; nylon stocking or stretch material; wool.

Make head and arms as for carton doll. Twist together the wires from the arms to make a waist and forming a triangle with the shoulders. Make legs in same way but slightly longer and twist remaining ends round waist. Finish as carton doll. For animals the wire should be longer according to size, e.g. about 72 in. is needed for a giraffe. Make as for doll, lengthening neck or body as required. Bend head back and legs forward, the end of the wire forming a tail.

Wired newspaper doll

Materials: 3 pieces of wire 12 in. long; newspaper; padding.

These figures do not need so much padding when formed. Wrap each piece of wire in a rectangle of

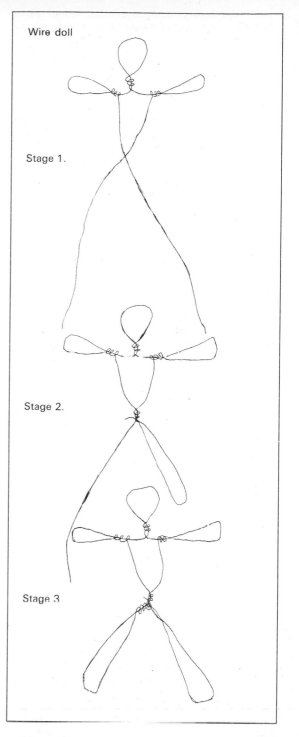

Wire doll

Stage 1.

Stage 2.

Stage 3

paper, Sellotaped firmly. Tie these three pieces together in the middle. Fold over the top of the middle piece for the head and the bottom of it for the body; the four remaining pieces form the arms and legs. This makes a flexible doll which can 'run', sit and hold positions. A little padding is needed for the head and body.

This form can also be used for a variety of animals, e.g. for a giraffe tie the wires in two places with the middle wire, which forms head and neck one end and short tail the other, placed higher than the others. For a crocodile the wire for head, body and tail should be twice as long as the other two pieces. Again tie in two places. Pad and paint or embroider features.

Dolly peg doll

Materials: Dolly pegs; wadding; nylon stockings or stretch material; pipe cleaners; wool.

Small dolls such as these can be quickly made from the old-fashioned dolly peg, the head padded with wadding and covered with nylon or stretch material; pipe cleaners twisted round the neck make arms; painted features; wool for hair. Push 'feet' into a balsa or plastic block to stand it up.

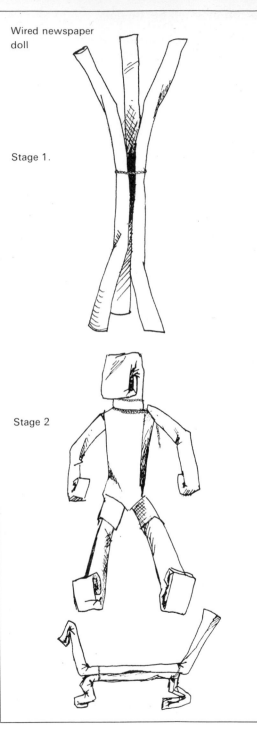

Wired newspaper doll

Stage 1.

Stage 2

Dolly peg doll.

Card doll

Materials: Stiff paper or card; glue; paper fasteners; staples; wool.

These are templates with movable arms fastened at the shoulders with paper fasteners, features painted and wool stuck on for hair. When made by young children they are usually very simply dressed — mainly for front show by sticking or stapling the clothes on, and are useful for pinning on to backgrounds of models to give a 3-D effect. All ages of children can use them to illustrate stories — rhymes for the younger ones perhaps, literature, history or geography for the older ones, with more elaborate and authentic costumes and greater attention to detail and finish. Paper patterns can be made by tracing round the shape, allowing generous turnings in cutting. Hats can be fitted on by cutting a slit along the brim. There is tremendous scope for experiment.

Card doll.

Chicken wire doll

Materials: A piece of soft 1 in. mesh chicken wire 18 in. by 15 in. (15 in. being the height and the firm edge being the base of the doll); a length of single core wire, or pipe cleaners; wadding; pale pink stretch material or nylon; wool or silk.

Moulded chicken wire forms a firm-standing, durable base for costume dolls. Much greater skill is needed in the use of stitches, fabric, style and planning when making such dolls which also require research for details of costume — research which often extends to homes, furniture, buildings, transport, customs of the period in history or the countries which the dolls will illustrate. Form the chicken wire into a cylinder, turning in the cut wires. Mould head and body, taking care to keep head small to allow for padding. Squeeze neck and waist in tightly, using pliers if necessary, to give an elegant figure. Form arms by doubling and twisting the wire, leaving a loop for hand. (Twisted pipe cleaners can be substituted here.) Pad and cover arms and twist into chicken wire at shoulders. Pad head and body with thin layers of wadding, keeping face (and shoulders if they will be exposed) smooth and free from wrinkles. Cover with pale pink stretch material or nylon. Paint or embroider features; make hair from wool or silk.

If a man or boy doll is required, before moulding cut wire up middle from base for about 5 in. (about one third of height) for legs. Form legs into cylinders and mould to shape. Continue as above.

Cylinder doll

Materials: A cardboard cylinder (e.g. toilet roll end); 4 pieces of string, 12–14 in. long; 4 newspaper squares, 3 in. square; 4 newspaper pieces, $1\frac{1}{2}$ in by $\frac{3}{4}$ in.; a dolly peg; padding; nylon stocking or stretch material; wool.

Pierce holes opposite each other at both ends of cylinder, wind one 3 in. square paper round one piece of string and Sellotape it (arm). Tightly roll up one of the smaller pieces of paper and tie at end of string (hand). Thread the other end of the string through both holes at one end of the roll. Make another arm and hand at the end of this string. Repeat with the other piece of string to make legs. Pad the dolly peg for the head and cover tightly with nylon. Embroider features and sew on wool hair. Slide legs of peg over taut string across end of cylinder and wedge in.

Newspaper doll

Materials: A double sheet of a large newspaper; wool or string.

Fold half newspaper sheet four times to make a neat strip for head and body. Make similar smaller strip for arms. Fold body strip in half, put 'arms' through 1½ in. below fold and tie body tightly above and below arms. Fold skirt piece once each way and join back. Gather along one long edge. Bind lower edge with Sellotape to make it stand firmly. Fold remaining quarter sheet six times and stuff between head folds. Pad head and paint features; sew on hair.

Stockinette or vest doll

Materials: Stockinette; stuffing; wool.

For a 7–8 in. doll a piece of stockinette material 10 in. by 6 in. for the head, body and legs is needed, and two pieces 3 in. by 2½ in. for the arms. Fold larger piece of material in half lengthwise and machine or backstitch as diagram, leaving one side open for stuffing. Stuff legs and sew across top to form a joint; stuff head firmly and tie tightly round neck; stuff body and sew up opening. Stitch and stuff arms; sew on across shoulder. Embroider or paint features (on lower half of face if baby doll); sew on wool for hair and dress.

Sock doll

Materials: A white or pale pink sock; stuffing; wool or floss silk.

Use a sock with no holes or darns in the back of the heel which forms the face. Cut off the toe at instep and cut lengthwise in two for arms. Fold sock so that the back of the heel is facing and cut up middle of welt for legs. Backstitch legs on wrong side, turn inside out and stuff. Stitch across tops of legs to make a joint. Stuff body, tie tightly round neck, stuff head very firmly and draw together cut edges at back of head. Sew and stuff arm pieces and sew on across top of shoulders. Embroider or paint features; make hair of wool or floss silk.

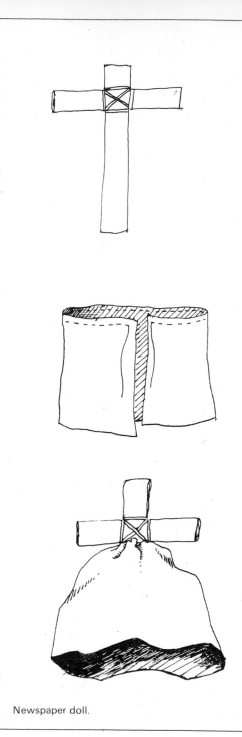

Newspaper doll.

150

Stockinette or vest doll.

Sock doll.

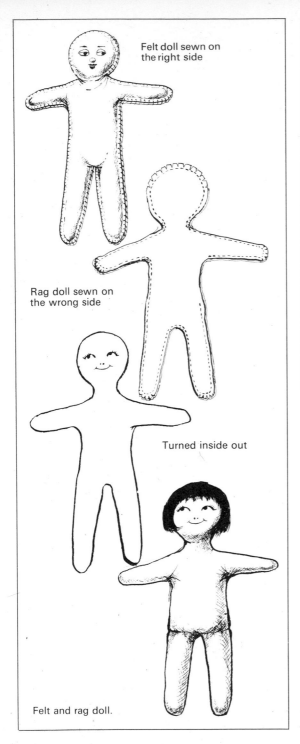

Felt doll sewn on the right side

Rag doll sewn on the wrong side

Turned inside out

Felt and rag doll.

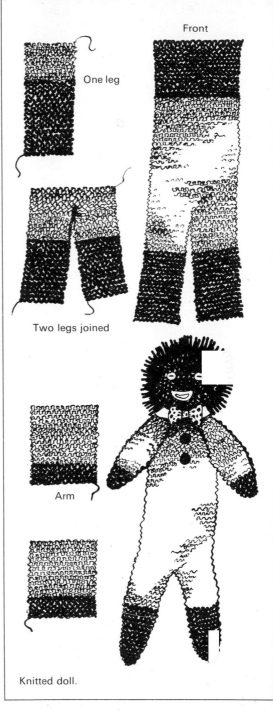

Front

One leg

Two legs joined

Arm

Knitted doll.

Rag doll

Materials: Pale pink or unbleached calico; stuffing; wool.

This is still a very popular doll. Trace from a template on to calico and backstitch firmly (or machine round) leaving one side open for stuffing. Cut small v's out of all curved edges and snip corners close to stitching to allow seams to lie flat when work is turned inside out. Again, paint or embroider features and sew on wool for hair.

Felt doll

Materials: Natural felt; stuffing; wool.

Using felt, cut out shape from template as for rag doll. It is not advisable to pencil the outline as marks on felt are not easily erased. Joining is done on the right side either by oversewing or stab stitch. Finish as rag doll.

Knitted doll

Materials: 4-ply or double knitting wool; stuffing.

Like the card dolls, these can be made by very young children as well as older ones and adults, starting from a straightforward golliwog or teddy bear for the young learner to the more elaborate pierrot, Puss in Boots, costume doll, etc. In each case the same basic strip of garter stitch knitting is used which can be varied in size by adjusting the number of stitches. Knit two legs and put both lots of stitches on to one needle. Now knit twice the length required for body and head, divide stitches and knit legs. Fold the strip in half and oversew firmly, being careful to match up stripes, and leaving opening for stuffing. Stuff and finish as required.

Many excellent books have been published on the making of dolls and stuffed toys containing good ideas, patterns and varieties of toy, and ideas for dressing (see bibliography page 245). Children can be encouraged to make their own templates and adaptations, e.g. the card doll template makes an easy glove puppet if the legs are omitted and the sides cut straight and wide to form a skirt. Templates can also be traced from toys and animals — ducks, dogs, cats, balls, bricks, etc. Children will contrive and experiment to

Knitted and dressed doll.

make successful dolls from a variety of materials other than those suggested here — pipe cleaners, string and rope, raffia, hanks of wool, wooden spoons; in fact, the more varied the materials made available for children to use, the more satisfying and surprising are the results.

153

Mobiles   Elizabeth Holder

It may be said that the history of the mobile began in 1678, the date of the earliest known chandelier. Movement, it is true, was limited but the basic idea was there. The mid-Victorian bead curtains and hanging lustres were developments of this idea. It was not, however, until the 1930s that the mobile as a moving sculpture became an art form, thanks to the inspiration of Alexander Calder. The purpose of a mobile is to give visual pleasure. It is purely decorative but if it is to give restful and interesting enjoyment to the beholder it must be well designed on aesthetic principles. The mobile can be a specialised form of craftwork in its own right but it can also be used as a means of displaying other techniques, for example, embroidery or weaving.

It is important that a mobile should hang freely so that it can move easily in small currents of air. As it turns it displays constantly changing designs in form and colour. The stringing and hanging of a mobile should be in character with its fundamental idea. For example, a mobile embodying the idea of flying birds or kites requires an airy effect and should therefore be strung lightly with invisible nylon thread. In contrast, a heavier droplet design needs, if it is to be aesthetically pleasing, to be balanced by horizontal wires and thicker, more showy supporting thread. A mobile constructed of interesting units, carefully designed and pleasantly coloured, can have a most soothing and enjoyable effect on a person watching its continuous, slow movement.

The simple and easily-available materials required for this craft make it one eminently suitable for the school or home.

Materials Scissors, pliers, wire-cutters; UHU glue or Bostick; needles; threads of various types, including invisible nylon thread; paper, card, foil, balsa wood scraps, string, etc.; scraps of fabric, felt and ribbon, beads, sequins, etc.; feathers, leaves, twigs, shells, etc.

Natural objects like shells can furnish ideas for mobiles as well as provide materials from which they can be made. In addition, the home or classroom 'bits bag' and other odds and ends offer numerous possibilities. Simple mobiles can be made from paper. Children would enjoy making one composed of a Christmas ring from which could be suspended single letters cut from variously coloured paper and making the words HAPPY CHRISTMAS.

A more interesting example is the spiral which is made of paper or card and, as it turns, gives a continuous climbing movement. The method of construction is given in Fig. 1. This circle 7 in. in diameter should be cut out in a brightly-coloured card. The thicker quality ticket card is suitable. Starting at A and cutting continuously until B is reached and the centre drops out, a spiral is formed. The card spiral may be hung on invisible thread through point C and will make an interesting, simple mobile.

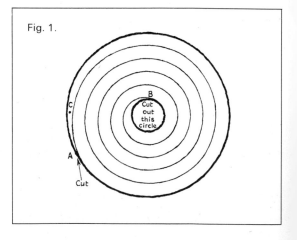

Fig. 1.

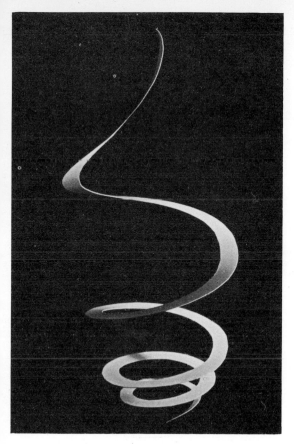

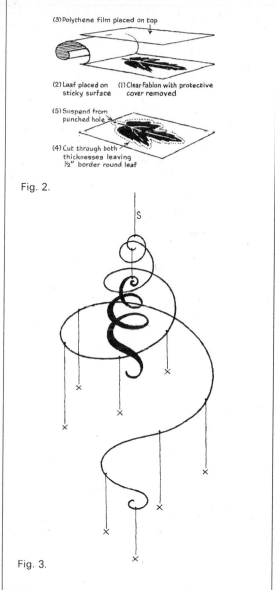

Fig. 2.

Fig. 3.

A development of this spiral theme is the 'shower of leaves' mobile. Colourful leaves of decorative shapes were pressed and then each leaf was made into a unit by mounting it between a piece of clear Fablon and a small sheet of polythene film. The adhesive of the Fablon held the leaf between the two sheets and thus a protective film was formed on each side of it. Fig. 2.

In this manner eight units were made and suspended individually from a spiral of copper wire of the thicker quality supplied by Dryad Handicrafts for toy-making at about 9p. per coil.

A twist of copper wire was suspended at (S) by invisible nylon thread (Fig. 3). In the centre of the large spiral a smaller spiral was hung to simulate a vine tendril. The wire of the second spiral was wrapped with florist's green parafilm, though green tissue paper would have been equally suitable, in order to give the idea of a grape vine with its leaves.

The various components of the 'shower of leaves' mobile were comparatively simply made but advanced craft techniques can be employed in the construction of more complicated examples. It should be remembered, however, that a mobile is a three-dimensional object intended to be viewed with equal effect from any and all directions.

The completed 'shower of leaves' mobile.

The stringing of a mobile is a factor as important as the design and colour of the individual units. Fig. 4 shows various ways of doing this but very often the theme of the mobile and the design of the units will suggest a method of stringing.

The struts to which the strings are attached can be wire as in (a), in which case coppered welding wire of an appropriate thickness is suitable Struts can also be made of thin wooden dowel as in (b).

The coil shown in (c) can be made from the springy toy-making wire mentioned above and supplied by Dryad Handicrafts. Sometimes the springing movement helps the play of the mobile. (d) shows how a large lampshade ring can be used as the main support of the units. (e) shows a restricted form of stringing by which the units are linked and the movement of one unit causes movement in the others.

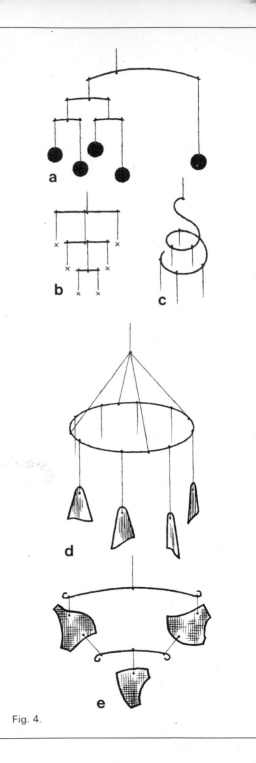

Fig. 4.

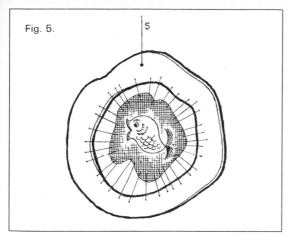

Fig. 5.

The photograph illustrates the use of string weaving, each unit being made of string on a framework of wire. (Aluminium wire obtained from a garage was used in the example.) The weaving can be made more interesting by the incorporation into it of pebbles or strangely shaped twigs or sticks. These are placed in the warp and woven into the weft. Aluminium wire is formed into a frame on which a warp of string is wrapped. The weft of the string weaving is threaded in with a large-eyed needle.

Machine embroidery is a craft appropriate for use in the making of more complicated mobiles. As the stitch is alike on both sides of the material the piece of work can be mounted to show both sides, and beads, sequins or hand decoration can be added on each face. The embroidery can be mounted between two thicknesses of card, plywood or polystyrene sheet, or stitched to holes in the framework as in Fig. 5. The completed units of embroidery in mounts are then strung in an attractive way. To mount a machine-embroidered panel the material is stitched to the tile with white embroidery cotton. The whole unit is suspended on invisible thread (S).

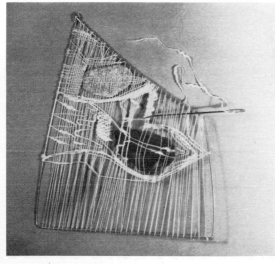

Unit in string weaving.

Fig. 6.

String is used to support glass drop forming one unit of mobile (Fig. 6).

A mobile with a banner motif can be made from woven material, without any wire framework, suspended from one end. Ideas for the decoration on each side of the material are infinitely variable but suggestions for a Christmas mobile are embroidered snowflakes or the Three Kings.

Since the making of mobiles is a comparatively new craft it affords considerable scope for individual choice and for experimentation, both in colour and design. The making of a mobile by the simple processes of cutting and gluing can give much satisfaction. Furthermore, the introduction of the idea of mobility to a traditional craft or technique is a means of opening up new fields of interest and possibility for the beginner to explore.

Model Making

G. Roland Smith

People have made models of various things, and for various reasons, from very early times. The ancient Egyptians, over four thousand years ago, made delightful toy-like models from painted clay or wood showing little figures busy using everyday objects. These miniature tableaux were left with the departed in the belief that they would somehow be of use in an after life.

Models have nearly always been made for some specific purpose. Unlike sculpture, they are seldom ends in themselves but generally convey, three-dimensionally, certain more or less precise information. They are not, strictly speaking, a medium for free expression, but are an applied art, not a purely creative one. Models undoubtedly have aesthetic appeal. For example, some model-making techniques are related to paper sculpture where the expressive quality of the material itself can be exploited to imaginative effect. These notes, however, refer to the practical applications of model making, simply as a means of handling factual matter constructively.

A model affords the opportunity of reviewing the elements of some large project simultaneously in advance. Town planners use models in this way, moving component buildings experimentally from place to place.

A model stage set enables the theatrical designer to put himself dramatically in the position of the audience while there is still time to make changes. In industry, model ships and aircraft can be tested in tanks or wind tunnels before going into production. Engineering problems may be solved with the help of mathematical models representing the stresses involved in construction (as in bridge building). Scientific ideas can often be best expressed by tangible models of crystal and cell structures, plant forms, and anatomical systems. Models are not necessarily miniatures: some are magnified versions of microscopic things. Making factual models from observation can further the study of basic design. Working models are used to demonstrate mechanical principles. Historical and geographical models reveal perhaps the military strategy behind some famous battle, or the geological formation of a land mass. Relief maps and topographical models can be photographed at close quarters, and have been used convincingly in film making. In all these examples accurate research and precision of scale are important. Museums make use of models. The Science Museum, London, has models of inventions, and the Maritime Museum, Greenwich, has famous ships marvellously reproduced in great detail. Apart from their instructional uses, such models appeal to the collector with limited space for preserving tangible records of historical objects — steam engines, veteran cars, furniture, etc. There is, moreover, the sheer fascination of making things small, as with the Lilliputian dolls' house, with the Victorian fort or cut-out theatre, with ships in bottles, and with the toytown world of childhood.

Educationally, model making provides an incentive to research. Before children can make factual models they must gather some facts. In schools, insistence upon perfect scale and craftsmanship is usually more trouble than it is worth. Children delight in making things well by their own standards. Professional techniques must be modified, and precise 'blue-prints' are out of place: they can be dangerous if they inhibit the spirit of practical enquiry which characterises genuine 'project' work. Models bring the environment into the classroom: they enable children to adopt a bird's eye view, and to take in at a glance things which might normally be encountered singly. As a technical pursuit, simple model making uses applied mathematics in an attractive form. There is no better way of learning geometry. Children

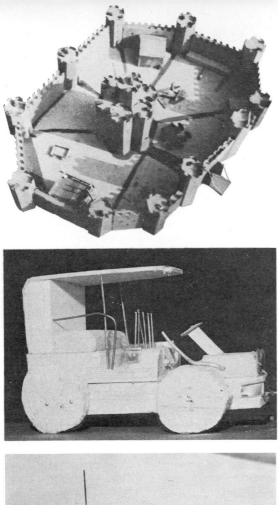

working in groups (on a dockyard, perhaps; a village, or a castle) develop social skills, and recognise each others talents. Farms or markets make excellent centres of interest to which various models can be effectively related. There is scope for the personal model also, maybe embodying some original design for a machine or a space ship. The experimental use of materials plays a vital part. Some school models are made strongly so that the finished article may be repeatedly used as a teaching aid. Temporary models take shape more quickly: their value lies in the activity rather than the end product.

The following briefly lists some materials commonly used for measured model making (distinct from free modelling or sculpture); wood, hardboard, balsa wood, plywood, light metals (aluminium, tin, zinc, etc.), clay (synthetic and natural), Newclay (self-hardening), plaster, wire mesh, expanded polystyrene, papier mâché (layers of tissue pasted over basic structures), Perspex, plastics, adhesive surfacing materials, dowel rods, cane, cork (lumps and tiles), gumstrip, paper (sugar paper, cartridge, etc.), paints (poster colour, powder colour, etc.), varnish (spirit, copal, Acrylimix, etc.), cardboard (probably the best general-purpose material — strawboard for sturdy construction; artists' line board for structures requiring a good painting surface; post-cards, bending board, or Bristol board for detailed structures).

Oddments may be useful, including: boxes, sponge, foam plastic, beads, sandpaper, wallpaper, cloth, corks, cotton reels, cocktail sticks, wooden spills, pipe-cleaners, lolli-sticks, leather, acetate sheet, canvas, pins, felt, Sellotape, raffia, wire, straws, veneers, etc. etc.

For children, the following tools will probably be adequate: small hacksaws, scissors, pencils, crayons, rulers, paint brushes, paper clips, stencil-cutting nibs, etc.

The teacher or professional craftsman may also require: guillotine, shears (bookbinders.), knives, pliers, stapler, tweezers, steel rule, file, drawing instruments, etc.

Adhesives include: vegetable glue (for general school use), impact glue (for strong fixtures), and cellulose paste (for paper coverings).

The following basic techniques relate to card-

Castle (top): A composite model built by a group of about 18 school children as part of a project on fortifications. It measures about 5 ft. 6 in. across, and is made mainly of wood and cardboard.
Vintage motor car (centre): A small-scale balsa wood model by a boy of 12. Length — about 5 in.
Liner (below): A small-scale balsa wood model by a boy of 12. Length — about 5 in.

Egyptian ship: A model made about 2000 B.C., found in a tomb, and now in the Science Museum, London

Roman merchant ship (left): The model itself is not old, but shows the sort of vessel once used for carrying corn. A fine example of the model-maker's craft to be seen in the Science Museum, London

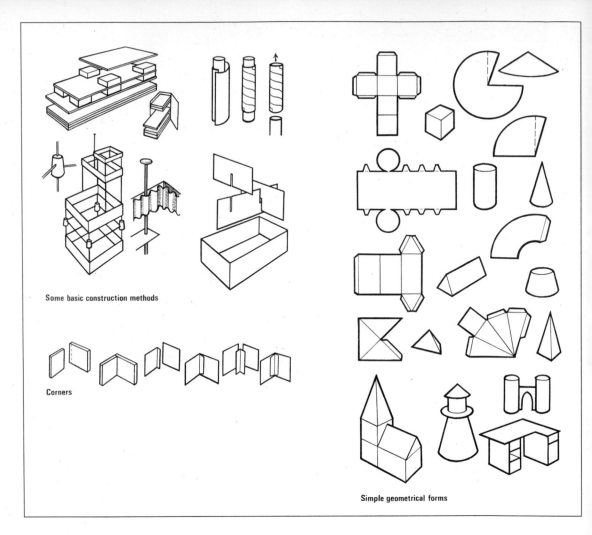

Some basic construction methods

Corners

Simple geometrical forms

board: blocks and platforms are made by 'sandwiching' layers together, or by introducing matchboxes or wood blocks in between (corrugated cardboard is helpful).

Hollow shapes are made by wrapping thin card round a former (e.g. broomhandle, jam jar etc.), binding with gumstrip, and removing when set. Skeletal shapes and open frames are built with knitting needles, dowels, lengths of cane or wire pushed into corks or inserted into punched or corrugated cardboard. Box-like shapes may be strengthened with intersecting internal partitions and the careful slotting together of wall sections. Corners are formed by butt jointing with thick

materials, by overlapping tabs, or using a sealing strip (e.g. gumstrip). Experience with uncomplicated mathematical solids (cube, cone, cylinder, pyramid, etc.) opens up unlimited possibilities.

There are usually four stages in model making: 1. Measuring and drawing, 2. Folding and cutting, 3. Assembling and fixing, 4. Decorating and finishing.

These are the basic steps. Subject and detail must be left to the model maker.

Modern Embroidery   Lavinia Everard

Until quite recently embroidery was regarded as the Cinderella of the crafts and not taken seriously. It has been looked down upon by artistic high-brows as merely a pastime for ladies with too much time on their hands or as a nerve-soother. It is, of course, a valuable subject for occupational therapy, but in this it is the simple repetitive performance of stitching which gives it its therapeutic value and not the creation of an embroidery design.

During the Middle Ages, particularly in the 14th and 15th centuries, English embroidery was famed throughout Europe and was, as a matter of interest, one of England's most important exports. The designs were mostly of religious subjects, and kings, noblemen, churches and monasteries paid large sums for examples which were so prized that they have been preserved to the present day. We can admire many of these, embodying incredible skill and beautiful design, in our own museums, in particular in the Victoria and Albert Museum. A very high standard continued into the Tudor period when the love of good living reflected itself in more secular subjects being chosen for embroideries. Lovely work was lavished on the clothes of both men and women as well as on articles for the great houses — bed drapes, coverlets, hangings, 'table carpets', and curtains, and also work for the powerful Livery Companies and Guilds.

The slow decline in quality which came with the Stuart and Georgian periods was unfortunately accelerated by another factor — the Industrial Revolution of the early 19th century. Fabrics could now be patterned so quickly and cheaply by machinery, and, alas, so tastelessly, that quality both in design and workmanship deteriorated and the demand for decoration by embroidery passed. Nevertheless women still embroidered as they had done through the ages, satisfying in some way a natural urge to create.

Jacobean embroidery.

163

Embroideries have been found in Egypt which are 3,000 years old and it is touching to think how, throughout history, women have stitched away their sorrows, found solace when waiting, and celebrated their happiness in weddings and christenings with embroidery. During the Crusades the ladies of the castles embroidered heraldic emblems, whiling away the long years whilst their husbands were away in the Holy Land. A quaint and spirited piece of embroidery still exists which was stitched by the delicate hands of Mary, Queen of Scots, who thus found solace whilst waiting in her grim castle prison for execution. During the alerts and air raids of the last war many women found relief from tension in embroidery notwithstanding that cloth was rationed and the supply of thread limited.

By the beginning of the present century the standard of embroidery had reached its lowest level and was generally spoken of as 'fancy work', but in the 'thirties a minor revolt, led by Rebecca Crompton, reacted against the prevailing boring and lifeless designs. It is true that there were strongholds of good technique in England in the form of guilds, colleges and schools, but good technique was rarely allied with original or lively design. The standard of commercially-produced transfer designs of this period degenerated into a dainty deadness; some of these are still stocked in the shops and look as if they were designed before the First World War. Rebecca Crompton's revolt was followed by the establishment of the Needlework Development Scheme which for fifteen years pioneered excellent work in sending out lecturers and in distributing well-produced leaflets, colour slides and books to schools, colleges and women's organisations and in the circulation of representative loan collections.

So now the outlook is completely changed and embroidery is, once more, a fashionable subject. There is, in fact, so great an interest in creative embroidery as a means of expression that, in the form of panels or hangings, it is accepted at the highest levels as a new art form — in fact it needs a new name. This revival is encouraged and helped by the ever-widening variety of inspiring new materials and threads, unconventional textures and effects now available. Smooth, rough, dull, shiny, knobbly, metallic, fluffy, shot, and in beautiful colours, bright, rich, intense, subtle and sombre — much of it due to the recently invented

Couched gold thread work.

man-made fibres. Better teaching has made people realise that embroidery is not merely the decoration of an article; it must be thought of, and thoughtfully planned, as part of it. An exciting piece of embroidery can exist in its own right. The finest examples of embroidery have been for the enrichment of religious and ceremonial articles but here are a number of everyday articles you could embroider today: Chair back and seats (try a stool for your dressing table) — rugs — cushions (how about a personal one for a special person?) — bedspreads — padded bedheads — curtains — door curtains or portières (well weighted and padded) — under-glass finger plates, paper-weights and trays — jewel boxes — fire screens — book covers for precious books — book-markers — needlebooks — work boxes — handbags — beachbags — belts — lunch mats — trolley cloths — runners — table cloths — draught screens — lampshades — tea cosies (or, for a different shape, a coffee-pot cosy) — egg cosies for both a single egg or several eggs — (Danish style) soft toys — babies' cot covers — christening robes — bonnets — bibs — children's clothes — adults' clothes (much discretion must be exercised here; consider the fashion angle and avoid 'arty-craftiness') — special greeting cards. I would like to add an idea which is Scandinavian in origin — special cloths and centres for the Christmas or Easter table.

All these are useful articles of which the embroidery is an embellishment, but today many embroiderers are attracted by working a panel or picture, which is glazed and framed, or a hanging. These require very careful consideration as, since they serve no useful purpose but exist solely as decorations, the design is all-important.

The craft of embroidery is coming back to the position of importance it once occupied. Influence from the Continent has been considerable, especially from Scandinavia where the heritage of traditional peasant art has been undisturbed by any industrial revolution, where nearly every woman embroiders and where good materials and designs have always been obtainable. Embroidery as now taught in schools is intended to develop the student's sense of colour and pattern, and to train the taste. It is also a subject in the General Certificate of Education examinations and is most popular as the emphasis is no longer on efforts to get painstaking skill from unwilling fingers (efforts which gave many girls a permanent dislike of stitchery) but on experiments in pattern, colour and texture arrangements. Classes for adults in evening institutes, adult centres and women's organisations have been backed up by articles on the subject in newspapers, glossy magazines and women's journals. A succession of inspiring and attractive books on embroidery continue to be published and there are frequently exhibitions of modern embroideries in the larger cities. From these work is often purchased by public or private collectors at high prices.

Do not fail to visit these exhibitions whenever you can — illustrations in books can never be the same as the actual work seen at close quarters. Look out for new books — you can request them from your local library and if, when you have seen them, you decide that they will help you, buy them; especially those giving technical information. They will serve you well. Many new churches have been built since the war; contemporary architecture needs contemporary furnishings and so some of the most exciting modern embroidery is ecclesiastic. Exploring churches in strange towns and villages may be rewarded by a fine altar frontal, a seat cover or a kneeler.

It is interesting to note that the excellent idea of putting original pictures in schools has extended to embroidery panels. Very often, because of their interesting techniques, they arouse more interest than paintings or prints, the reason probably being that children respond more readily to the direct appeal of varied textures of actual cloth and threads.

All this is very encouraging, but still a beginner may be uncertain how to start on the creation of an original design and doubtful if she will be able to carry it through to completion. 'Oh! I cannot draw' is so often heard. Whilst an ability to draw certainly helps, lack of it is not a bar as there are many other ways of evolving a good design. In fact, skill in realistic drawing can sometimes be a handicap as a pictorial treatment is not suitable for the limitations of embroidery. Here I am leaving out those examples of embroidery laboriously worked in long and short stitch which set out to imitate paintings, for the admiration which they evoke is purely on account of the industry and patience involved. They do not exploit the various stitches.

In every craft no design can be attempted without some knowledge of the techniques and tools particular to that craft. Stitches are the words, so to speak, the various methods are the grammar and the tools make it possible to work correctly. So, first, collect your tools and materials:

Stitch book The few stitches shown here will do to start with but later, acquire a more complete vocabulary.

A selection of varied needles It is so important to use the right needle for the job in hand as the pleasure of working depends on it. Fine and coarse, with round eyes and long eyes, crewel needles and some thick chenille needles, also tapestry needles (blunt ended), all in various sizes.

A thimble If you have grown up without having learnt to use a thimble, as so many women have, it will certainly be difficult to take to one. Perseverance, however, will pay off as no rhythmic regular stitching can be done without one. Though a fine needle is more accurate, you must remember that the needle has to make a hole sufficiently large to draw two thicknesses of the thread through it. Too long a needle, e.g., a darner, is awkward so use a chenille needle instead.

Fine embroidery scissors Really sharp and cutting right to the tip.

Medium sized scissors

Stiletto For piercing holes.

Embroidery frames A small ring embroidery frame, called a tambour, will be useful at first. Later, a large square frame called a slate frame for canvas work will be needed. Avoid ring frames of plastic which have a tendency to slip, or frames without a screw for adjustment. If the material in the circular frame slips, or if the outside ring is too large, bind one ring with a strip of binding or tape. Instruction on dressing a frame is given in many good books on embroidery. The ultimate luxury when working is to have the frame fixed to a stand; this also looks quite interesting when standing in a room in the same way as a spinning wheel does. (Frames are a good idea for a gift which will give life-long pleasure.) Square frames are of two kinds: one with pegs and holes for adjustment, and the other with large wooden screws. The latter is well worth its extra cost as it can be adjusted more accurately.

Chalk (dressmaker's), or the same substance in pencil form; a fine sable brush (No. 0 or 1) and tubes of water colour, Chinese white and black.

Drawing paper, Dressmakers' carbon paper, graph paper and tracing paper The last is very useful for laying over your work when trying out corrections.

Background fabric This is all-important as it sets the mood and the style of the work. A fabric with a really interesting texture and colour can arouse your creative spirit. Select a material not too cheap in quality or you will be discouraged by the result. Never stint money on background fabrics — your time is too precious to waste on poor material. The idea that anything will do to start with is completely wrong, as even well-executed stitches will fail to achieve a completely successful piece of work. This is just the stage when you need

all the help a good material can give you. The background fabric should be firm or it will pucker and be less easy to hold. Not too tightly woven, like poplin or grosgrain, or the needle will not pass through it easily, especially if the thread is thick. If you have to tug each stitch this will disturb the rhythm and pleasure of stitching. The fabric should not be stretchy or too loosely woven. Avoid furnishing fabrics, especially rayon, unless of expensive quality. They mostly have a loosely woven surface into which the stitches will sink and are too often coarse in texture.

Make a firm stand against 'mud' and neutral colours to start with; you will find that your ideas appear quite different on, say, a deep, rich, coloured background worked in lighter tones. Historic embroidery had perforce to be chiefly on a pale neutral background because natural fibres such as linen and wool were usual, and these could not easily be dyed in the length, and silk which could be coloured was rare and therefore costly. Time has darkened the examples in our museums and so it has come to be accepted that embroidery tended to be on neutral coloured backgrounds.

Suggestions for background fabrics are: Woollen fabrics, which are most excellent and sympathetic, such as flannel, Viyella and smooth woollen dress materials; dress linen; good quality dress cottons, and even-weave linen. Felt has neither warp nor weft threads to strengthen it, and has moreover a boring texture. Cloth with an even weave or easily counted thread is helpful for getting stitches evenly spaced on a sampler. (This kind of fabric helps the timid and the counting of threads, serves as a prop to your morale and helps you along.) Hessian is difficult as its uneven surface can be a hindrance. However, a good quality and evenly woven type is suitable.

Threads Assemble your 'palette' of threads; a good collection is inspiring. Fine and thick, smooth and rough, silky and woolly, and also some experimental threads such as string, raffia, unusual and knobbly knitting and weaving yarns, metallic threads, mohair angora and even plastic.

Regular Embroidery Threads

Stranded cotton Skeins of divisible threads of six strands, mercerised and so moderately shiny. Clark's Anchor and D.M.C. (French) with better colours. Made in more colours than any other thread. It is worth searching for the special, muted, tapestry colour range.

A single thread is easier to manage than a stranded or multiple thread and knotted or looped stitches are unsuccessful using several threads in the needle. It is hard to see why stranded cotton is so universally used. The advantage is that it can be used in any number of threads from one to six. Probably the real reason is that it is all that many shops are able to offer and comes in more colours.

Coton â broder Similar to the above but a single thicker thread. Easier to use though not quite so many colours.

Soft embroidery cotton Thick, smooth, soft and completely matt.

Oiska Rayon Imported from Denmark. A little thinner than above, loosely twisted, lustrous, and in very attractive colours.

Pearl Cotton In balls, shiny, medium coarse and twisted. Sold in two thicknesses (5 and 8) and in a moderate range of colours.

Linen thread Coloured, not very fine, loosely twisted and slightly uneven.

Lace threads Very fine in white and natural.

Perlita (Anchor). Very heavy, shiny and cord-like.

Fresca (Anchor). Even thicker and matt. Both this and Perlita in limited colours.

Crewel wool Two-ply, best for canvas work. Use as many threads as needed to fill holes in canvas — this varies with the chosen stitch.

Tapestry wool Four-ply thickness. Other wools are: knitting wools and double knitting crochet yarns; uneven yarns such as bubbly poodle, looped mohair and angora can only be couched.

Twisted embroidery silk Very shiny, loosely twisted, medium thickness.

Filo Floss Smooth and glossy but difficult to handle with even slightly rough hands.

Buttonhole silk for fine, even work.

A variety of metallic threads, of which Lurex is the least expensive, generally have to be couched.

A comprehensive range of colours and threads is only collected with difficulty. If you know other embroideresses living in your area, members of a local class for example, then try persuading your local shop to stock a wider selection, or at least the various shade cards from which thread supplies can be ordered. Alternatively, write for your own shade cards and order what you need through the very knowledgeable and reliable people who run postal services for embroidery materials. Their addresses can be found in the magazine 'Embroidery'.

A note regarding threads. If threads are kept for a long time in a tangled mass, constantly turned over and rubbed together, they will suffer — mercerised cottons lose their lustre, silks get snags and wools get matted. So keep them well, either in boxes or — a better idea — in plastic bags of separate colours, or, though it is more trouble, in a roll-up cotton holder. A good way is to take strips of cartridge paper folded four times into long sleeves, like a smoker's spill, about 1 in. wide. Cut your skeins into even needle lengths, fold in half and place between the folds of the 'spills' with the looped ends showing, secure the 'spill' with a rubber band and write the shade number of the thread on the outside. To withdraw a thread you hold the 'spill' firmly and pull out one loop — the rest will stay undisturbed.

Beads, etc. Develop a squirrel-like addiction for small beads, sequins, bugle beads, cords and simple braids. (Elaborate braids do not mix with hand-worked stitches.) These can be added to your stitches to give contrast and interest. Your friends' button boxes, junk shops, Oxfam shops and old evening dresses are some other sources. You can sometimes buy bags of mixed beads or 'sweepings' from the wholesale firms who supply the couture trade. This is far cheaper than buying in separate packets where you get far too many of one kind.

Stitches Instead of the usual dull sampler of stitches, chalk out a simple motif of, say, a sprig of flat leaf shapes and/or a flower on a piece of fabric about 7 in. square and try out several stitches on it. You can test your sense of arrangement and colour at the same time.

An axiom to encourage beginners: no stitch in itself is difficult to execute and some are extremely easy — the hard part is the even repetition. Practice here makes perfect. Never work a fresh stitch straight on to a piece of work as the relationship between the texture of the background, the thickness of the thread and the chosen stitch will be different every time. Also you need to get your hand in to get the stitch going evenly. Look through your stitch book and make a collection of stitches which appeal to you on different fabrics with assorted threads. The same stitch looks quite different in a thick thread compared with a thin thread worked to the same size. Looking through this collection later will, perhaps, give you an idea for a complete design. Consider the suitability of the stitches for the work in hand, for instance a few of the most handsome do not take washing and ironing. Others will not stand up to wear or friction such as on a cushion or chair seat, but are possible on a hanging or under glass.

Surface stitches are those which are not influenced by the weave of the background and can therefore go in any direction on the surface of the fabric.

Stitches can be broadly tabulated. Here is a selection from each type:

Line stitches are those where the needle travels in a single line.

Running	Many variations of these can be
Back	threaded and whipped singly or in blocks.
Pekinese	Based on back stitch. Contrasting colour can be used for the interlacing thread.
Stem	Quick and flexible but does not turn sharp curves easily.
Chain	Can be whipped or back stitched.
Magic chain	Worked with two or even three colours.
Cable	More open than chain stitch.
Coral	Interesting, thin line stitch.
Couching	One method is shown here but it is not difficult to devise other ways.

Band stitches are wide stitches worked across two lines. Many have an interesting shape or silhouette. Heavier than the previous group, they can be in parallel rows to make good fillings but generally look better with a narrow space between each row.

Buttonhole	Many varieties, open or closed. Blanket stitch is not the same stitch.
Twisted chain	Pretty. Semi-line stitch.
Open chain	
Broad chain	Thick.
Double chain	Complicated, scaly.
Feather	Single (like slanted buttonhole), double or triple.
Rosette	Best worked in single, smooth thread. Effective in outward curves but in single thread.
Crested	Very complicated appearance
Cable chain	
Chevron	A close cousin of herringbone stitch.
Cretan	Versatile, open or closed, can be graduated.
Fishbone	Can be graduated, open or closed.
Leaf	Very like fishbone stitch.
Fly	Either vertical, sprig-like or horizontal points.
Thorn	Lovely for sewing down a metal thread or cord which cannot be pulled through fabric.
Wheatear	Lacy.
Satin	Appears deceptively easy — the needle just goes in and out — but actually one of the most difficult stitches with which to get good results.
Herringbone	Worked from left to right.
Braid	Worked from right to left, makes an effective border.
Loop	Can be adapted to fill a shape.
Scroll	Most suitable under glass.

Filling stitches are mostly best worked in a frame.

Wave	Worked from right to left, makes an effective border.
Couched	Contrasting thread can be used to tie the 'lattices'.
Sheaf	Handsome, heavy and slow. Does not take easily to narrow curves. Single thread.
Interlacing	Two lines of superimposed herringbone form base which is laced.

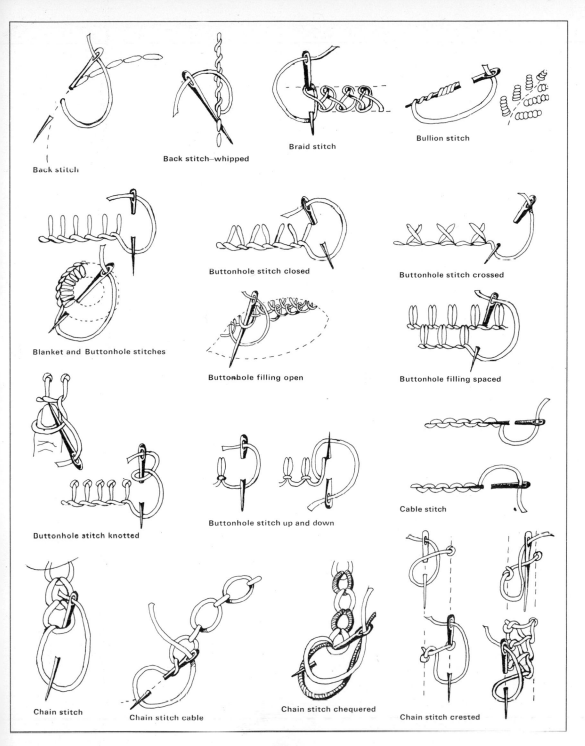

Back stitch

Back stitch—whipped

Braid stitch

Bullion stitch

Blanket and Buttonhole stitches

Buttonhole stitch closed

Buttonhole stitch crossed

Buttonhole filling open

Buttonhole filling spaced

Buttonhole stitch knotted

Buttonhole stitch up and down

Cable stitch

Chain stitch

Chain stitch cable

Chain stitch chequered

Chain stitch crested

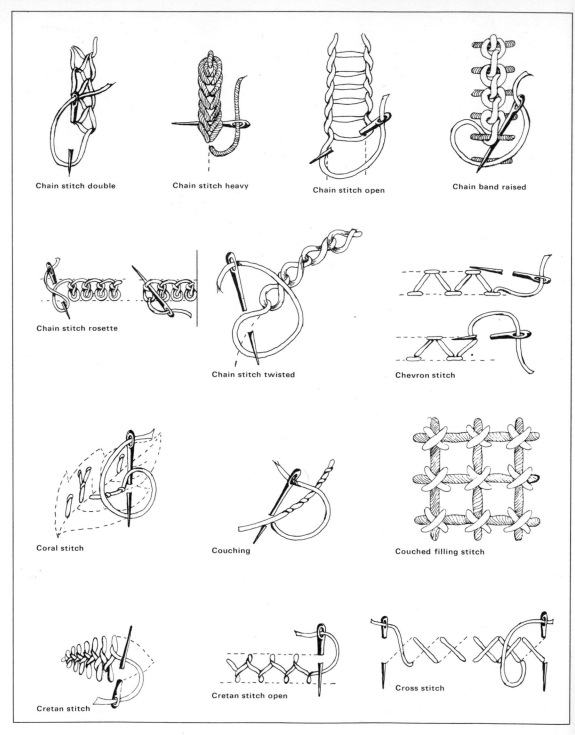

Chain stitch double

Chain stitch heavy

Chain stitch open

Chain band raised

Chain stitch rosette

Chain stitch twisted

Chevron stitch

Coral stitch

Couching

Couched filling stitch

Cretan stitch

Cretan stitch open

Cross stitch

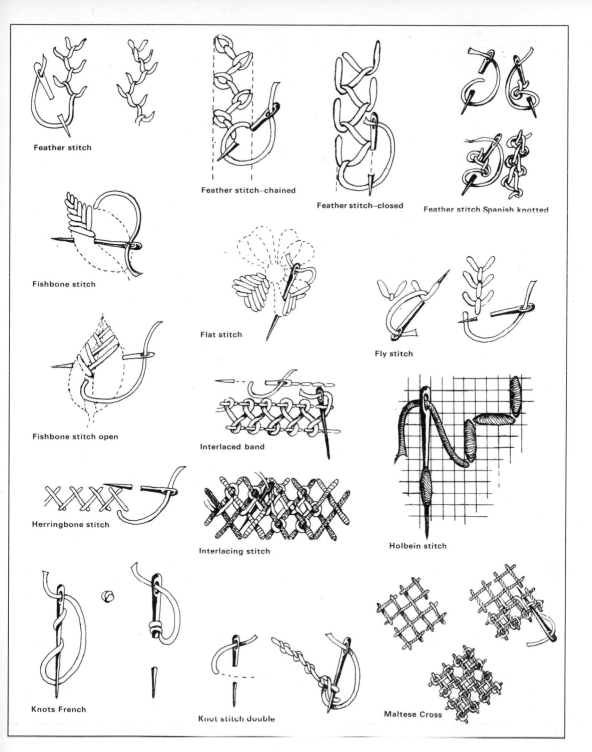

Feather stitch

Feather stitch—chained

Feather stitch—closed

Feather stitch Spanish knotted

Fishbone stitch

Flat stitch

Fly stitch

Fishbone stitch open

Interlaced band

Holbein stitch

Herringbone stitch

Interlacing stitch

Knots French

Knot stitch double

Maltese Cross

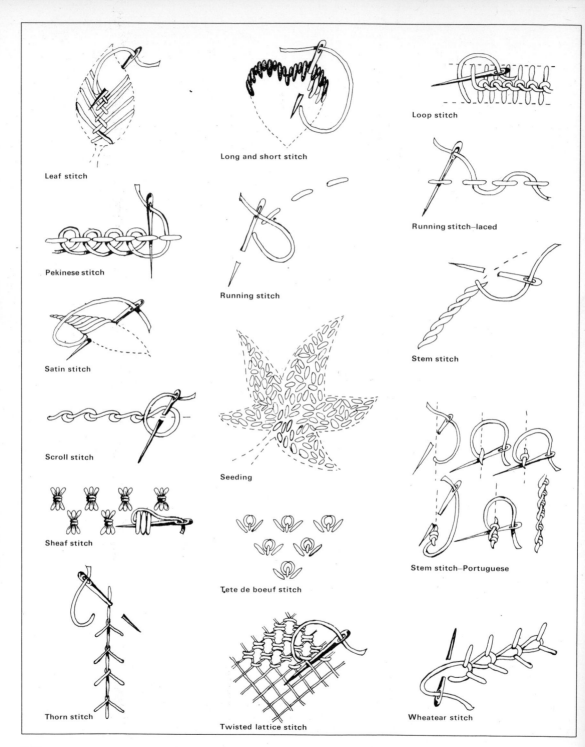

Leaf stitch

Long and short stitch

Loop stitch

Pekinese stitch

Running stitch

Running stitch—laced

Satin stitch

Stem stitch

Scroll stitch

Seeding

Sheaf stitch

Tete de boeuf stitch

Stem stitch—Portuguese

Thorn stitch

Twisted lattice stitch

Wheatear stitch

Maltese cross	An embroidery 'show-off' — a development of the previous stitch.
Seeding	Keep stitches of even length but place at random.
Long and short	Like satin stitch, deceptively difficult.
Raised honeycomb	Avoid too heavy a thread.
Raised chain band	Single thread. By making the horizontal bars longer several parallel bands may be worked on them.
Guilloche	Single thread. Comprises stem stitch, satin stitch, and interlacing stitch and French knots.
Interlaced band	Also known as Herringbone Ladder. Filling stitch.
Tête de boeuf	Pretty filling stitch.

Net embroidery.

Stitches can also be classified into 'families' as follows:

Flat stitches
Running; Back; Stem; Long and short; Fishbone — closed and open; Leaf; Chevron; Thorn; Cross; Couching; Feather; Buttonhole; Closed feather; Loop; Scroll.

Looped stitches
Buttonhole; Crossed buttonhole; Closed buttonhole; Spaced buttonhole; Cretan stitch; Up and down buttonhole; Detached buttonhole filling.

Chained stitches
Chain; Magic or chequered; Twisted chain; Open chain; Broad chain; Double chain; Rosette; Crested; Cable chain; Braid; Wheatear; Tête de boeuf.

Knotted stitches all need single strand of firm thread.
French knot; Bullion knot; Coral knot; Double knot.

Composite stitches
Interlacing; Maltese cross; Pekinese; Threaded back; Cloud filling; Twisted lattice; Cretan filling; Raised honeycomb filling; Sheaf; Raised chain band; Guilloche; Interlaced band.

Different kinds of Embroidery

Workers of various tastes and abilities can find a method to suit them. One can work extremely finely or very boldly, in work of one colour such as 'white work' where the texture of stitches make the design not the colour. One can stitch in the entire background as in canvas work, or work to the counted thread. The latter imposes limitations and a discipline which helps the stylisation of the design, and many people feel safer with an even count of thread to help them.

Traditional methods have been given vitality today as people are experimenting with the old rules. For example, 'white-work' — so called for it was always worked with natural-coloured linen or cotton and matching threads — is now often worked in strong colours with contrasting threads. The scale of stitches in one piece of work can be varied, or two or more methods can be combined.

There are many detailed books available and Anchor and Coates both publish attractive, inexpensive booklets with clear directions and good designs. The following notes suggest some of the many ways in which these stitches may be used.

Counted Thread First we will consider methods based on the counted thread. It is essential to use a cloth with the warp and weft threads of even thickness. You should be able to count the threads and it should not be so tightly woven that a blunt-ended needle (called a tapestry needle) cannot pass between the threads. This needle is always used to avoid piercing the background threads or

173

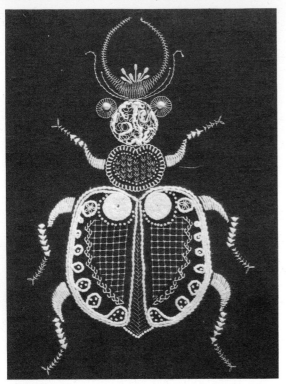

White work on a dark slub background and using varied thicknesses of thread, by Mary Roberts.

thread work does not make many demands on design abilities — just space the lines well. Threads should be same thickness as background threads.

Drawn Fabric or Pulled Work The second name is the more descriptive one. No threads in the background are withdrawn but the background threads are pulled apart by different stitches to make patterns of holes. A great variety of textures can be obtained by working on a loosely woven linen or cotton. The sewing thread should match exactly and be the same thickness as those of the fabric. Again, a contrasting coloured thread looks confusing.

Hardanger This originated in Hardanger Fjord in Norway and is a fairly coarse type of work. Formerly 'white-work', today we often stitch in white on a coloured background. Finely woven linen or cotton must be used but the best results are obtained on specially woven Hardanger cloth, the threads of which are woven in pairs. Pearl cotton, either No. 5 or No. 8, is used and the design is built up with rectangles of satin stitch called Kloster blocks, generally over four or five threads, using the thicker No. 5 thread. Spaces of four threads are left between the blocks; the threads on the inside of the blocks are cut and those of the spaces left. This leaves open squares which are sometimes filled in with looped stitches, and the remaining background threads are woven into bars using No. 8 thread. Picot loops can be added. In spite of the heavy technique the finished effect can be lace-like. Designs have perforce to be geometric, and traditionally have always been so, but it is possible to stylise a flower, figure or bird motif with charming results. Surface stitches worked on the counted threads can be introduced, but the best designs exploit the light and dark character of the holes cut in the fabric.

the sewing thread. These fabrics are specially made, ranging from 16 to 34 threads to the inch, and are listed in embroidery catalogues. Try them out and do not attempt to work on one too fine for your eyesight. You can obtain a magnifying glass to hang round your neck, or half-lenses in three magnifications to clip on to your existing glasses. Some people find an engraver's glass useful — this is a magnifying glass on a 'goose neck' stand. It is better not to work too long with these aids but they are certainly useful to get a stitch started or to sort out a mistake.

Drawn Thread Essentially patterns built up of lines of openwork and much used for table linen. Threads are withdrawn either from the warp or weft. This weakens the lines of cotton so threads are replaced decoratively to strengthen them. Where the lines cross a square hole is left and this is filled with webs to prevent the openwork from being torn by the tip of the iron. Contrasting coloured threads are rarely successful. Drawn

Cross Stitch The entire design is carried out in cross stitch over an even number of threads. Of course, all the crosses must cross in the same direction but unless the work consists of fairly solid masses of stitches it tends to look thin and straggly. Denmark is the real home of this work and specialises in delicate, naturalistic flowers finely worked. A bold stylised design can look effective in one colour on a strongly contrasted background, say, white thread on a deep blue or red. From the 'fashion angle', this could be acceptable used on a dress without looking self-consciously, arty-craftily 'hand-embroidered'.

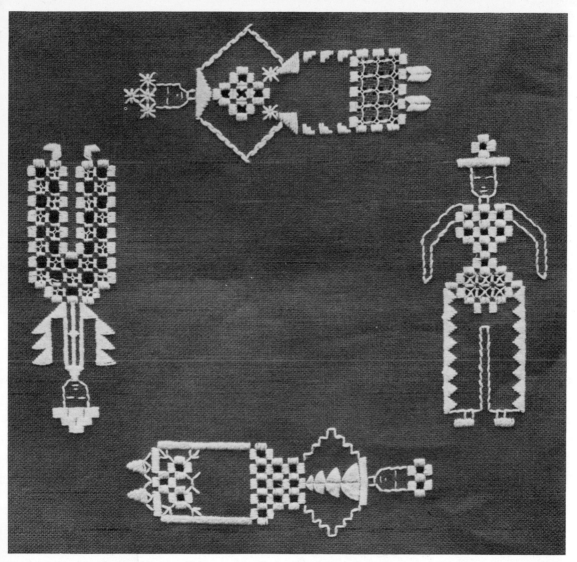

Hardanger work by Blanche Moseley. The central motif of a table cloth.

Assisi Work This is allied to cross stitch in that the design is outlined in double running stitch and the background is filled in with cross stitch in another colour leaving the shapes open.

Patterned Darning A sort of damask as the embroidery thread weaves in and out of the background in a regular pattern. Each part of the design has a different texture and the weaving threads follow the warp or weft. Tone contrasts can be obtained by heavy or light filling. In addition to plain even-weave linens and cottons, a coarse fabric called honeycomb and one rather finer, huckaback, are inviting to work on, as thick threads such as soft embroidery and pearl cotton can be woven through the surface loops and knots only, making easily built-up borders. Good for dressing table runners, mats and guest towels.

Pattern darning by M. Woodhead

Needleweaving This is very limited in use as it is composed of borders and rectangles only on the straight of the grain of the cloth. It is generally found on peasant costumes in bright colours on natural linen or sometimes worked finely in white on white cloth. Threads are withdrawn from the background in wide bands, the ends being neatly darned in. Next the top and bottom of the border are hemstitched dividing the threads into equal number of groups. These groups are woven with contrasting threads in figure of eight blocks. The weaving thread passes from one block to the next in steps leaving vertical slits between each and making a geometrical pattern.

Needleweaving has possibilities as dress decoration on linen or coarse woollen dress material. The wool would have to be of the handwoven type or the threads would not be strong enough to withdraw. It is also suitable for end runners, curtains, place mats, aprons, etc. It is not suitable for curves.

Blackwork This work was first introduced into England in the 16th century and we see it on the clothes in Elizabethan portraits. A black thread is used on white linen with fine lacy filling stitches worked on an even number of threads horizontally, vertically or diagonally. The worker can follow designs in books and then devise her own patterns. Today you can try out colour on colour or light stitches on a dark background. Avoid a design of small shapes as you will not be able to fit in enough repeats. Formerly rather naturalistic, curved shapes were outlined with heavy line stitches such as chain, double knot or twisted chain, and then the shapes were simply filled in with blackwork patterns, presenting a nice balance of light and heavy fillings. Today the designs are composed of shapes with more regard for the angular nature of the work, using as much as possible horizontal, vertical or diagonal lines. The designs look more interesting if they are not always outlined.

Double Running or Roumanian Work This is in Holbein stitch giving a lacy effect or that of delicate ironwork. It is a running stitch under and over an equal number of threads. On the return journey the stitch is reversed to fill in the spaces so that the work looks the same on both sides — useful for table linen which must look well on the back. To start and finish the thread is neatly darned in along a line of stitches. Traditionally the thread is black on white linen, and the design is embellished by squares of one stitch on each side

filled in with satin stitches in, say, red or bright green or yellow. The diagonal direction is worked in right-angled steps. It is best to work out your design on graph paper.

Canvas Work (Often erroneously called 'tapestry' work. True tapestries were woven on a loom.) Here the method differs from other embroideries as the entire background must be filled in. It is worked on strong, open-meshed canvas, fine to coarse, from 10 to 32 threads to the inch. Some of the coarser counts are woven with double thread.

It is very hardwearing and so is used for chair seats, church kneelers, handbags, footstools and similar articles. Many people think of this work as entirely worked in a single slanting stitch (tent stitch, called gros point, when on double canvas, or petit point when on single canvas) but there are at least fifty canvas stitches producing the most diverse effects. Embroidery shops have ample stocks of ready-made packs complete with design, canvas and wools. The canvases are either already painted, in which case one just fills in with the coloured wools provided, or they come with a chart to be counted out on the canvas (very tedious), or a design ready trammed — the ultimate in uncreative, repetitive work since all that is required is to work tent stitches over already laid coloured threads. How much more rewarding to make or adapt your own ideas!

Draw the design on paper in thick black ink, lay the canvas over it and paint the design on with ball point, felt pen or oil colour. There is no need to work the design on graph paper for the stitches will make their own outlines. However, it is very boring to use the same stitch over the whole of the work when there are so many to make variety of texture.

If the article is to be sat or kneeled upon it must be very firm; it is better to use 2-ply crewel wool as then you can vary the number of strands in the needle according to the stitch. Tent stitch on, say, 16-thread canvas would need three strands, but rice stitch or long-armed cross stitch would need four. Try out all your stitches on a sampler and keep it by you for reference. Tramming (the laid threads referred to above) is not necessary unless you work with single 4-ply tapestry wool on double canvas. Wool is usual but some sparkle can be added by working a few points such as centres of

Blackwork using three thicknesses of thread to give a shaded effect, by Anne Shepherd.

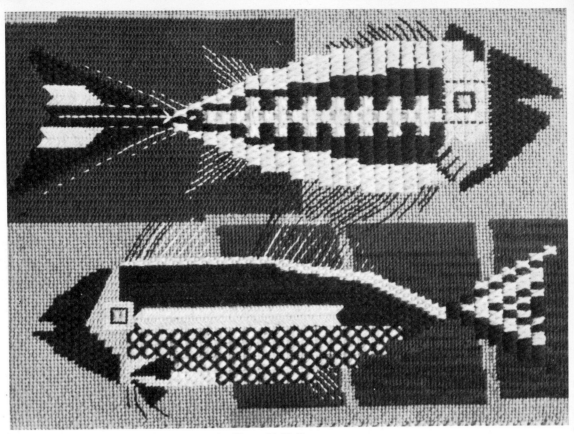

Canvas work using eight different stitches, by Moyra McNeill.

flowers or eyes of animals in mercerised cotton or silk.

Cut Work Interesting for lampshades but it must be backed with an opaque pale or white fabric, or one of the new plastic materials, so that the filament of the lamp will not glare through. It is used also for table linen and cushions and in colours for dress decoration. For this work use a firm linen or cotton which will not unravel easily when cut. The design must be composed of masses, crowded into the area to be filled, with not much background left. The shapes are outlined with plain buttonhole stitch to match the background with the head of the stitch on the outside (so avoid thin shapes or there will not be much left). Then the background material is neatly cut away. If the background spaces are large the results will be unsuccessful. It is necessary to bridge the cut spaces with worked bars to keep the work firm for washing and ironing. These bars *must* be worked before the background is cut away.

Broderie Anglais This is a more delicate form of decoration. The design is built up of very small holes, or eyelet ovals or rounds, connected by fine lines of whipped stem or chain stitch. The material is fine, firmly woven cambric or fine linen and it is worked with tiny running stitches, then very small eyelets are pierced with a stiletto and the edges finely and closely overcast over the running stitches and raw edges. Larger circles and ovals are cut horizontally and vertically in a cross and again overcast with the material turned over to the back. Any surplus material is then cut off.

Build up your own design with masses of eyelets — if you use them sparsely, and rely on stitched lines, the effect will be feeble. It can be used on babies' and children's clothes (when worked

178

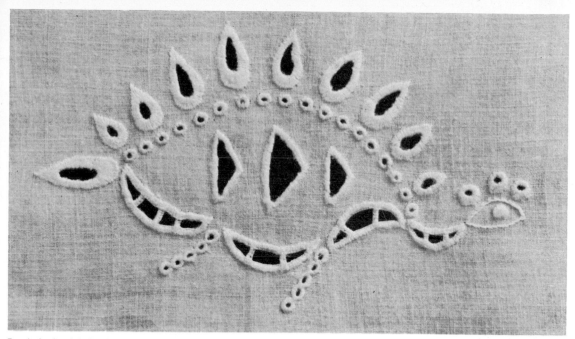

Broderie Anglais by M. Woodhead.

boldly in colour) and also for adults' dresses. Lampshades and table linen look interesting when worked in unexpectedly rich colours.

Net Embroidery Another counted thread method. Fine or coarse net is tacked over the drawing of the design and the design is then darned on to the net in various stitches. You can use fine net for such articles as delicate table mats, babies' over-dresses and wedding veils, or coarse net worked in very thick thread for curtains. Two things to remember: the thread is wholly visible so stitches which cross elaborately on the wrong side look muddled (herringbone, for example, looks like figures of eight), and much can be done with 'tartan' arrangements of straight lines. Starting and finishing is awkward so do as much of the design in a continuous line. Avoid small isolated motifs or spots. Hexagonal nets are used which have three straights on the grain so the lines of the stitches should follow these. Contrasting coloured threads are less successful.

Shadow Work This is worked on transparent materials—cottons, organdie, nylon, organzas, voile, very fine cambric and linen for table cloths, lampshades, babies' clothes, pillows, coverlets,

blouses and fine dresses, and for the charming American idea of 'cloud' cloths—a large organdie cloth thrown lightly over a laid tea table or buffet to keep it fresh if it has to be prepared some time in advance of the function. The cloth can be lightly decorated with shadow motifs and the edges weighted here and there with china beads, though I cover these with padded cloth so that they will not damage delicate china.

This embroidery is composed of long, narrow shapes or circles worked entirely in close herringbone stitch, also called double back stitch. The embroidery is worked on the wrong side so that on the right side one sees the outline in back stitches and the shadow of the crossing of the threads.

It looks particularly lovely worked in white thread on white, but I have discovered that you can use almost any colour combination for this technique. Connecting lines in the design can be in stem or back stitch. To prepare the cloth the design is pinned under the transparent material and then painted with a fine brush and water colour.

Quilting, Smocking and Patchwork These

Shadow work by the author. Photographed against the light to show the stitches used.

and chest of a working garment and at the same time keeping the work elastic. To achieve this the stitches must be worked zig-zag across 2 lines. Smocking survives today in young children's dresses. Occasionally fashion permits its use for women's clothes — round waists and wrists and also for waists of aprons. The smocking is done before the garment is made up. If the band of smocking for a baby's dress comes below the armhole level, it is neater and easier to deal with if the rectangle of material for the front and back is smocked straight across, the armhole cut into it and then the armhole seam double machined.

Smocking must not look skimped — you should allow 3 times the finished width. First prepare the work by putting in lines of dots. These can be marked by a ruler or by iron-on transfer. It is fun (and quick) to use a checked, striped or spotted fabric, then, provided the pattern is woven, you

originally were functional methods and not strictly embroidery.

Quilting Used originally for warmth; a layer of combed out or carded lamb's wool was enclosed between two layers of cloth and then stitched in lines to hold it in place. The stitching soon developed into decorative patterns and today, in addition to wool, you can use nylon or terylene wadding which do not go flat and can be washed. Avoid choosing a realistic design as the wrinkles of the padding will confuse it. Do not put several lines close together or the padded look will not survive and it will become flat and stiff. Do not use contrasting thread or thick embroidery stitches — running or back stitch is best. This work can be done in a frame. The traditional quilted bedspreads made by the miners' wives of Durham were worked in large frames, the designs being scratched on the cotton surface round traditionally shaped templates.

Smocking Originally smocking was a decorative way of releasing fullness needed across the back

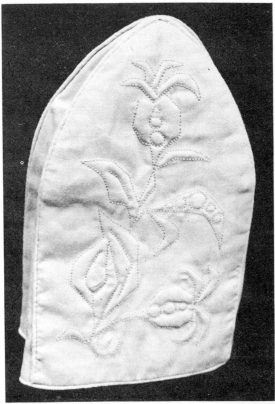

Quilting on fine embroidery linen using padded linen quilting, by A. M. Pilcher.

do not need dots — if printed it is rarely straight on the weave of the fabric. Next put in a gathering thread along each line of dots and draw up tightly — pull it to set the pleats and release slightly.

If you have a cloth with a distinct weave so that you can keep a straight line, iron the dots on the back as sometimes they can be messy or show on the front.

Pick up a small stitch under each dot on the back then the draw thread will lie at the base of the pleats and is less likely to be caught up in the embroidery.

If, on the other hand, you have a smooth fabric and the dots must be on the front to act as a guide line, then iron lightly and pick up a large stitch under each dot so that again the draw thread will not get caught up by the smocking.

Test the heat of the iron carefully, too cool and the dots won't mark — if this happens in a few places fill in the gaps by pencil. If the iron is too hot the dots will run and make a mess.

You can now pin the gathered-up work to a stiff paper or stay, especially if the smocked area is to be curved round a neck. Then twist the long ends of each pair of draw threads, figure of eight way, round pins at the end of every two rows. You are now ready to start smocking. The first row is best non-elastic so work 2 lines of stem stitch from pleat to pleat, carefully adjusting spacing and tension. This stitch being non-elastic sets the width for the rest of the work which has to have stretch and 'give' so all subsequent lines are worked up and down in various ways.

There are very few different actual stitches in smocking — variations on stem stitch, chevron and feather stitch are mainly used. Variety is obtained by the direction of the stitches As the general appearance is quite complicated avoid using too many colours or any attempt to embroider flower forms.

A neat and decorative edging for a smocked sleeve or top of a waist apron or dirndl skirt is to hem the edge and smock through the hem. This has the advantage of a cuff of being elastic and is therefore better than finishing with a binding. A skirt or apron top will need a stay band of the material to prevent stretching.

Patchwork Early patchwork grew out of the necessity of utilising small scraps of valuable cloth. In the 19th century it was a favourite occupation of groups of ladies — a large bedspread, for example, being an ideal community work since each one could make up a section which was later joined up to the background patches.

The cloth of each 'patch' has to be tacked over a stiff paper or thin card shape which must be accurately cut from a metal template. The patches can be squares or equal-sided triangles or combinations of both — the most popular is the five-sided hexagon which builds up like a honeycomb. A three-dimensional effect can be obtained by using the diamond template and dark, medium and light-toned cloths. The most difficult to use is the 'scale' or 'shell' pattern. Use a razor blade and cut on a piece of thick cardboard which being grainless is better than a wooden cutting board. Good quality stiff notepaper, old playing cards, etc. can be used for the paper shapes. Aluminium templates can be purchased in several sizes in all the shapes. The patterns can be built up geometrically in motifs — you make a large number of patches in each of the colours you are using; then you arrange them before you start to sew. Do plan your bedspread, cushion, tea cosy, etc. before you start. A haphazard collection of patches never looks well. The patches are joined by oversewing neatly on the extreme edges on the back. Try and use a thread to match at least one of the sides you are joining.

Do not mix different types of cloth. Keep the work all cotton or all wool or all silk. Templates for wool should be large. Use plain colours or very fine patterns, unless you have fun with a printed pattern by cutting one little motif to come in the middle of a patch. Make a careful choice of your colours — even though sometimes sentiment may govern your choice. (You might make a cushion composed of bits of some of your favourite dresses you remember with pleasure — or a cotton bedspread of bits from all your children's dresses.) You can embellish your patchwork by embroidering a tiny motif in the middle of some of the patches.

There is another form of patchwork called 'Log

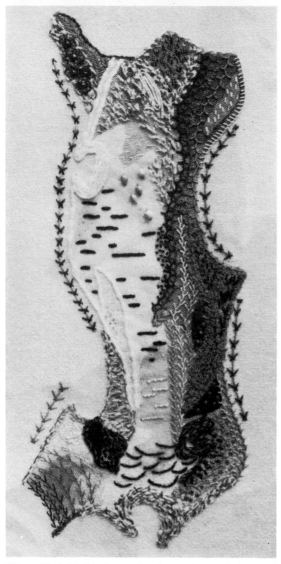

'Silver Birch Bark'. A panel using various stitches and threads, by Sheila Hodgkins.

Cabin' which is formed of overlapping folded strips of cloth. If the colours are graduated in tones it can look unusually subtle, but unless very well done can have an untidy appearance.

Design

So far all this is teaching the embroideress the means of expression, but what is she going to say? Technical ability does not produce a design and to do so is difficult for those who are not gifted or trained as designers. But the more the embroideress practises stitches and methods, and experiments with a variety of threads on different fabrics, the more ideas will germinate, because stitches do a lot of the work and make much of a simple design. Never use your thread just to draw the lines of a motif. For example, you are developing something feathery or furry — the plumes in a bird's tail, angel's wings, a fox's brush or a girl wearing a shaggy coat — then employ such stitches as fly, feather, herringbone, etc. Others such as buttonhole, back stitch, chain or couching will suggest the firm, hard edges of buildings or furniture; Holbein or interlacing — ironwork; the legs of a bird, or of furniture, stem stitch; for something firm but slender, consider open chain or closed feather stitch.

Knobbly twigs, tree bark, crustacea — use coral knot, double knot or Portuguese knotted stem stitch.

Centres of exotic petals and leaves — look up border stitches with a rich complicated silhouette, such as raised chain, band, crested chain or wheatear.

Surfaces of water, meadows, patterned robes, etc.; wave filling, trellis, honeycomb stitch.

Throw a handful of exciting coloured threads on to an interesting piece of cloth. Take out and add colours until you feel they are right. Try a very few strong colours backed up by neutral tones and see what results. That yellow woollen with those lovely greens and oranges could develop into a giant tiger lily, a stylised lion or an interesting group of haystacks with patterns of ploughing around them. Keep the shapes simple and flat. Now get the best references you can — drawings, photographs of the real thing. Reject second-hand ideas of design (which we have seen so many times before) and remember that in embroidery and the crafts generally a realistic rendering is disastrous.

Design, briefly described, is a matter of assembling some shapes in a given space in a satisfying arrangement. So it is essential to start by setting out the shape you have to fill — either draw it the exact size, or smaller but in proportion, on brown or tinted paper. Then in newspaper (for contrast) cut out quickly and roughly the shapes of your motifs and arrange them on the brown paper. You can move them around until they are right and then with a thick soft pencil or a felt pen scribble any lines or textures. Newspaper is plentiful so by using it you won't be inhibited as you would if you used a more costly paper.

Cut out flowers — their shapes are so variable; birds — adding wings and tails; animals — refreshing your memory from zoological or natural history books; things seen around the house — quaint little chairs, vases, coffee pots, utensils, garden implements; the flat façades of interesting buildings; look at the proportions of windows, arches, domes and steeples and assemble a group. Children's books today are a great source for motifs. They show a high standard of design ready stylised in excellent and unusual colours. Children's own drawings have a directness, and express the basic character of the subject, which can often be translated in an embroidery design.

Study the best of modern commercial art. Posters, especially those of London Transport and British Rail, and travel brochures are all rich sources of ideas. So are advertisements from good magazines and newspapers. Make a collection of your own or your friends' Christmas cards well edited. Start a scrapbook to which you can constantly be adding ideas.

At this point it will be useful to know how to enlarge a design, either your own or one you have copied or traced. You will need also to know:

How to dress a square frame.
How to transfer a design from the paper to the cloth.
How to stretch a finished embroidery professionally.
How to mount it.

All these methods can be found in most of the numerous good books on embroidery which are in the bookshops or you may find some of them in your local library. (See bibliography page 245.)

Musical Instrument Making

William Prince

There must be many people who have thought of of the pleasure it would give to be able to make and play one's own musical instrument, but have never attempted such a venture as it appears to be much beyond the scope of the average home craftsman. There are, however, many instruments which range in quality up to professional standard and which have been constructed by painstaking amateurs who have had no training in the art of the luthier. If you can use wood-working tools reasonably well I can think of no more rewarding task than to apply your talent to the making of a musical instrument.

Guitars It is doubtful if any other instrument in musical history has had the popularity which has been accorded to the guitar during the past ten years, so it must be the first on my list.

To produce the range of notes a guitar has shallow, metal strips inserted at varying intervals across the fingerboard. These are called frets, and all instruments so designed are called fretted instruments. On the classical and flamenco guitars there are usually 19 or 20 frets. On the wire-stringed instruments — which include electric, cello-style, 'country and western' and Hawaiian steel guitars — there may be up to 24 frets.

Like most stringed instruments, the guitar has an open sound chamber over which is attached a soundboard. On this soundboard depend the vibrations of the strings which are transmitted through the bridge, which rests upon it, and which in turn produces the music. The soundboard, therefore, is the most important part of the instrument and must be fashioned with great care. Soundboards are made from 'quarter-cut', straight-grained spruce or fir from Europe or North America. The remainder of the sound-chamber of the guitar is made of hardwood to give the stability which is necessary for amplifying the sound. Concert

Victoria and Albert Museum

Guitar decorated in engraved marquetry of tortoise-shell, ivory and pewter with floral patterns and figures. Made by Joachim Tielke, Hamburg 1693.

guitars are made of rosewood, although in many good instruments European walnut, maple, Cuban mahogany and pearwood have been used.

The necks of these instruments are, of long practice, made from what is commonly called Spanish cedar. The light-weight mahoganies are also used.

The flamenco guitarist's instrument is like the concert guitar in shape but is often fitted with wooden pegs instead of metal machine-heads. This is traditional but it is in keeping with the lightness of construction which is an essential feature of this kind of instrument. Instead of rosewood the body of the flamenco guitar is made from the wood of the Mediterranean cypress tree which is very light and imparts the special timbre which is required in the music.

To make a Spanish guitar we shall need a mould some 3 or more inches deep with the inner section cut out exactly to the shape of the completed sound-box. It is usually of softwood and may be made from solid timber or built up of laminations glued together.

First the ribs (sides) are prepared, a bare $\frac{1}{12}$ in. in thickness and, after soaking for 10 or 15 minutes in water, they are bent over a hot 'iron' and fitted into the mould. There they are clamped or wedged into place and allowed to dry out.

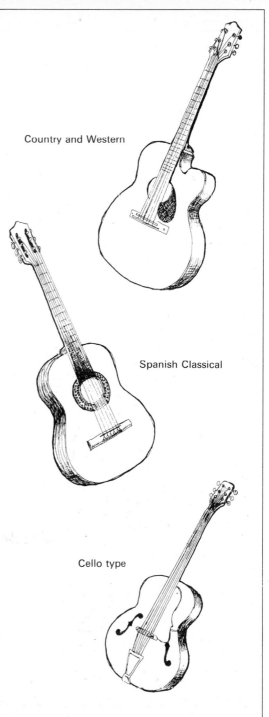

Country and Western

Spanish Classical

Cello type

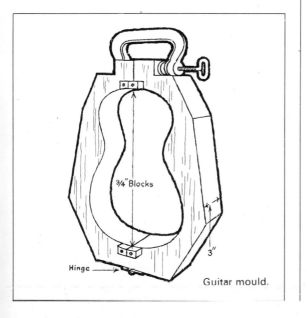

3/4" Blocks

3"

Hinge →

Guitar mould.

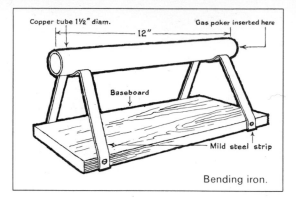

Copper tube 1½" diam. Gas poker inserted here

12"

Baseboard

Mild steel strip

Bending iron.

The next process is to glue in place, on to the ribs, blocks of softwood at the shoulder and tail ends of the body. Into the shoulder block will be dovetailed the neck, after the sound-box is finished.

Fillets of softwood, about $\frac{3}{16}$ in. by $\frac{1}{4}$ in., are next bent and glued inside the back and front edges of the ribs. These are to give a sufficient gluing surface on which will be fixed the back and soundboard of the instrument. Back and soundboard are prepared to about $\frac{1}{12}$ in. thickness and then roughly to shape some $\frac{1}{6}$ in. larger than the finished size. They are given a slight curvature by gluing to them the supporting struts which have been shaped beforehand. For the back there are 3 struts spaced about equi-

distant at right angles to the centre line. The soundboard has 2 similar struts, above and below the soundhole, but the large area over which the bridge is glued on the outside is strengthened by a number of small, thin struts placed in the shape of a fan. They are fixed after the bridge has been glued in place. First the back, then the soundboard (after cutting out and decorating the soundhole) are glued in placed while the assembly is in the mould. The body is then removed from the mould, the edges trimmed and the hardwood binding fitted to front and back edges.

The neck of the Spanish guitar is often made from wood about $1\frac{1}{6}$ in. in thickness with pieces glued together to make the 'heel', to the depth of the body, and the head is jointed on and cut to shape afterwards. The slots, for the passage of the strings, and the holes for the machine-heads are made at the same time. The neck is made with a dovetail which is then jointed into the 'shoulder' block.

The guitar fingerboard should be prepared $\frac{3}{12}$ in. or $\frac{4}{12}$ in. in thickness and to extend from the 'nut' to the soundhole. It is marked out and the fret positions scored across before it is glued into place. After the frets are fitted the whole instrument is glass-papered to a fine surface before polishing, or varnishing, and attaching the nut, machines and strings.

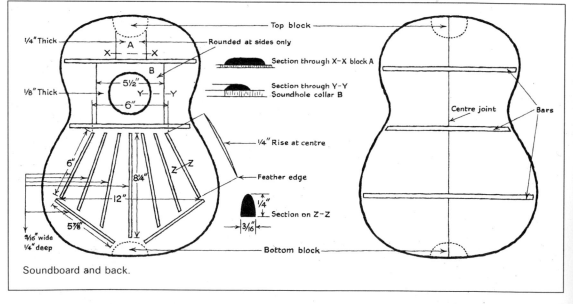

¼" Thick Top block Rounded at sides only Section through X–X block A X A X Section through Y–Y Soundhole collar B ⅛" Thick B 5½" Y Y 6" Centre joint Bars ¼" Rise at centre 6" Z Z 8¼" Feather edge 12" ¼" Section on Z–Z 5⅞" 3/16" ³⁄₁₆" wide ¼" deep Bottom block

Soundboard and back.

186

Guitar neck.

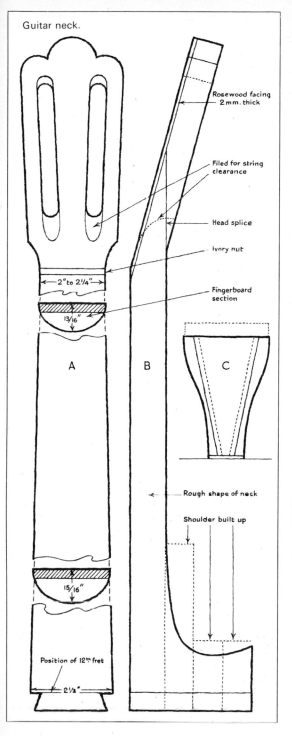

Rosewood facing 2 mm. thick

Filed for string clearance

Head splice

Ivory nut

2" to 2¼"

Fingerboard section

13/16"

A   B   C

Rough shape of neck

Shoulder built up

15/16"

Position of 12th fret

2½"

The author with one of his Spanish classical guitars. Back and ribs: Indian rosewood; Soundboard: European spruce; Fingerboard: Ebony; Bridge: Rosewood.

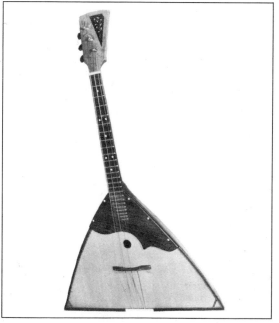

Prima Balalaika made by the author. Soundboard: Canadian spruce; Fingerboard: Ebony; Fingerplate: Indian rosewood.

This general outline may be used as a basis for making other instruments which include plectrum or 'folk' guitar, Hawaiian guitar, electric/acoustic guitar, ukulele, tenor ukulele, tenor guitar and 'flat-back' mandolin. Although the round-backed mandolin and the balalaika are made by a different process from that described both these instruments are within the scope of the home craftsman.

187

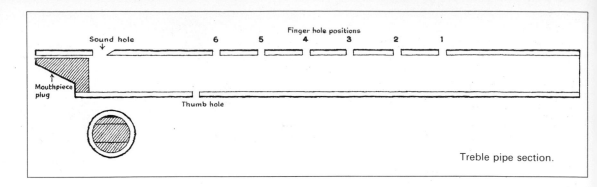

Finger hole positions

Sound hole

6   5   4   3   2   1

Mouthpiece plug

Thumb hole

Treble pipe section.

Wind Instruments Quite a variety of simple, but sweet-sounding, wind instruments may be made by the spare-time craftsman and the materials used can be so cheap as to permit experiments in order to produce perfect articles. Instead of using the laborious techniques of hollowing wood from the solid piece, such as is necessary in the making of clarinets, oboes and kindred instruments, we can find suitable tubing in wood, plastic or light alloy which will well serve our purpose. Depending on the bore of the tube we may make pipes and recorders pitched at treble, alto, tenor and baritone, thus being able to form a full consort of instruments. A start could be made with a treble pipe as follows:

From a piece of jointless bamboo with an internal diameter of about $\frac{3}{4}$ in. cut cleanly a length of $11\frac{5}{12}$ in. and make a hole, $\frac{1}{4}$ in. by $\frac{1}{6}$ in., some $1\frac{1}{6}$ in. from the mouthpiece end. To this hole, which has its shortest measurement across the tube, should now be cut a sloping channel which follows the curve of the bamboo and ends in a fairly sharp edge on the inside. The angle of the slope will depend on the thickness of the bamboo wall and about 40° should be tried at first. The final angle may be decided after the mouthpiece has been made and tried.

In order to set the pitch of the instrument the mouthpiece must now be made and this is done by cutting away the end of the tube so as to leave about one third of the rim, where the lips are applied. The lower saw cut is made $\frac{3}{4}$ in. from the end of the tube and less than half-way through its diameter. It is joined by a slanting cut from the end to remove the waste material. A plug of cork or balsa wood is now fitted firmly into the mouthpiece, being shaped externally to match the tube

and extending inside to a point a little higher than the soundhole. From the soundhole to the upper part of the mouthpiece should be cut, in the tube, a straight, shallow channel (about $\frac{1}{24}$ in.) and this will correspond with a shaving which will be taken from the top of the plug.

It is usual to have these pipes tuned to C or D and the pitch is determined by the length. When a clear tone is achieved tune the pipe with the aid of a piano. If it is sharp reduce the length slightly until the pipe plays the desired note correctly. Now measure the distance from the end of the pipe to the centre of the sound-hole and put a mark a quarter of this length from the end of the pipe. There will be the first hole. Then from the soundhole centre measure $2\frac{1}{6}$ in. and mark the position of the sixth hole. The remaining four holes are marked at equidistant intervals between the first and the sixth. Each position is bored and tuned separately before starting the next one. A small hole is made and gradually enlarged to produce the required note. The last hole, which is for the left-hand thumb, is made on the side opposite to the finger holes at a position a few millimetres nearer to the mouthpiece than the sixth hole.

A final smoothing with flour-grade glass-paper and a coat or two of clear varnish to the exterior surfaces — except the mouthpiece — will complete the instrument.

Simple Percussion Percussion effects give the amateur, perhaps, the greatest scope for ingenuity, and from cheap components can be contrived the most exciting rhythms. Indeed, some famous jazz bands have built their reputations around the sound of metal thimbles striking the corrugated surface of the old-fashioned washboard.

During the 'skiffle' craze many groups used the *tea chest bass* which is made as follows. A tea chest, or other box similarly made from plywood, placed upside-down has a springy broom handle, or other rod of hardwood, bolted firmly on one side in a vertical position. A bass string is then attached to the top of the handle and the bottom of the inverted chest — somewhere near the centre — by a metal eye-fastening at each end. By bending the handle inward with one hand and slapping the string with the other, as sometimes played on the string bass, various frequencies of sound may be obtained.

Simple but effective *drums* can be made out of many hollow objects. Small round wooden casks, heavy plastic and pith-fibre drain pipe and heavy cardboard packing tubes can be made into drums and bongos. Drum heads, which are obtainable from musical dealers, are soaked in water to make them pliable and then fastened over the upper end of the drum. Tuning is varied by the length of the drum; the longer the cylinder the lower the pitch. By sawing the tubes into different lengths one can make a very versatile rhythm section.

Another simply-constructed percussion instrument is the *marimba* and this may be made from hardwoods or softwoods. To get the most pleasing results may entail some interesting and rewarding experiments. Supposing you have some material about $1\frac{7}{12}$ in. by $\frac{7}{12}$ in., cut two pieces about $21\frac{8}{12}$ in. long to form the side pieces of the marimba bed. To the narrow edge of each piece now fix, with a tack at each end, a piece of thick twine which must be stretched taut from end to end. Stand the pieces side by side, with the twine uppermost, about $5\frac{5}{12}$ in. apart at one end, and $10\frac{1}{4}$ in. at the other. To hold them in this position lightly tack a piece of lath across the ends.

The keys are made from the same material and you will require 8 pieces for this one-octave instrument. They will lie flat across the bed spaced about $\frac{7}{12}$ in. apart. The natural key of C is a good one to start with, so cut the first key, which will be the lowest one, long enough to protrude some centimetres over each side of the bed at the wide end. Sound it with a light, wooden hammer, such as you will make for playing the instrument, and tune it with the piano to C natural. It will probably be too low at the start and the tone is sharpened by shortening the key slightly or paring away on the

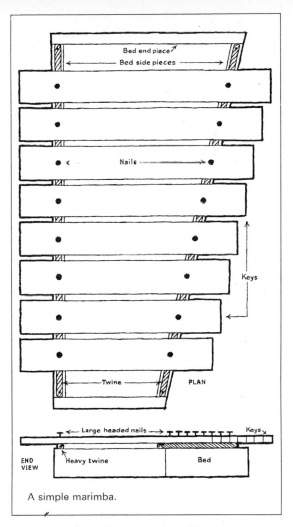

A simple marimba.

underside between the sides of the bed. Remember it is simpler to sharpen the keys than to flatten them, so start off each one with a good overlap.

By the same method make each key up the scale until you have the full octave. Now take off the pieces of lath and sound the keys, with adjustments to the angle of the bed pieces, until the best alignment is found. Then permanent pieces are fixed at the ends to complete the bed. Holes are bored through the keys at the centre of the point where they rest on the bed and through these are gently hammered wire nails to keep the keys in position. The nails must not in any way restrict the vibration of the keys.

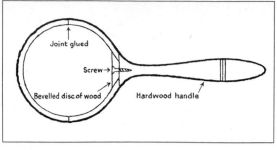

Section through a maracca.

A great variety of percussion instruments are used in Latin American bands and some of these effects may be easily copied. Coconuts make excellent *maracas*. With a fine-toothed saw cut the nut across into two halves, remove the flesh and dry and smooth the shell with glass-paper. Attach a wooden handle to the end, either by gluing into a hole or screwing on from inside. Place inside a few split peas or similar 'seeds' and glue the halves together. Decorate the maracas with enamels to taste. Other hollow objects could be used in the same way.

The Latin American rhythm sticks called *claves* are made from pieces of hardwood about 7 in. long by 1 in. in diameter. They are played in pairs, one being cupped loosely in the hand and struck with the other one.

In an article of this length only a general description of making can be covered but it is hoped it will, in conjunction with other publications and much observation on your part, enable you to make a start on producing your own musical instruments.

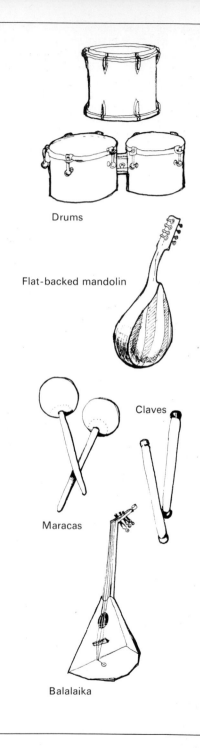

Drums

Flat-backed mandolin

Claves

Maracas

Balalaika

Plaster and Polystyrene Plaques

Leon Metcalfe

This section is concerned with the making of plaques from two essentially different yet readily obtainable materials – plaster of Paris and polystyrene. Certain basic knowledge is, however, common to both materials and this should be fully appreciated before work commences. It includes such considerations as size, shape, design and colour. Useful working sizes for plaques fall in the range of 6 in. to 12 in. across, but it is necessary to consider the thickness of the work in relation to the overall size. Strength and a certain amount of aesthetic satisfaction can come from a well-proportioned piece of work, and the thicknesses for the sizes given above should range between $\frac{1}{2}$ in. and 1 in.

Basic shape can enhance and influence the appreciation of the completed work, and in this respect it is best to keep to simple geometric shapes such as circles, squares, rectangles and pentagons. Avoid fine points and angles as these are fragile and difficult to protect. When the design of the motif or decoration is under consideration simplicity is again the key factor, and bold, simple designs and colours will always be found to be the most successful.

Plaster

Materials Plaster of Paris is cheap and can be obtained from most chemists in white powder form. It is mixed with water to a creamy consistency and poured into greased moulds where it will set quickly. Tin lids, which are made in a variety of shapes and sizes, form useful moulds, but others may also be made from Plasticine or cardboard. The basic white colour can be changed at the mixing stage by adding a powder paint colour, and this will then be the base colour for the plaque.

Before the plaster has set it is advisable to introduce a reinforcing agent. The larger the plaque the

more important this becomes. Any form of open-weave material, such as bandage, is useful for this purpose, and strips of this should be pressed down into the mixture so that they are completely submerged. A final strip of material can be looped and the ends inserted into the plaster for hanging the completed work. The grease in the mould should enable the plaque to be turned out easily, when it will be ready, after cleaning and dressing, for the addition of the chosen design. The dressing and smoothing of the surface can be accomplished with fine glass-paper, and sharp corners can be rounded off into pleasant curves.

Plaster plaque. Badge of Culham College, Oxon.

Polystyrene plaque. Section of the Bayeaux Tapestry.

A bas-relief technique is imposed on the surface of the work by means of lino cutters or similar small cutting implements. Plaster can be decorated with almost any type of paint, ranging from powder colour to enamels, depending on whether a matt or shiny surface is required. A final protective layer of varnish can be painted over the completed plaque.

Polystyrene

Materials Polystyrene is widely used as a packing agent for fragile goods and this source should not be forgotten, as it can be the cheapest way of obtaining the material. Most hardware shops and builders' merchants stock both sheet polystyrene and also prepared wall tiles. Tiles are most useful for plaque-making as they require no initial cutting or shaping and they have neat, chamfered edges.

To cut a basic plaque shape from sheet poly-styrene, a hot knife is the best tool to use. The blade of the knife can be heated in the flame of a Gaz or similar picnic stove. Alternatively use the heated tip of an electric soldering iron. The cellular structure of this material does not lend itself to fine detailed work and this should be avoided.

Sketch the basic design on the surface of the polystyrene with a felt pen, and hatch those areas of the design which are to be removed to produce a bas-relief effect. These low-relief areas can then be 'burnt' away by using an electric soldering iron or the heated knob end of a steel knitting needle.

Painted decoration of the design can be added using most types of paint, except cellulose which has an unfortunate effect on the polystyrene. Any final dressing of the work can be done either with the hot soldering iron or with fine glass-paper sticks.

Printmaking

Gerald Woods

The printmaker need not be contained within the limitations of one particular method; he can select from four main techniques, which come under the collective title of printmaking. These are wood-cutting, etching, lithography, and silkscreen printing, with many variations and extensions of each process. A combination of two or more processes may sometimes be used to create a single print image, but usually the technique selected as an area of specialisation is that most suited to one's particular requirements.

Printmaking can be defined thus: an autographic means of programming the production of a number of copies of a single image, for the purpose of distribution. This means that a print is created using a preliminary plan; if the print is to be in four colours, then a separate plate or block must be made for each colour, and the colours must be registered in the correct position on the printing paper. The main interest of most artists and designers lies in the special graphic qualities of the print processes; that is to say, an artist would select a printmaking process to achieve an effect not possible in any other medium. For example, lithography is best used for its soft and atmospheric qualities; etching is concerned mainly with linear and sculptural effects; woodcutting and silkscreen printing are basically used for hard-edged designs and broader tonal qualities.

Three of these processes are based on mechanical principles, but lithography is a chemical process. On a professional level prints are usually made with the aid of special printing presses and equipment but there are many techniques which can be used at home or at school without presses or expensive equipment. This section is mainly concerned with processes that can be carried out without the use of a printing press. The following is a brief outline of each printmaking process:

Relief Printing Woodcuts and linocuts come into this category. The non-printing areas of the block are cut away with a sharp gouge or knife, the parts of the block that remain are in relief and will therefore receive printing ink from a roller pushed over the surface. This process is the oldest and perhaps the best known of all the printmaking media; most people have at some time made a linocut or a potato-cut—a basic form of relief printing. In schools linocuts are often used for repeat or multiple images and also for printing directly on to fabrics. A print taken from a relief block is recognised by the characteristic simplicity of the cut or gouged shapes, and the tonal weight of the image, which is inherent in the medium. It is a craft which requires a certain amount of control, especially in the use of cutting gouges.

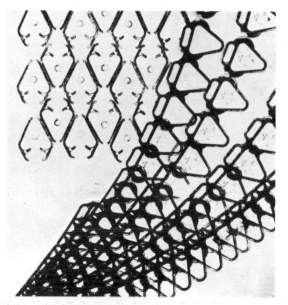

Offset print from a plastic electrical plug.

193

Stencil Printing Silkscreen printing is founded upon the basic principle of stencil printing and was developed by the fabric industry as a means of producing printed designs on woven material. A piece of silk or organdie is tightly stretched over a wooden frame. The frame contains the printing ink which is forced through the weave of the stretched material by a rubber blade called a squeegee. Parts of the weave are first blocked out with a water-soluble glue or paper stencil so that the ink forced through the weave forms a positive image on a sheet of paper beneath the screen. The stencil or glue blocks the weave in those parts of the design that are to remain clear.

Incision Printing This process is really a reversal of the relief process because the areas of the plate that are taken away act as a reservoir for the printing ink, the parts of the plate in relief being wiped clear of printing ink.

A metal plate made of zinc, steel or copper is covered with a fine layer of specially prepared wax-ground; this is done while the plate is hot so that the wax can be rolled into an even layer with a leather-covered roller. The wax-ground surface of the plate is held upside down in a hand-vice and smoked black with lighted tapers, taking care to rotate the tapers continually so that the wax is not scorched or burnt.

The drawing is made using a steel needle which exposes the base metal through the wax-ground. When the drawing is completed, the back of the plate is protected with an asphaltum-based varnish and the plate is immersed in a bath of diluted nitric acid. The acid bites into the metal in those areas where the wax has been removed by the drawing needle. The wax-ground forms an effective acid-resist in the remaining areas. The depth of the line to be bitten can be controlled by removing the plate at various stages to paint out delicate lines with varnish. When the etching stage has been completed, the plate is taken out of the acid bath and washed with water before clearing away the wax and varnish with turpentine substitute; the plate is then ready for printing.

The incisions on the plate (the drawing) are filled with a heavy-pigmented ink while the plate is kept warm on a hotplate. A leather pad is used to force the ink into the incisions and the surface of the plate is then wiped with a pad of fine canvas, taking care not to remove the ink from the incisions. Finally, the plate surface is wiped with the palm of the hand until the drawing appears as a crisp line on the shiny surface.

Operating the etching press.

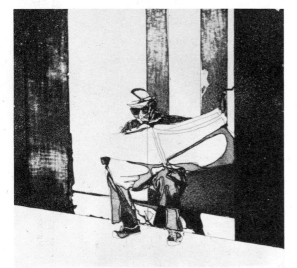

'Man with newspaper'. Etching showing aquatint.

The plate is warmed again to keep the ink moist and laid on the steel bed of the mangle-like printing press. A sheet of damp printing paper is laid down on top of the plate, followed by a sheet of blotting paper to absorb the excess moisture and a set of felt lengths which help to force the paper into the incisions on the plate when the bed moves through the steel rollers under great pressure. As the paper is forced into the incisions, the ink is transferred to the paper. When the print is lifted from the plate the inking procedure must be repeated to take further copies.

A wide tonal range can be obtained by using lines of varying depths. A two-colour print can be made by filling the incisions with one colour, and rolling a second colour over the surface of the plate. Tones can also be made by melting particles of fine resin dust on to the plate; and etching between the particles, forming a pitted texture that will retain printing ink. This is called Aquatint.

Planographic Printing In the process of lithography the image is taken from the surface or plane; metal tools are not required, the drawing being made with a brush and ink or a wax crayon. It is perhaps the most spontaneous of the print-making processes since one can paint directly, using the medium with the same degree of lucidity that one might use on a canvas or in a sketchbook.

The process is founded upon the mutual repulsion of grease and water. Originally drawings were made on blocks of a calcerous limestone quarried in Germany which is particularly receptive to grease. Now zinc and aluminium plates have almost replaced the use of stone except in specialist establishments. The plates are mechanically grained and chemically treated so that grease and water will have anchorage on the surface of the plate. Crayons and ink are made from greasy substances such as soap and tallow; the ink can be diluted with either distilled water or turpentine to make half-tone washes on the plate. Any mistakes made at the drawing stage can be corrected during processing.

When the drawing has been completed, the whole surface of the plate is covered with a fine film of liquid gum arabic. The gum arabic de-sensitizes the plate and acts as a protective stencil to contain the grease drawing. An area of grease penetration forms beneath the drawing and, as the gum hardens in the surrounding areas, provides a smooth aqueous surface. The grease drawing is dissolved with turpentine leaving only the area of grease penetration within the grain of the plate; this is strengthened with asphaltum solution before the plate is finally washed clear with water and evenly damped with a sponge.

A roller charged with a special printing ink is rolled over the surface of the plate; the ink on the roller will adhere only to the grease image on the plate because the fine film of water applied with the sponge will cause the ink to be rejected on the remaining areas. When the image has been built up to full strength with printing ink, a sheet of paper is placed on the plate and the first print can be taken. Successive prints can be taken by re-damping the surface of the plate and rolling-up with ink.

Inking-up a lithographic plate on the press.

Colour lithographs are made using a separate plate for each colour. The colours are registered by means of a small mark which appears in the same position on each plate and is also to be seen at opposite edges on the printing paper.

Basic Printmaking Techniques

Collage relief blocks The first requirement is a stout baseboard made of either strawboard or hardboard; the size of the baseboard will determine the image area of the completed print. A good plastic adhesive is needed for securing 'found' materials to the base and for coating various materials to give them a suitable surface for the retention of printing ink.

No cutting tools are required for this system of printmaking; any article or piece of material that will readily accept a layer of ink from a printing roller can be arranged on the baseboard and finally secured with the adhesive. The *height* of the collective fragments on the block should be as equal as possible. Certain objects are quite unsuitable for this method; coarse woven fabric, cloth and lace are particularly suitable. String and rope can be formed into patterns on a board that has been coated with adhesive and left in the arranged position until the adhesive dries. (Most cloth and similar materials should be totally immersed in the adhesive before being laid down on to the baseboard.) Leaves, silver paper and flattened-out packages are also useful in creating a collage.

Direct print from screwed-up paper and hessian.

When the collage is completed, sufficient time should be allowed for the adhesive to set really hard, otherwise the roller will tend to lift off certain fragments as it is moved across the surface of the block.

An interesting extension of this technique is the use of the adhesive itself for retaining impressions of textured materials. The baseboard is given a very heavy coating of adhesive and, when it is almost dry, objects can be pressed into the surface; the imprint will remain as the adhesive hardens and will print as a negative image. One can work to a particular theme using this method — signs of past events, footprints, tyremarks, etc.; or mechanical objects — flywheels, screws, nuts and bolts.

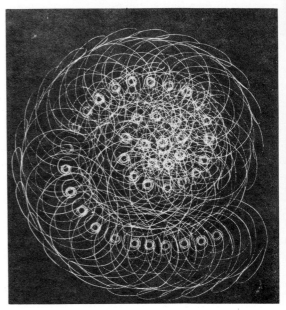

Negative print of a metal spring.

Descriptive Printmaking A great deal of depth research has been carried out by Michael Rothestein in the extension of relief processes. In a recent lecture he described the uses of printmaking techniques for visual narrative. By taking apart a commonplace object such as a wooden crate or tin can, it is possible to produce a visual description of each surface or facet, inside and out, by rolling-up the surfaces with ink and taking prints. In this way we develop a total understanding of the object more accurately than if a pencil drawing or photograph is made of it.

A search for suitable objects could be centred around industrial-waste areas where any number of found artefacts would be suitable for graphic analysis.

One of the simplest methods of making trial prints is the use of an offset technique; for this method a large gelatine roller is necessary in addition to a standard size inking roller. The surface of the object is rolled-up with ink and the gelatine roller is allowed to rotate slowly over the inked surface until the limit of the rotation is reached. The image is then transferred from the gelatine roller to paper.

Woodcuts and Linocuts The drawing is usually made directly on to the surface of the block, or on a sheet of thin paper which can be pasted in reverse on to the block. At the drawing stage one must decide if the drawing is to appear as a negative or positive image in the completed print; for a positive image one must cut around the contours of the drawn line, for a negative image the line itself is removed. A brush or fibre-tip pen is ideal for drawing on the block; a pencil or pen line is difficult to interpret in terms of even the finest cutting gouge.

The cutting action is always directed *away* from the body; a wooden bench hook is useful for keeping the block steady. Broad flat gouges are used for clearing away large areas of the block and the finer 'V' tools are employed for detailed cutting. Lino is much easier to cut if it is warmed slightly. Lino can be etched by using a diluted solution of caustic soda which is painted on the surface of the lino directly. The areas of the lino to remain smooth are protected with an acid-resisting varnish. The caustic solution forms a granular texture on the lino. Rubber gloves should be worn to protect the skin from the solution which can be quite harmful. A variety of timber can be used for woodcutting; the most popular wood is Parana pine, although some of the harder woods are more suitable for detailed cutting. Pear has a particularly good surface.

Printing by burnishing and with a simple press There are several types of inexpensive printing presses available and very often a visit to a printer's sale is a worthwhile expedition. Bookbinders' 'nipping' presses are also good for giving a direct pressure, or the Farley proof press which has a simple roller-pressure.

Burnishing is the simplest technique for taking prints but can be tedious if a large number are required. The ink should be rolled out into a fine film on the inking slab before a fine layer is rolled over the block. Over-inking will spoil the print and

Inking-up a relief block on the bed of an Albion press.

cause some of the finer textures to fill in. A sheet of printing paper with an absorbent surface, such as a soft cartridge paper or imitation Japanese paper, should be placed carefully on to the inked block and a metal weight of some kind should be placed on top to prevent the paper and block from moving. The burnishing is done with a wooden spoon or similar object using a circular movement as pressure is applied. The metal weight can be shifted from corner to corner as the burnishing progresses and a corner of the paper lifted to judge the effectiveness of the burnishing. The tonal qualities can be controlled by the amount of pressure applied with the burnisher. A clean hard printing roller and a flat cold iron are alternative tools for burnishing.

Printing in Colour To make sure that the colour is registered accurately on to the sheet of printing paper, a simple registration system can be planned. The best method is to make a registration sheet which can be used throughout the printing of all the colours. The sheet should have a margin over the size of both the block and printing paper. Lay marks are drawn on the sheet for the correct positioning of the block and paper. For burnishing techniques a more substantial registration system is necessary, comprising a wooden base with slats of wood fixed to the surface for positioning both block and paper.

When the first colour has been printed sufficient time should be given for the ink to dry before printing the second colour. The effects of over-printing are lost if a wet colour is printed over a wet colour. Printmakers are limited in the number of colours that they can use and tend to take full advantage of overprinting, e.g. yellow overprinted on blue makes a green at the area of overprinting, but the yellow and blue retain their value as colour primaries where they are printed directly on to the white paper. If a set of four blocks are used in producing a print it is advisable to make a set of colour proofs, amending the colours if necessary.

Large blocks may use quite a lot of ink; when rolling-up large areas of colour make sure that no roller marks are left in the ink.

Monotypes The fact that only one print can be made makes this technique less popular than others, but it is an ideal medium for exploring preliminary graphic ideas. There are two basic methods:

A slab of glass is covered with a fine layer of ink which should be blotted several times with waste paper so that it is not too tacky. A sheet of cartridge paper is then placed carefully on the glass and the drawing is made with a ballpoint pen or pencil. Whilst drawing the hand should not rest on the paper at any time. The point of the pen or pencil forces the paper into contact with the ink remaining on the glass and the ink will adhere to the under side of the paper at the point of pressure. When completed the drawing is lifted from the glass and the inked drawing will appear on the reverse side, together with perhaps an overall half-tone film of ink which is difficult to avoid but often lends to the tonal composition of the print. The glass can be cleaned with turpentine and a different colour may be used for further additions to the print.

The second method is to paint directly on to a clean slab of glass with dilute printing inks or oil paints; the ink can also be dribbled or smeared with a cloth. When the drawing reaches a satisfactory state, a sheet of paper is pressed on to the glass to remove the surplus ink or paint and a final print is taken on an absorbent paper, burnishing with a soft cloth.

Stencils The basic stencil process is an interesting one that is too often ignored, and is open to development, although it has been replaced to some extent by silkscreen printing. The stencil is made preferably from a thin card such as 'oiled manilla card' which is very strong and will not be broken up by the viscosity of the printing ink. The shapes are cut away with a sharp knife and the stencil sheet is placed on top of the printing paper. The ink is rolled through the cut-out shapes to meet the printing paper surface. A soft rubber composition roller is recommended for this purpose.

Silkscreen Techniques One of the main reasons that silkscreen printing has achieved a prominent position in the field of experimental techniques is that it is a highly versatile medium which does not require the use of machinery. Most of the materials can be bought at very little expense in any town.

Although it is a medium that is founded upon simple apparatus, it is possible to produce a wide scale of tonal values. The printing frame is constructed from wooden slats 2 in. by 2 in. In making the frame a margin of at least two inches above the print area should be allowed, to act as an ink duct. The frame can be joined with metal brackets, nails or a standard woodwork glue-joint.

For basic experiments the frame can be covered with organdie, a material which is available in most soft furnishing stores, but for fine precision work a good quality Swiss silk is recommended. There are a number of ways of stretching the organdie or silk tightly over the frame. The use of a staple-gun is the quickest method, but has the disadvantage that the staple marks eventually damage the frame. The material should be stretched like a canvas, tacking the centre pieces first and then tensioning the remaining sides. This must be done without causing the material to tear. It is possible to stretch silk using gummed paper tags only, but the most ingenious system that I have seen is the use of a bicycle inner-tube which is stretched around the outer edges of the frame; the silk is then tacked over both frame and inner-tube, and is finally tensioned by inflating the tube with a bicycle pump.

When the silk is firmly stretched over the frame it should be washed with warm soapy water to remove any dirt or grease. The print area should be centred and indicated with a pencil line on the silk screen; the remaining areas are masked off with gummed tape both outside and inside the frame. The gummed tape can also be given a coating of shellac to seal the edges properly.

Using a squeegee on a silkscreen frame.

The screen itself is hinged to a baseboard with an attached support bar to keep the screen in a raised position when laying down printing paper. The squeegee is made from a length of wood which has a rubber blade slotted-in on one edge. The width of the squeegee should overlap the width of the print area so that an even layer of ink can be forced through the weave of the screen.

Having prepared the screen a stencil can be made by one of the following methods:

Paper Stencils A stencil can be made from any type of thin paper, even newspaper. The shapes can be cut away with a knife, or torn-out to give a softer edge to the printed image. The thicker the paper stencil, the heavier the deposit of printing ink, so that even for flat areas a thin paper such as newsprint is quite adequate. One should bear in mind that the shapes cut or torn away provide the apertures through which the ink is forced after penetrating the weave of the silk, thus forming a positive image on the paper beneath the frame.

Newsprint or paper stencils are fixed to the open screen just as the printing commences. A sheet of printing paper is placed in position on the baseboard with the stencil on top, the screen is then brought down on top of the stencil and a film of printing ink is dragged across the screen area with the blade of the squeegee. The ink will pass through the open stencil shapes to the printing paper and the remaining ink will cause the stencil to adhere to the screen. Since screen ink dries rapidly (about 10 minutes) the stencil is firmly fixed to the screen, the only disadvantage being that the silk cannot be used again.

A special stencil paper is marketed by a number of graphic supplies firms, the most popular being one called Profilm. This is a thin paper coated with gelatine. It is transparent and can, therefore, be placed over an original design in order to trace the main shapes of the colour to be printed. The shapes are cut out with a knife or razor blade. The stencil paper is attached to the screen by laying the gelatine surface of the paper in contact with the underside of the screen. A hot domestic iron is run over the silk on the inside of the frame, causing the gelatine to melt and adhere to the screen. There are also several different types of self-adhesive stencil papers which are quite useful.

Glue-Stencils Water-soluble glue can be painted directly on to the screen with a brush, filling the weave of the screen, so that the printing ink will not go through the screen wherever the glue blocks the weave. A number of manufacturers

199

Surface print of grass, leaves and a safety pin.

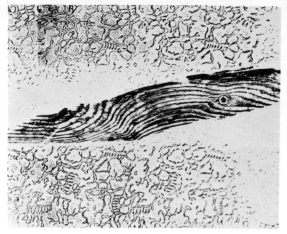

Print from plastic adhesive combined with wood grain.

produce effective water-soluble screen fillers, and interesting effects can be achieved by spattering glue on to a wet screen or by diluting the glue with water to obtain half-tones. The main advantage of this technique is that the screen can be used several times providing that the screen is cleared of ink and the glue removed with warm water.

When working on the screen the original design can be placed underneath the screen and the main outlines traced on to the silk with a soft pencil. When the painting-out of shapes with glue has been completed hold the screen up to the light to check for pinholes which may need retouching with glue.

Wax-Resist Method For direct linear work a wax, lithographic crayon and lithographic drawing ink can be used to draw and paint on the screen. Make sure that the screen receives a heavy deposit of ink and crayon pigment so that the weave is filled. On completion of the drawing stage the whole screen surface is coated with screen glue and allowed to dry. The drawing is then dissolved with turpentine. The screen will thus be clear wherever the drawing is dissolved and blocked in the surrounding areas by the glue which is not disturbed by the turpentine. This means that at the printing stage a *positive* image will appear on the printing paper because the line drawn with the wax crayon or ink is eventually the only clear part of the screen weave.

For poster work transfer dry lettering can be

burnished to the inside of the screen and protected with the special fixative to prevent damage when using the squeegee.

Note: Most of these methods can be employed for printing on fabrics (see page 132) but a special ink dye is required for permanency on fabric and the screen should not be hinged for printing.

Printing Preparation for silkscreen printing is a critical task because once the actual printing operation begins it must be done without pause or interruption; the fast drying ink will clog the screen if it is left for half an hour and may be very difficult to remove.

Organise the printing table so that paper is easily at hand and have the ink, ready mixed, in a spare container. Ideally it is a good plan to have an assistant to handle the paper while you are doing the squeegee work on the screen. The paper can be registered on the baseboard with simple paper tabs as lay-guides for two corners of the paper. The paper being in the correct position on the baseboard, rest the screen flat on top so that the paper is sandwiched between the baseboard and the screen. The ink is then spread in a line on the margin opposite your standing position and within the gum-paper margin. Holding the squeegee with two hands, put the rubber blade immediately behind the line of ink and drag the ink towards you, remembering that the ink must be forced evenly through the screen mesh. The squeegee action should be sharp and brisk and it should be held at

200

an angle of approximately 45°. Before lifting the screen make sure that the squeegee does not fall on the screen into the ink, then lift the screen and remove the paper which will contain the printed image. Register the next sheet of paper and move to the opposite side of the screen for the next screening. Add more ink to the screen as may be necessary.

When the printing is completed, place a wad of newsprint underneath the screen and scrape out the surplus ink with a palette knife; finally clean the screen with turpentine and soapy water.

Additional colours can be overprinted the same day. By the time you have cleaned up your first screen the prints will be ready to receive the next colour. Colours can be either transparent or opaque. The ink can be extended by adding reducing medium.

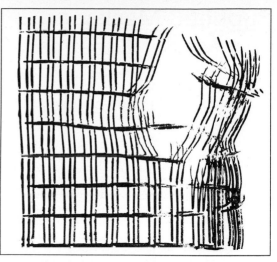

Direct relief print from a metal grid.

Puppets, Masks and Model Theatres

Stuart Robinson

Puppetry is more than a craft. Not only can it be enjoyed as an improvised activity but it can be studied as a serious craft with most advanced techniques. It is particularly useful with shy and retarded children as an excellent way of releasing the inner tensions that often produce and foster such disabilities. As imaginative play it affords a true example of integrated work in the classroom as it involves different methods of creative expression including painting, modelling, story telling, acting, speech, lighting and effects which will delight both the creator and the beholder. All this and yet the operator is still hidden from the spectator.

To start with, quick methods and simple materials are essential as it is the use of the puppet that is important rather than the making. Whichever type of puppet is employed it should evolve from the actual materials available. This will make it seem logical and individual with a life of its own. From these characteristics the puppet will perform in a certain way which will give rise to a sequence of action and so to the plot which will be the result of free play. Since it is so important to retain the spontaneity of performance a script of cues rather than a written-down dialogue will give the best results. The best way to start puppetry is not to plan and write scripts, but to make a puppet and use it. Everything else will grow from this. It is not until the fun of making and playing has been experienced that it becomes possible to make the puppet to suit an existing character or play.

It is useful when planning a public performance to have one member of a group as a producer and cue prompter (actions rather than words) who will guide the flow of the action, look after lights, curtains and special effects such as music and noises off, see that properties are available and generally manage without imposing too much control. Producers can often be a link-man or narrator or commentator who brings the audience into the action. They can see that the performers speak out clearly and loudly but that the backstage workers keep their directions to a whisper.

It is quite feasible to start a group project, integrated work or centre of interest from a number of puppets rather than the more usual topics such as tea, transport and so on. A group of explorer puppets each of whom goes off, finds something and enacts his voyages and discoveries with other characters in one scene of a production. Research and written records will be needed, pictures, scenery, models and writing can all be easily linked to a real, live performance. Each separate scene may use different kinds of puppets most appropriate to the action. More than one stage can be set up and action flow from one to another. There is no end to the possibilities arising from the imaginative use of puppetry. The following sections give the basic techniques, ideas and sources. The only extras necessary are imagination, enthusiasm and inspiration, the stock-in-trade of most children and many teachers.

Shadow Puppets

Materials required for simple shadow puppets A bright light from a window or a reading lamp (keep 'bayonet' fittings out of reach of little fingers). A picture frame which should be covered with some semi-opaque material such as an old sheet, thin white cotton, linen, tracing cloth, etc. Whichever is selected should show clear shadows but not the performers who are behind. The frame can be held or fixed to a table with 'G' clamps or tied between chairs.

Some brown Kraft paper or postcard thickness card (old exercise book covers, thick Christmas cards, offcuts), stiff dark paper or card. A stapler, scissors, a six-hole punch, Sellotape, paste, push-through paper fasteners, black book cloth, coloured cellophane sweet wrappers.

Method

Cut or tear the brown paper or card into any simple shape.

Use a stapler, or sew on a support of folded stiff paper, wire or card (Fig. 1).

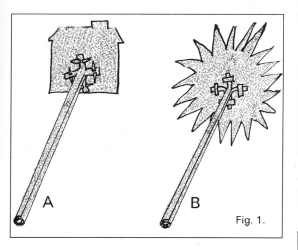

Fig. 1.

With the light behind and either above or below you, hold the shadow up to and touching the screen. As you press the puppet against the screen the shadow appears darkest, as you hold it farther away it will seem lighter and larger.

Play with the shadows on the screen letting them fly, fall down, move away and so on as you wish. Set up a mirror at an angle to see the shadows as they are made (Fig. 2).

Fig. 2.

Invent simple situations as the puppets suggest and voices to suit them. Set up a mirror at an angle in front of the screen so that you can watch your own performance.

Now devise two characters and some suitable props, cutting or tearing from stiff card. Eyes, etc. can be made with a six-way punch. Play on the screen with them and allow a small incident or plot to develop. Simple scenery can be fixed to the screen with Sellotape and can include coloured cellophane from sweet wrappers for eyes, buttons, faces, sun, flowers, etc.

Moving shadows

To make the figures move try only a few joints at first, one or two per figure as you only have two hands to hold *and* manipulate the puppet. One hand can hold a wire from the body and the other hand work the legs which move, together with the head, on the second wire.

After further experiment it will be found that four or five supports can be operated by one person at the same time.

Fig. 3

More permanent shadows

For these use a stiff card which cuts cleanly, such as shoe and stocking boxes. Cutting directly without preliminary drawing gives a much livelier result and is to be encouraged. Allow sufficient circular overlap at joints and place these to give the maximum amount of controlled movement. Push-through paper fasteners are the easiest form of fastening and punched holes allow free movement.

After jointing, the supports to hold and work the puppet must be added. Galvanised or coppered wire of about 16 gauge; thin wood rods, umbrella or cycle spokes are all suitable, Fig. 3. Fasten to the appropriate part of the figure. The holding support that will take the weight of the figure must be very firmly attached by sticking and sewing to give rigidity of control. Sometimes legs or other parts can be left free to dangle. Where it is necessary to prolong the life of the puppet, cover with a dark, matt bookcloth, using a rubber gum such as Copydex.

Further experiments

A more rigid or permanent screen allowing greater scope for experiment will soon become necessary if any advanced work is to be attempted.

Card puppets can combine with plywood, metal sheet (such as zinc, aluminium or tin) or clear acetate. The last material can be coloured with thinned oil paint, coloured tissue, or coloured inks. It can also be used as a full-size sheet of transparent scenery with the setting painted on in opaque black ink and/or transparent colours and then placed immediately behind the screen.

Torches are useful as suns, moons, car headlights, bonfires, etc. Tinsel, sequins, pieces of mirror, with edges protected by Sellotape, and similar material hanging near the light source produce a magic sparkling background.

Puppets can recede and advance right up to the screen. Necks can be made of expanding material. Heads and other parts can be controlled separately from the rest of the body and figures can come apart and be rejoined incorrectly.

Shadows should be stored flat taking great care not to allow the supports to tear away from the actual body.

Ideas for play production and an all-purpose stage are given on page 216.

Glove Puppets

Materials required for simple glove puppets
Some pieces of plain or patterned fabric (old large handkerchiefs, curtain and dress samples), about 18 in. square. Assorted size elastic bands, 'magic' markers or felt pens, card rolls cut to about 1 in. or $1\frac{1}{2}$ in. length rings. Assorted trimmings, beads, brooches, curtainings, net, lurex pieces, fasteners, feathers, embroidery silks, gummed paper shapes, ribbon scraps, etc.

Method

Place a card ring on first finger, cover whole hand with a piece of cloth, Fig. 4, slip an elastic band over the card ring 'head' and down the neck, and others over thumb and second finger, Fig. 5.

Play with the puppet facing you over your other arm. Talk to it and make it answer back. Pick things up and hand to your neighbour's puppet.

Use a ball point or felt pen to draw eyebrows, eyes, nose, mouth, etc. Fig. 6.

Trim the puppet with beads, etc., make a paper cone hat, use wool, string or unravelled pan scrubbers for hair. Fasten waistcoats, coats, aprons, etc., with glue, push-through fasteners, staplers or by stitching.

Fig. 4.

Fig. 5.

Fig. 6.

Make props from counters, pillboxes, doll's jugs, cups, brooms, cutlery, etc., a 'treasure chest' from a small box full of beads, and similar items.

The puppet described above is excellent but inevitably comes to pieces after the performance. A more permanent glove puppet may be made as follows. The body is the operator's hand. The clothing is a simple 'T shirt' glove as in Fig. 7.

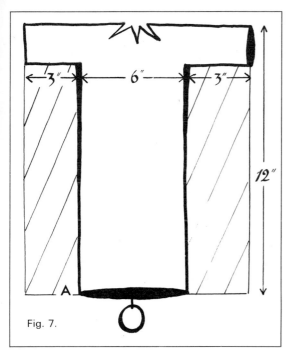

Fig. 7.

The head can be made from a match box; pulp cup, flower pot or egg tray; milk or yoghourt containers; old rubber or tennis balls; plastic containers; old sponge or plastic foam pieces; carved potatoes or soap. Eyes from beads, buttons, fasteners, hair from wool, string. Even a paper bag can be used for a complete puppet. The head can be further improved by making a tube of paper to fit the forefinger, crumpling or winding paper strips around it, pulling a nylon stocking over the head to obtain a much smoother skin effect and fixing this into the neck of the glove. The nose may be pulled out and stitched in place, scraps of felt or buttons sewn on for eyes and mouth, features drawn or painted.

This type of glove puppet is one of the easiest to

make and quickest and most satisfactory to use since it is easy to alter and is light in use.

More permanent glove puppets The 'T' shape glove shown in Fig. 7 may be joined to a wide variety of heads, some of which are shown below. Whatever material is used for the actual modelling it may be built upon a modelling base (A) such as an old light bulb; plastic or glass container; ball; stone; potato; paper-stuffed toe of an old sock, stocking or leg of a pair of tights (these also give a convenient glove already attached to the head); a small balloon, etc. The base is best greased, oiled or painted with a liquid detergent before covering with a $\frac{1}{4}$ in. or $\frac{1}{3}$ in. layer of the modelling material (B); allow to dry out between layers if these are more than $\frac{1}{2}$ in. in total. When dry, slit up heads (on other than sock, stocking, tights or balloon bases), remove base (C), insert a finger tube (D), stick slit together or paste over with pieces of thin paper or bandage. Allow to dry and attach to glove (F).

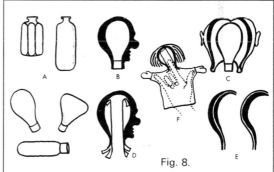

Fig. 8.

In the case of sock bases, remove stuffing when head is dry; with a balloon base let down balloon and pull out.

Prime the face with white or slightly tinted emulsion paint or tempera colour and use felt markers for features; string, cotton wool, rug wool, pan scrubbers, frayed out cotton, straw, etc. for hair, eyebrows, moustaches, beards, etc. Ears, noses, and chins can be modelled or stuck on afterwards, as can sequins, buttons or paper fasteners for eyes.

Modelling materials for heads
Sawdust heads from a mixture of Polycell, water and sawdust.
Paper pulp heads by preparing pulp from news or

soft paper, torn into small pieces, soaked in well mixed Polycell paste.

Sawdust with paper pulp mix may also be used. Two ovals or circles of coloured felt stuffed with cotton wool around a tube and sewn together.

An old mitten converted into a head or glove.

Egg-shaped balls of polystyrene foam, sponge, loofah or balsa wood carved into a head with a finger tube inserted and then dipped into a Polyfilla mixture.

Paper or cloth pieces or strips built around the modelling base with Polycell. This may also be built up directly on the finger tube although this gives a slightly heavier head, but is, of course, much tougher.

A very tough permanent head may be built by modelling on Plasticine or clay as in Fig. 9. First model the head in two halves (A and B). Rub with vaseline or oil, press on strips of thin cloth (bandage, butter muslin, old handkerchiefs), work in a layer of paste (Polycell or Casco), build up alternate layers of paper and cloth strips pasted into a 'skin' six or more layers thick. Build up features as required (C and D) and leave to dry. After removing Plasticine or clay, insert a finger tube (E), join head together (F) and paint, add hair, etc. (G).

Puppet with paper pulp head by S. Haywood.

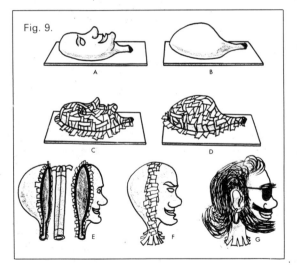

When in use hang glove puppets upside down from hooks set around the stage frame using a curtain ring sewn at the lower back hem of the glove. Store by pulling the glove inside out and back over the head to reduce the rubbing of the face paint.

String Puppets or Marionettes

Materials required for simple string puppets
Thread, string, peanuts, beads, foam rubber lumps, matchboxes, cotton reels. cord-spools, conkers, balls, tins (avoid jagged edges or holes), small weights, Sellotape, decorative scraps of material and trimmings, felt markers, elastic bands, small screw eyes, card, Le Page glue dotter, paper clips, coloured foil and cellophane sweet wrappings.

Methods
String together about a dozen peanuts or cotton reels or any other items as listed above. Keep joints loose with washers to give free movement. Clip on simple clothes with elastic bands and use small pieces of scrap metal to give sufficient weight to feet, hands or seat to enable the puppet to move correctly. Fig. 10.

Cut out a flat head, body, arms, legs from card, loosely tie together with short knotted ties, hang and move with two lengths of string or thread.

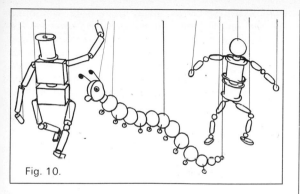

Fig. 10.

A simple rolled paper shape puppet is shown in Fig. 11. It is made from stout paper cut and rolled to give cylinders and cones or folded to cubes and other geometrical forms. Fasten with a Le Page glue dotter or Sellotape and add some weighting as necessary.

Fig. 11. Puppet made from paper cones.

More advanced string puppets

Controls for string puppets should be made from a smooth soft wood such as deal which will take hooks, eyes, screw holes, etc. easily and without needing complicated tools. In the following Figs. 12 and 13 the same key has been used.

Other strings may be fitted for special purposes including mouth strings, elbow strings and strings to special properties such as hats, 'standing-on-end' hair and juggling items.

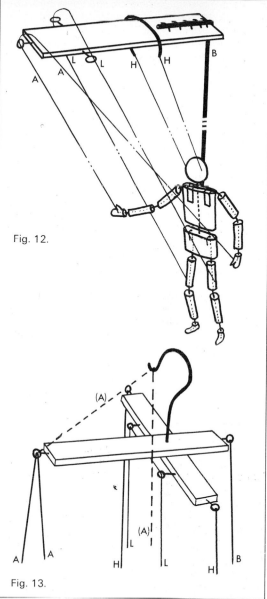

Fig. 12.

Fig. 13.

H — Head — this is the first string to be attached and is fastened to the top of the head. Where two strings are used, attach one to a screw eye behind each ear.

A — Arm — a loop which passes through one or two screw eyes on the control, and is attached through a hole in the centre of each of puppet's hands and tied round the hand.

207

B – Back – a wire joining to shoulders and down the back of the body or a string joining to just below the waist.

L – Legs – usually a free running loop which is best tied above the knee joint.

NOTE: In the preceding set of diagrams the screw eyes are not completely screwed down and the controls are shown diagrammatically and not in the true perspective, in order to represent more clearly the details of construction and stringing.

NOTE: Since marionettes are the form of puppets most used by professional puppeteers, many other variants of the above controls have been devised. Other and more complicated versions will be found in the books listed on page 245.

Stringing the puppets is best done from a jumping stand, adjustable science retort stand, a rod, a bar or a specially made gallows, adjustable to various heights. For the actual string, use macramé thread or fine fishing line. It should be noted that some types of nylon and terylene can be difficult to knot securely.

The point at which you hang the control must of course be at the overall correct height from the stage floor of your puppet when in use. The usual practice is to fix the head string(s) to the control at a point well above the eye level of the audience. Take care that there is sufficient play to allow your puppet to sit or lie down and still keep your hands and the control out of sight. With a detachable leg bar, keep it on the peg or hook. Make arm strings slightly overtaut to prevent arms hanging lifelessly at the side of the puppet when your fingers are busy with other things.

Work in this order – head, shoulders, arms, legs and then any other strings. The simplest control and the fewest possible strings is a golden rule. Walking-on characters can often get by with head strings only. The strings should all be taut when the figure is standing normally. Use small screw eyes or pass thread through a hole and knot on the other side. (A drop of Evostik or Durofix on the knot will avoid the tragedy of knots becoming untied during the performance.) Take the thread right through the clothes to the screw eye beneath.

Much trouble often arises from poor weighting of the hands, feet and hips. Hands that are too light tend to float about; feet not correctly weighted will not walk properly, and the puppet will not be able to sit down unless hips are heavy enough. Hands and feet may be cut out from sheet lead and covered with plastic wood. At the hips attach sheet lead around the seat.

Walking is one of the most difficult actions to do smoothly. Practise in front of a long mirror, although, of course, in a performance you will have to judge from above.

If the strings become tangled, do not cut or unscrew the eyes, but concentrate on releasing one string only, and this will often release the rest. When your puppet is strung and ready for use it will need to be hung from a rack. On the stage back there should be a rail or hooks to take the puppets waiting their turn.

If you have to pack your puppet and wish to prevent tangling the strings, then:
Hold the control and gently turn the puppet around several times, so twisting the strings together.
Next take the control and carefully roll it down the strings until it lies on the puppet.
Secure with a large elastic band or tape.
Undo in the precise reverse of the way you did up, and your puppet should be ready for use.

A simple string puppet constructed from newspaper as in Fig. 14

Materials required for a 15 in. to 18 in. puppet.
Two or three newspapers, tissue paper (paper handkerchiefs, toilet paper, etc.), macramé thread, Polycell paste, Le Page tube glue, $2\frac{1}{4}$ yards $\frac{1}{2}$ in. white tape, elastic bands, beads or washers, odd scraps for clothes, hair, etc.

Method: Head
Cut 2 ft. 6 in. of tape, and tie at halfway fold with about 1 ft. of macramé thread (A).
Fold half a page of a large newspaper to give a folded strip about 12 in. by 3 in. (B).
Paste this around the tape just below the knotted fold, leave the threads hanging out and about 8 in. ends of tape below (C). If necessary hold with elastic bands until dry.
Fold another half page of a large newspaper to

give a folded strip 6 in. by 1½ in. and paste over top (leaving threads out) as shown in (D).

Build head and neck up with paper strips about 4 in. by 2 in. pasted on. Use alternate layers of newspaper and tissue to build the required size. Pieces of thin rag, muslin, etc., can also be used to fill out noses, eyebrows, chin, etc. Leave thread coming out at ear position and tapes hanging out below neck (E). Exaggerate any prominent features.

Upper body

Separately fold two or — for a flat puppet — three pieces of newspaper as for head above, and wrap around a ruler, pasting as you wrap (F). Withdraw ruler, leaving centre hole clear of paste. Use elastic bands down the body to hold together during drying.

Lower body

As in upper body, but use a folded strip of newspaper 12 in. by 2 in. to produce a smaller section (G).

Arms and legs

Take four 12 in. pieces of tape and eight single strips of newspaper each 12 in. by 3 in.
Crease each tape into half and stretch out.
Fold and paste strips of newspaper around the tape as shown in diagram H. Each strip gives half an arm or leg. Leave ½ in. for elbow and knee joints.
For arms, fold one end of tape in half and tie 6 in. of thread to fold. Use pasted paper to build up hand over folded tape (I), trap a small piece of lead inside hand if possible.
For legs, fold over tape as before (but do not tie on a thread), including in foot, if possible, a small piece of lead, a small metal button, ball bearing, metal bead or similar heavy scrap to help weight feet (J).

Putting together

Thread head tapes down through a bead or washer and then through the upper body (K).
Thread leg tapes up through lower body (leaving ½ in. between top of legs and body) over top and glue down back of lower body (L).
Thread head tapes that are hanging from upper body down through lower body leaving about ½ in. at waist, fold round bottom and glue up back of lower body (M).

Glue loose ends of arm tapes into the slits on top of shoulders, leaving ½ in. tape free for shoulder joint between upper arm and upper body (M). Use an awl or compass point to make a hole in each upper leg just above knee and tie 6 in. of thread to each leg (N).
Now paint puppet and dress.
Fix stiff wire to back of puppet by drilling a hole through upper body and inserting wire, or take down neck and bind on to body with thread (O). Attach end of wire to control and string puppet as suggested on page 207.

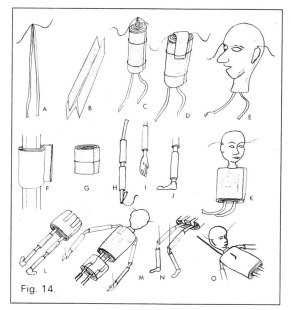

Fig. 14.

A simple wood block puppet as in Fig. 15

Materials required for a 15 in. puppet. Pieces of wood and dowelling of various sizes, sheet lead or heavy metal buttons, screw eyes, glue.

Method Cut out and assemble as shown. Hands and feet may be modelled from wood, balsa wood, corks, or plastic wood around pipe cleaners.

A simple modelled wooden puppet as in Fig. 16 Materials required for a 12 in. puppet. Pieces of wood and dowelling of various sizes. Sheet lead, screw eyes, wire, twill tape or shoe laces, glue, short panel pins or tacks and cord.

Fig. 15.

Fig. 16.

a

b

Method Cut out and assemble as shown. The head can be made from any method previously given. The upper arms and legs are made from a cloth tube or strips. Hands and feet are modelled from plastic wood built on to a base of cut-out sheet lead (a). Lead is also used to line lower body for extra weight. It is usual to make heads solid and (b) shows the basic wire or wood armature necessary to give secure anchoring points for the string screw eyes.

Ideas for play production and an all purpose stage are given on page 216.

Rod puppets

Materials required Card or strawboard, $\frac{1}{4}$ in. to $\frac{1}{2}$ in. round or square dowelling, wire, small screw eyes, wire, scrap materials.

Vertical wire controls as in Fig. 17. The first (A) has a vertical support carrying the body and head and controlled by strings.

(B) has a head made from a ball, potato or plastic container, and a coloured crepe paper costume. (C) shows developments.

A   B   C   Fig. 17.

Glove and fully modelled head as in Fig. 18.
(B) shows a glove with fingers in legs, the body held up by a rod and the jointed arms worked by wires. (C) shows methods of attaching wires. (D) gives ideas for animals, each of which will set its own problems to be solved.

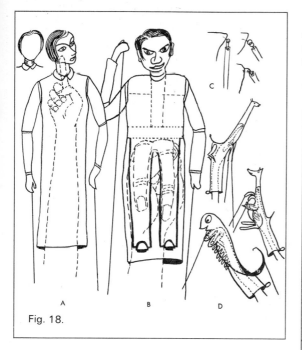

Fig. 18.

Peep-Shows, Toy Theatres and Push-on Puppets

Everyone finds peep-shows fascinating. The intriguing view through the tiny hole punched in the end of a shoe box, together with the mysterious light filtering through the coloured tissue paper covering the holes cut in the lid, can open up a miniature world of delight.

The easiest 'beginner's' peep-show uses figures, animals, trees, buildings and all the necessary scenery cut from magazine illustrations and arranged within the shoe-box in layers going back from the peep-hole to the far end. The strategically arranged holes in the box top or sides allow shafts of daylight or torchlight to fall on important parts. Pieces of coloured tissue or transparent sweet wrapping paper give interesting effects as in Fig. 19. Some boxes have other peep-holes to give different view points. Others have strips attached to the figures which slide in and out of slits cut in the box sides. A development is the use of all sorts of pebbles, shells, sponges, twigs, toy soldiers and the like.

Different types of boxes give different effects. If it is possible to obtain circular hat boxes, these have great possibilities for varied views of a central topic which has certain parts hidden from some peep-holes. Long but narrow boxes give corridor views and the insertion of small pieces of mirror set diagonally to the peep-hole enables one to see around corners and into buildings.

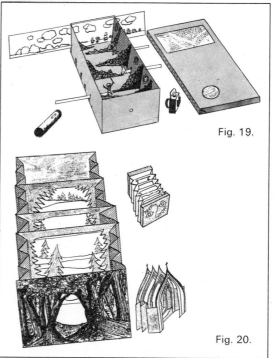

Fig. 19.

Fig. 20.

The peep-show in a concertina or folding form has been in existence from a very early date, probably the middle of the 18th century, or even earlier. In essence it consists of a back scene, a number of cut-out sheets forming a series of layers between the back and front and a front panel cut either as a proscenium arch or with a peep-hole. The concertina sides of paper or linen have the cut-out sheets joined in them, and each sheet has the middle cut away so that a sky or building strip ties the top, and the ground strip ties the base to the sides. The whole can be folded away easily. Some are so designed that the back scene is on the inside of the base of a box and the front on the box top, the whole closing into a shallow box for storage (Fig. 20).

Another development was the Victorian Toy Theatre constructed from paper. Still in existence is Pollock's 'Penny Plain, Two Pence Coloured' Theatre. Examples may be seen at Pollock's Toy Museum, 1 Scala Street, London, W.1, a most exciting museum of antique toys, dolls, games, magic lanterns, foreign toys, toy theatres, and many other bygones, where toy theatres (of the type first sold in the mid-19th century) can be bought (Fig. 21). Pollock's 'Penny Plain, Two Pence Coloured' Theatre may also be obtained from the toyshop, Tridias, 44 Monmouth Street, London, W.C.2, together with a wealth of other toys.

Pollock's Toy Museum

Fig. 21.

The "Regency"

The simplest toy theatre to build consists of a box with a proscenium front and the set built up in a series of cut-out card flats placed between the proscenium and the back cloth. The properties, figures and scenery may be manipulated by wires, rods, card or acetate strips from underneath, through slits in the sides and back, or by strings from above. Narrative theatres are useful for group work in a large class. Four or five children can work on one theatre which will tell a part of the complete story. The adventure type of story is most effective for this, e.g. 'Cinderella', 'Dr. Who',

'Into Space', 'Captain Nemo', 'Voyage of Columbus', etc.

If the theatre is used with slide-on rod puppets, a very versatile form of puppet theatre becomes possible. A simple walking device for a flat or padded push-on figure is shown in Fig. 22. In (A) the leg circle is cut out to the dotted lines position for the four legs and feet and a hole punched in the centre. The figure is cut out and the legs piece joined to body with a push-through paper fastener so that legs revolve easily (B) and (C). The figure can be made from stiff card in three layers, the centre layer being for the top half of the figure only. The legs piece goes between the outer layers which have been stuck to centre layer at top The rod for pushing the figure may be fixed at waist or above.

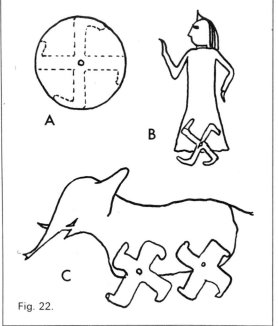

A

B

C

Fig. 22.

Masks

Note: Under no circumstances should plastic bags be used for masks because of the extreme danger of suffocation

Many of the methods given in the glove puppet section are suitable for making masks, and reference will be made in the appropriate section. It is

Fig. 23.

Fig. 24.

Fig. 25.

not always advisable to make a full face mask. Often a half or three-quarters mask which allows part of the wearer's face to show (such as a nose and chin) is much more alive in use than a full mask.

Simple masks

Paper and cloth bag and carton heads as in Fig. 23 where it can be seen that any large enough and strong enough container (not a plastic one) can be adapted into a most effective mask (A), with strings to work parts (B), inner straps to rest on shoulders (C) and a number put together (D).

Paper plate masks as in Fig. 24

Materials Paper plates, scissors, stapler, fasteners, a variety of cardboards, paste or glue, newspaper for paper pulp, paints and trimmings.

Method Push holes through for eyes, nose and mouth. The nose can be cut as in diagram (A). Paint face, model eyebrows, cheeks, chin, etc., add hair, beard, ears, etc. If required chin may be cut away. This allows the plate to wrap around the face as well as giving the mask animation.

Mount on a stick or wire if it is to be held up, or fix elastic strip if to be worn on head.

Wire frame masks, simple flat mask

Materials Stiff wire, cellophane, paper, cloth or card for covering, thread, fasteners, stapler, adhesives, paint, trimmings.

Method Bend the wire into required shape. A number of suggestions for full or half masks are shown in Fig. 25. Stretch covering material over and fasten by sewing, sticking, stapling or with fasteners. Cut holes for eyes, nose and mouth. Turn back any resulting flaps on to the inside of the mask and fasten down. Brush Polyfilla or Casco over both sides of whole mask and leave to set. Repeat if necessary and, when dry, paint and decorate.

Folded and fastened paper or cloth masks

Materials Stiff cartridge paper (90 lb.) or 6 sheet card or buckram, sharp knife, scissors, fasteners, adhesives, paint, trimmings.

Method The simplest forms of these are constructed as in Fig. 26. Using careful slitting and cutting, together with decoration, quite elaborate but rather fragile masks may be made. A development is to construct the main section from thin acetate sheet (plain or coloured, fully or semi-transparent). This can then have trimmings added using such adhesives as Evo-Stik, UHU, or Le Page's clear adhesive or by painting on.

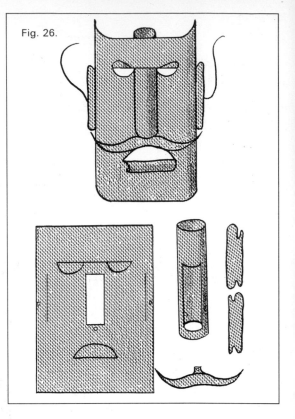

Fig. 26.

More elaborate masks

Masks and heads built upon a balloon

Materials Large balloons, newspaper and other soft paper, old thin fabrics, paste, scrap materials, string, paint, trimmings, as required.

Method Blow up a large balloon, tie neck with string, paint with a liquid detergent or apply oil or thin coat of grease. Tie to a chair or heavy object to hold in place. Use long strips of newspaper (12 in. by 4 in.), toilet paper, tissue, paper handkerchiefs, etc., to cover all over and paste on top. A second layer is prepared by soaking in paste strips of muslin, bandage, old sheet, scrim, old stockings or any thin fabrics available. These are then placed crossways on top of the first layer. Repeat alternate layers of paper/cloth/paper/cloth up to eight or nine layers for a tough head. Use a good waterproof paste such as Polycell or Casco Casein glue Grade A, and finish off with a well-soaked layer of fabric.

Leave top third of the face for the forehead and use a crumpled piece of paper for nose, and paste fabric over in several layers; thick cord, string or rolled paper covered with pasted fabric for chin, eyebrows and lips; shaped card covered with pasted fabric for ears; extra paper/cloth layers are added for cheeks (as Fig. 27). Alternatively, all features may be placed on to the balloon before first layer is spread over.

When thoroughly dry, undo string and remove balloon. Paint and decorate after cutting a hole or slitting for insertion of head, as shown in diagram (B). If powder paint is used for decoration, fix with a spray of charcoal fixative or rub over with a matt wax polish. For masks only, a different face may be built on the back and front of the balloon. After removing the balloon, and splitting up the sides, two masks will be obtained.

Of course, any of the previous mixes suggested in the glove puppet section such as sawdust, paper pulp, etc., may be used. It is, however, wiser to start with a layer of thin fabric and finish with another one, both well soaked in paste.

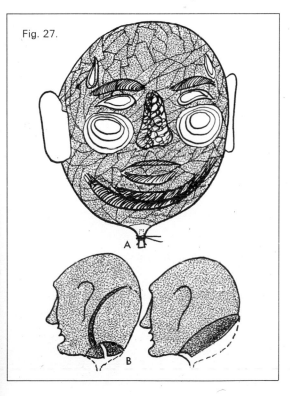

Fig. 27.

A

B

Masks and heads built on a Plasticine or clay shape

Materials As for balloon masks, plus clay or Plasticine.

Method Proceed as recommended in the glove puppet section using the method employing cloth strips described on page 206, and of course making the mould of Plasticine very much larger.

Use a large stone or upturned dish, cover with a thin layer of Plasticine, build up features, etc., and proceed as before. The mask should be designed about $\frac{1}{2}$ in. larger all round than the face it is to fit, to allow for shrinkage during drying. After all trimming, painting, etc., is complete, punch holes about an inch in from edge of mask behind the ears, and attach a piece of elastic to go round the back of the head.

Masks taken from the face

Materials Sheet aluminium foil (as used for cooking), newspaper and scrap cloth, adhesives, paint and trimmings.

Method It is essential to have two people to make this type of mask. Place a sheet of foil on the face you wish to use as a mould, press in and around the features. Take care to press gently, particularly over the eyes. It is necessary to remove the foil after a few moments to insert nostril holes so that your model can continue to breathe! Use sufficient foil to fold around and up to the ears, try to avoid a crumpled effect, and obtain as smooth a finish as possible. Remove very carefully, and if necessary, trap side folds with Sellotape. Take care not to push in the face. Sometimes it is possible to strengthen the foil whilst it is still on the model's face, with pieces of Sellotape across folds or other points of weakness.

Next paint the surface with a liquid detergent or thin oil and cover with strips of cloth (or alternate layers of paper/cloth/paper/cloth, etc.), building up as smooth a surface as possible with plenty of paste. For a very exact likeness, put six or seven alternate layers of tissue paper and pieces of old stockings, preferably of the stretch variety. When dry, remove foil, paint, trim and add elastic band, and your facsimile mask is ready.

Play Production

Keep the mechanics of a production as simple as possible. Do not become over-ambitious. Use only a cue script and avoid the reading of dialogue so as to retain the free spontaneous quality so essential in puppetry. Allow the play to develop from and around the interplay between the characters. The audience will need only the fundamentals of an idea to build upon this in their imagination. Encourage the audience to join in by referring to individuals by name and asking them to warn the puppet when someone else appears, and so on. It is always important to remember that puppets, and particularly string puppets, are not meant to compete with humans. They are not just little people but can do what no human can; they can fly, leap higher, float in space, come to pieces, be entirely abstract, as they please.

Over-statement, melodrama, caricature are all well suited to puppetry. Play with the voice and try to make it suit the character. Most people have a far wider range of voices than they realise. The screen hides the operator and soon removes any feeling of self-consciousness. Music and sound effects add a great deal to any performance and these can be very simply produced. The rumble of thunder can be reproduced by shaking a large sheet of tin or aluminium; falling rain is produced by rattling dried peas over a piece of metal mesh or hardboard. It is possible to borrow or hire records with various sound effects of birds, trains, cars, water, etc., or the actual sounds can be taped.

Play Situations

Simple ideas to start action with a puppet: It has a sleep, but is disturbed by a dog or wasp; telephones; is a magician, a policeman, mummy, teacher; has toothache, etc.

Story starters for young children: The naughty child is found out; 'It's no good, I can't stop falling down', and so on. For older children: Elephant boy; parade of the soldiers; father washes up; at the circus; a puppet revue (clowns, pianist and so on); the birthday party, etc.

Further ideas might be developed from: Nursery rhymes; fairy stories; fables; children's classics and other stories, including science fiction; poems and ballads; songs and descriptive music. Maurice Maeterlinck's 'Three Little Dramas for Marionettes' may be of interest. There is endless scope.

Note: Public performances may require permission in writing from the author or his agent.

Simple stages are shown in Fig. 28. A, B and C show an improvised stage using tables and curtain across an open door. D is a more elaborate form with jumping stands, a blackboard trapped between stout tables, all lashed together with string. E shows stage dimensions for a 12 in. puppet. Lighting points are shown at X and Y in Figs. 28 D and E. Obtain an experienced electrician to set up permanent lights. With young children use cycle lamps and torches and as much natural light as possible.

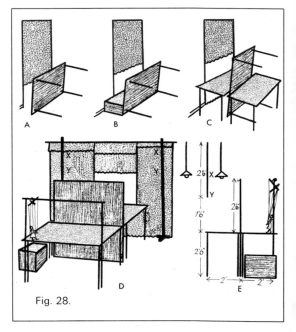

Fig. 28.

A Multi-purpose stage

Materials One large three-wing clothes horse. Two curtains the same height as the clothes horse, and one curtain half the height of the clothes horse. These should be pleated and pinned or stapled to laths or dowel rods. When ready for use each should be as wide as one wing; the rod joined to the top of each curtain should be 3 in. wider each side than one wing.

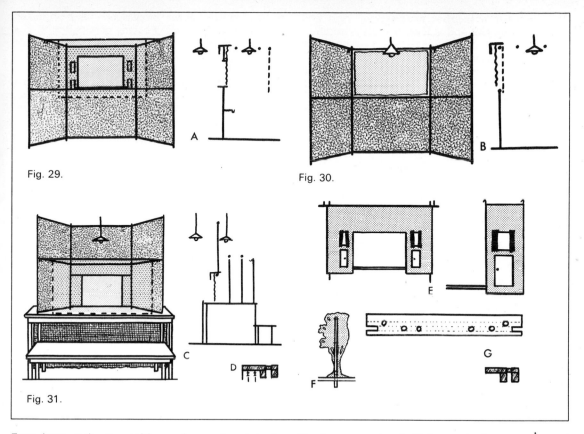

Fig. 29.

Fig. 30.

Fig. 31.

Four long rods at positions shown by dots in diagram (A) for glove puppet scenery, (B) for shadow puppet lights, and (C) for string puppet scenery which can also stand on the floor.

One shelf as in diagram (G) with strips of wood set underneath. These lock the shelf on the front centre bar for use with glove puppets. A few holes in the shelf will enable scenery such as trees, beds, tables, to be fixed so that they do not fly into the audience if knocked during the performance (F).

One shelf (D) with curtains and rails attached to lock on top front bar for glove and shadow puppets, and on centre front bar for string puppets.

Large elastic bands will be found useful to hold the various bars, etc., in place.

Method

Shadow stage Arrange side and front curtains.

Hook on curtain shelf, hang shadow screen and rod for lights (B). Fig. 30.

Glove or Rod Puppet Stage Transfer shadow screen to back-cloth position, hook on shelf and scenery rods (A). Side window pieces as shown in (E) are useful for by-play between glove puppets. A further useful luxury is an inside shelf to clip on below stage shelf on which to store props, scenery, etc., with hooks along front edge from which to hang glove puppets (A). Fig. 29.

Marionette Stage Re-arrange front curtain by raising the half curtain to top rail, drop curtain shelf to centre front rail and also backcloth and scenery rods (C), remove centre shelf. Fig. 31.

This form of stage folds right away and stores flat. It can also be used for a shop or Wendy house. The various curtains are easily cleaned, and the puppeteers are hidden.

217

Curtains for a puppet stage Deep reds and blues are excellent and at least twice the width of the proscenium arch should be used to allow plenty of centre, bottom and side overlaps. Fig. 32. gives details of simple home-made versions. If it is possible, use a plastic rail and runners; this will give a very quiet pull. The rail should be hidden behind a pelmet attached to the curtain shelf.

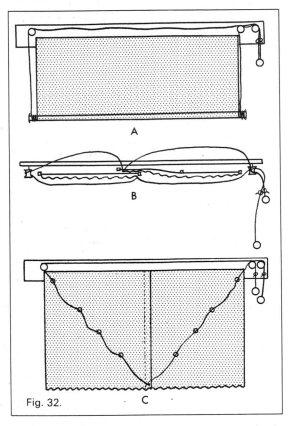

Fig. 32.

Fire-proofing scenery or costumes It is possible to buy aerosol sprays or ready-to-mix powders to fireproof scenery, etc. If you wish to make your own, mix $1\frac{1}{2}$ lb. borax, 1 lb. boracic acid, 2 gallons water. Dip or spray but do not rinse. Check that colours are not affected before dipping the whole article. For information on materials generally available, see page 246.

Bookshops catering for puppeteers K. R. Drummond, 30 Hart Grove, Ealing Common, London W.5, although stocking, obtaining and selling all new and secondhand books on arts and crafts also specializes in puppetry and produces admirable catalogues. Foyles, of Charing Cross Road, London W.1, have a section on puppet books.

Puppet films and film strips Instructional strips may be obtained from Common Ground Ltd. (distributed by Educational Supply Association, The Pinnacles, Harlow, Essex).

Instructional films may be hired through the British Film Institute, 4 Great Russell Street, London W.C.1 (including the delightful Lotte Reiniger Shadow Puppet Films). Films are also available on Glove Puppet Making (British Instructional Films Ltd.); Russian Puppets (Workers Film Association Ltd.); The Lanchester Puppets (Douglas Fisher, c/o Wellcome Foundation Film Unit).

Societies Catering for Puppeteers

The Educational Puppetry Association A vigorous group which has a special interest for teachers at all levels from kindergarten right through to college.

Aims of the Association:
To present and develop the full educational possibilities of puppetry as a creative and dramatic activity with important social values.
To encourage experimental work in puppetry in the education of retarded, subnormal, and maladjusted children.
To assist adult rehabilitation.
To exchange ideas and information with similar organisations in other countries.

The Secretary, 23a Southampton Place, Bloomsbury, London W.C.2 will send full details of the many amenities and activities available to members upon receipt of a s.a.e. These include instructional leaflets; a lending library; advice on technical matters; headquarters open to visitors on Mondays during school terms from 6.30 p.m.; evening and vacation courses; a regular journal, 'Puppet Post'; and many other advantages.

The British Puppet and Model Theatre Guild Aims to advocate the use of puppets and model theatres; to raise the standard of puppetry in all its forms; and to form a means of communication between its members, the amateur and professional puppeteers of Britain, and its overseas members in all parts of the world.

Some advantages of membership are:
Monthly newsletter and quarterly journal 'The Puppet Master'.
Panel of experts who will give advice on puppetry.
Free use of the library.
Sales section.
Frequent meetings for discussion, puppet demonstrations and lectures.
Participation in exhibitions and festivals.

Membership is open to anyone in sympathy with the objects of the guild; all applications are submitted to the council for approval. Application forms for membership may be obtained from the Secretary, 7 Lupus Street, London S.W.1, upon receipt of a s.a.e.

Museums with Collections of Puppets
(A full list will be found in 'World of Toys' by Leslie Daiken, Lombarde Press.)

England
The British Museum, London – outstanding Raffles collection of Javanese shadow puppets. The Victoria and Albert Museum, South Kensington, London – particularly good shadow puppets. The Horniman Museum, Forest Hill, London – good masks and shadow puppets.
The Pitt Rivers Museum, University of Oxford – shadow puppets and masks.
The Kingston-upon-Hull Museum – old English marionettes.
Pollock's Toy Museum, London – Toy theatres and other forms of puppetry.
The Toy Museum, The Grange, Rottingdean, Sussex, many toys showing an affinity to puppets.

Scotland
The Museum of Childhood, Edinburgh.

America
Detroit Institute of Arts – outstanding Paul McPharlin collection of all types of puppets and information about puppets.
The following museums have collections with above average interest to puppeteers.
American Museum of National History; Cooper Museum for the Arts of Decoration, New York; Brooklyn Museum, New York; Museum of Fine Arts, Boston.

France
Musée de l'Homme, Paris – excellent collection and a most interesting museum.
The Museum of Lyons – good puppet collection.

Germany
The Museum of Munich.

Russia
The Moscow State Puppet Theatre under the direction of Sergei Obraztsov is outstanding as a professional company presenting opera, plays and the full-time performances of a flourishing repertoire of puppet plays.

Materials

Adhesives For sticking on hair, trimmings and general joining of fabrics, fabric and paper, paper – Copydex. PVC glues for making paper pulp or sawdust mix – Polycell, Polyfilla, Casco Casein Glue Grade A. For sticking plastics and small repairs between wood, china, glass and metal – Araldite. For sticking card, thin wood, thin plastic – UHU; Evostick; Marvin medium. For simple joining of thin materials Polycell; Le Page's Glue Dotter. For sticking balsa wood – Le Page's Balsa Cement. For sticking polystyrene – Le Page's Polystyrene Plastic Cement.

Lead weight Shot, sinkers, round dress weights, sheet lead and plain solder – fishing supply stores; gunsmiths; large hardware suppliers.

Screw eyes Steel or brass, size $2\frac{5}{8}$ in. is an average small size.

Thread Macrame thread or tested fishline in black or grey nylon is practically invisible.

(The publishers are grateful to Mills and Boon Ltd., publishers of *Exploring Puppetry* by Stuart and Patricia Robinson for permission to use a number of the illustrations which appear in that book among the illustrations to this section.)

Sculpture in Various Media

Glenn Hellman

It is paradoxical that although we exist in a three-dimensional world most people think visually in only two. This you may at first discount as ridiculous but ask someone with no training to make a sculptural object. The chances are that the result will be a collection of views (usually two or four) each one thought of separately, with no conception of how it affects the others, no internal logic or structure and no understanding of how the object affects the space it exists in and defines.

The production of a self-existing object which is the externalisation of an experience in formal terms is a rather catholic definition of sculpture. People tend to have preconceived standards against which 'art' is measured and judged. Unfortunately, these conceptions stand in the way of enquiry, are an excuse for mental idleness and, as such, are barriers against a great deal of exciting and pleasure-giving experience, not only when looking at art but also in everyday life. These same preconceptions judge whether an object or situation is worth the effort of really looking, and at the same time filter out those judged to be unworthy. We all need these censors — such is the complexity of life — but they should be servants not tyrants.

The process by which an experience becomes a formal idea takes place mostly in the subconscious and is generally a lengthy process. Before an experience can be used it must be totally absorbed into the personality (when it reappears its source may be unrecognisable). This process cannot be forced. The effectiveness of the assimilation and metamorphosis depends on how well the experience is understood. (It must be remembered that an emotional experience, as far as sculpture is concerned, can only be expressed in terms of mass and space.) Beautiful objects, driftwood, stones, mechanical waste, etc., cannot be made into art

just by putting them on a base and smoothing the edges (but see Marcel Duchamp!).

For a start try these two seemingly simple exercises which, if carried through beyond the obvious, will be found to be rather difficult:

1. Take a piece of thin card, 12 in. square for convenience, and using only variations of one geometric shape make an all-over pattern, random or repetitive. Then cut the pattern so that pieces of it can be bent out on either side. You now have a two-dimensional pattern which has extended into the third dimension. Now stick on more card, using the appropriate shapes, until the flat plane of the original piece is lost and what is left is a totally three-dimensional model.

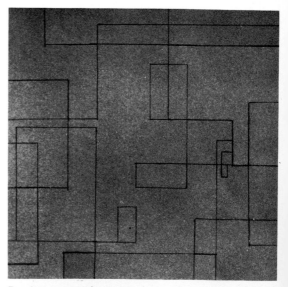

Random geometric pattern drawn on card.

The 'pattern' extended into three dimensions.

Exercise in cutting cubes of clay.

2. Make a dozen or so small cubes of clay or similar modelling material (2 in. x 2 in. x 2 in.). Take one and cut into it, using only variations of the cube, to make a design in three dimensions. As you find out what happens in the first cube work on through the rest developing in subsequent cubes ideas and forms that appear, making larger cubes as your ideas become more complex. Continue until you have exhausted all your ideas and then force yourself to try again.

It should be emphasised that these exercises are not intended to show you how to make sculpture, but to introduce you physically to some of the problems of working in the round.

A craft is important to an artist in that it allows him to communicate clearly in the specific manner of his choice: it is the means only. The more the master of his craft an artist is, the more precise can be his statements, but craft ability should be developed alongside the exercise of creativity, not as something separate. Superior craft is no substitute for creativity, just as the finest ideas are useless

unless they can be translated into some external form.

The understanding and feeling for a material or technique plays a large part in the creative process, just as the physical act of making a piece of sculpture plays a part in its evolution.

Casting and building up Plaster is perhaps the most useful of sculptural materials, although seldom used professionally for the final product because of its fragility and surface deadness. Whether for modelling or casting there is one type of plaster superior to others: Superfine White Industrial. It is very strong, has useful setting characteristics and a very fine texture. Plasters called 'pottery' or 'casting' are not suitable, being very much weaker and coarser; neither is plaster of Paris as sold by chain chemists, as it sets too quickly. The latter is quite suitable however for filling small moulds.

Art shops sell a vast range of plaster tools, mostly

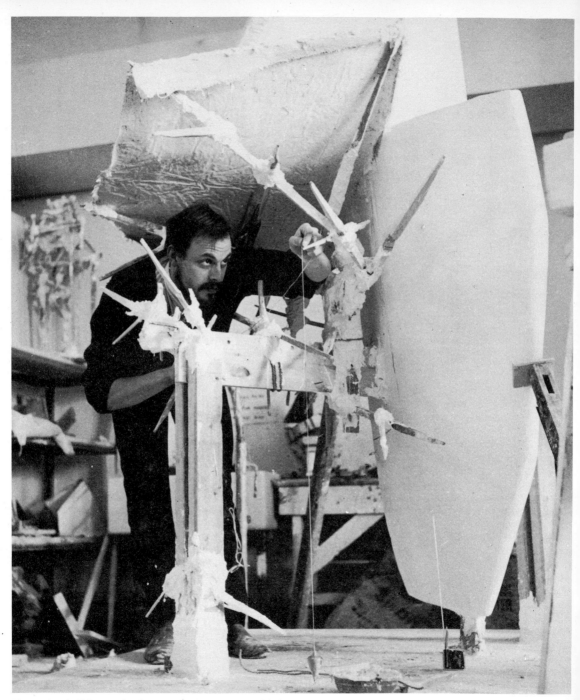

The author building up in plaster using an armature of wood and scrim.

superfluous. You will find that there are various everyday and domestic tools which in many cases are as good as or superior to these (especially for larger work) such as plastic salad spatulas and cheese graters. A tool you will have to make is a plaster axe. This is most useful and can be tailored to your requirements.

When working directly some form of armature is needed. This can be skeletal or surface or a combination. Steel rod and chicken wire are often used, either separately or together, but, should a drastic alteration be necessary, it is very difficult to cut through plaster, wire and steel rod. The use of wood and pre-stiffened scrim is to be preferred as it can be easily attacked with a wood saw or axe. (It is most important not to feel restricted by the mechanics of the medium.) Pre-stiffened scrim is made by smoothing plaster over the scrim so that it impregnates the fibres. The scrim is then lifted to remove the plaster from the gaps and laid flat elsewhere to set. When set it can be cut, bent and fixed with plaster to the wood armature, forming a surface on to which plaster is then modelled. Scrim in strips dipped into plaster is used to bind the wood together. This method is very useful when enlarging. A substance such as expanded polystyrene sheet can be built over, requiring no other armature. The disadvantage of this is that expanded polystyrene has no great strength and the plaster tends to break away from it. However, its use does enable formal statements to be completed quickly — very useful when making maquettes.

When it comes to enlarging a maquette into the chosen material, there are two schools of thought. One says that the maquette will not work in the new scale if enlarged exactly, and alterations will have to be made anyway, so that it is un-necessary to go to the trouble of an exact enlarge-ment. This has the disadvantage that, if it does look wrong in the new size, it is impossible to decide why in relation to the maquette. The other school of thought says enlarge the original and then, if it looks wrong because it cannot take the new size (which is by no means always the case) any alterations can be made with confidence. It is then easy to incorporate the scrim and wood-building method into an enlarging method so that the ends of the sticks represent significant points on the surface equivalent to points on the maquette.

There are two types of plaster mould: piece and waste. Today, piece moulding has been largely superseded in sculptural use by flexible moulding materials. A waste mould, as its name implies, is destroyed in order to remove the cast from inside. Also, in removing the mould from the clay the 'original' is destroyed. It is when moulding from a hard substance that piece or flexible moulds are made. The mould is there to take the impression of the 'original', not to entomb it. The less plaster, the easier it is to chip out, strength is obtained by reinforcing with iron, wood or scrim.

After suitable treatment, the mould can be filled with plaster or plaster-like materials (e.g. Terrosa Ferrata, an artificial stone looking like terra cotta), with cement and ciment fondu (a black aluminous cement setting in about twelve hours) both with either sand or fibreglass mat as aggre-gate, or with resin and fibreglass; with any of these as backing, a thin layer of metal can be sprayed into the mould first. If it is simple and purpose made, plastic sheet can be formed into it. In all these cases the actual filling does not need a great thickness. It is possible to make a cast of ciment fondu and fibreglass mat as thin as one of resin and mat, and even cement and sand need not generally be thicker than $\frac{5}{8}$ in. For large casts, a permanent steel bracing can be fixed inside to give extra strength.

A form of casting which is useful for small objects is clay pressing. If done carefully, accurate and sensitive casts can be obtained. It is really most useful for the quick reproduction in plaster of objects that cannot be worked on in their original state (i.e. stones, bones, bits of machinery, tools or even other maquettes) so that the ideas they suggest can be developed by carving and model-ling.

Just as cement and resin can be cast so too can they be built up direct like plaster. In these cases it is simpler to use a surface armature and, be-cause of the length of time they remain plastic, a rigid material is needed — expanded steel or close mesh chicken wire. A certain control over the surface is obtained by the aggregate used; resin, by the addition of appropriate aggregates, es-pecially to the surface, can be made to look like practically anything.

Modelling wax can be made from a mixture of

Fig. 1.

Fig. 2.

Fig. 3.

Fig. 4.

Fig. 5.

Fig. 6.

Fig. 7.

Clay pressing.

Fig. 1. The object to be cast, block of clay and talc. The talc is rubbed on to the object and acts as a parting agent.

Fig. 2. Press object into clay up to half its width. Dust top of clay with talc.

Fig. 3. Thin slab of clay pressed tightly round object and then built up to equal other block.

Fig. 4. Completed mould with sides cut square and top cut flat to ensure a good register when replaced.

Fig. 5. With object secured, pouring spue is cut in both halves which are then placed together. Make sure all edges are registered before pinching seams lightly together.

Fig. 6. Pouring in plaster mixture.

Fig. 7. Cast object with spue still attached. Mould is still good for further use.

paraffin wax and microcrystalline wax. Cast into slabs, sheets and rods it can then be cut up as needed and used to construct smallish sculptures. It can be modelled in a similar manner to clay but is rather laborious to use as each little bit has to be melted to the right consistency. Car styling wax has been developed for ease of modelling and ability to take a smooth surface. It really is almost like clay to use. It cannot be melted down and cast as it breaks up at fairly low temperatures.

(If it can be obtained, a copy of 'Modelling and Sculpture' by Albert Toft, Seeley Service Co., 1929, is invaluable for its wealth of technical information.)

Metal Sculpture

Steel sculpture probably started with Julio Gonzalez (1876–1942) and until recently had few practitioners. Although it would seem that an extensive workshop is needed for working in steel, a great deal is possible with surprisingly little equipment. Obviously one must have access to oxyacetylene welding and cutting equipment. The rest of a very basic tool kit is completed by a strong vice, a steel bench, a heavy ballpein hammer, a heavy piece of flat metal to hammer on (or an anvil), a pair of mole grips, and something to grind the welds with (this can be managed with a partly worn angle-grinder disc on a fast electric drill). 'Head' below was made using no more tools than these. It is not hard to add to this list. Such items as an arc welder 100/200 amp. 100/50 volt range, angle grinder, bench grinder, bench shears, bench drill, a whole selection of G cramps and grips soon find their way into the studio. As with all tools, let the need arise before buying, then you get the right tool for the job and not one that might do any number of jobs but is never actually used. The most attractive and expensive welding set or tool is not always the best. It is instructive to find out what the Local Education Authority issues to its colleges.

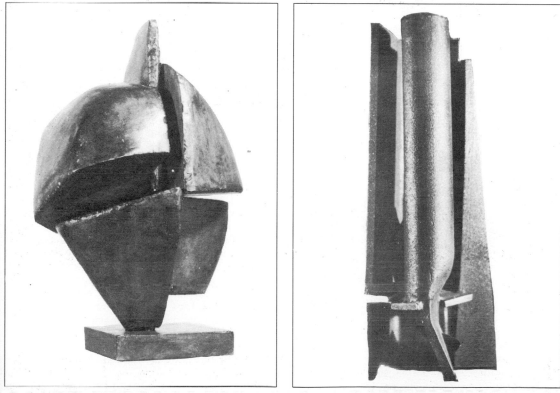

'Head' 1964. Made in steel by the author, 13″ high.

'2 Forms II'. Made in bronzed steel by the author.

'Polarity'. Painted steel sculpture by Robert Adams, 98½ high.

Coll: R. Nasher, U.S.A.

Some sculpture springs immediately from the form of the steel. Although not recognisable as such, Fig. 8 is made from standard (pipe) sections. 'Polarity' and '2 forms II' also depend, in varying degrees, on standard steel forms for their conception. Whereas, though 'Head' gains strength from being steel its form is in no way dependent on the material. Just because a material is difficult there is no necessity to become simplistic and limited in formal conception when using it. Obviously steel, as other materials, makes special demands of its own, but these should be incorporated and not allowed to dominate.

When making sculpture that requires a lot of sheet manipulation it saves time and steel if, in the first place, a maquette is made and then paper patterns made from this of the more straightforward

Fig. 8. Sculpture by Brian Bishop.

The selection of sculpture illustrated makes no pretence of comprehensiveness but each does represent a different approach:

226

'Ritual' 1969 by Antanas Brazdys, winner of a competition sponsored by the Hammerson Group.

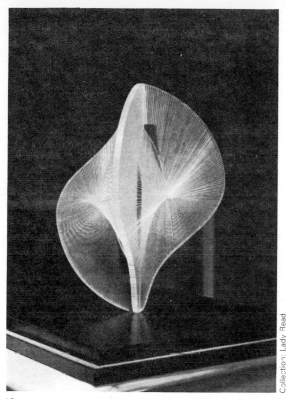

'Construction in Space with Crystalline Centre' by N. Gabo.

surfaces. It will be found that most working can be done cold and the rest can be done by local heating with the oxyacetylene torch. If these resources are beyond reach then quite a lot can be done with tinplate which is easily soldered.

The problem with ordinary mild steel is that it rusts. There are several treatments to prevent this, the easiest of which is painting. If it is going to be polychrome anyway it might well be better to use self-coloured resin in the first place. Some other treatments, all industrial processes, are shot-blasting and zinc spraying, which can be left plain or another more decorative metal sprayed on top, galvanising and plating. With this last it is difficult to obtain successful results, and certainly not on large sculptures. A blue-ish finish can be obtained by burning oil on to the surface, but this does not have a very long life outside. Small pieces for inside are very effective if polished and clear-lacquered.

Plastics

Those plastics mainly in use are the hard acrylics (such as Perspex), the softer thermoplastics for vacuum forming (polystyrene) and the thermosetting plastics (polyester resin with glass-fibre as reinforcement).

As previously mentioned, polyester can be made with any colour or surface; a fact which has taken a long time to be exploited because, when first introduced as an art medium, it was canvassed as a cheap substitute for cast bronze! It is ideal for exploiting colour in sculpture. Such sculptures if composed of several similar shapes are best cast from fibreglass piece moulds taken from a plaster original. If not repetitious but still simple then casting sheets of resin on to glass or hardboard, which gives curves, and joining them as appropriate with similarly coloured resin will be found easier and more effective than building up on an

Plastic sculpture by Stella Fagg depending for much of its effect on the lighting.

armature. It may be that a combination of methods is needed. As making sculpture is not like making furniture from plans and written instructions, a sound understanding of the principles of the processes and qualities of the materials involved and ingenuity are needed for success — aesthetics apart.

It is perhaps the ambiguity and immaculateness that people find so attractive in Perspex. It is very difficult to make anything more than simple (i.e. in one plane only) bends and curves in it without recourse to industrial machinery. However, it is its light-passing and reflecting qualities which have been exploited from the beginning. The makers of Perspex (I.C.I.) provide comprehensive information on all aspects of handling their product, which is not all that difficult. The photographs show some of the possibilities but there are very many more. With the greater use of electronics,

and the prevalence of environmental sculpture, a great vista for the future is opened up. Very little equipment is needed; a coping saw and sheet saw with appropriate blades (see maker's instructions), a drill and cement. Cleanliness is essential as the surface is easily scratched, so if used in conjunction with other materials its protective covering should be left on as long as possible; this can be rather awkward. It should be noted that Perspex is a trade name for I.C.I. and there are other manufacturers.

Further mention should be made of vacuum forming. Of the thermoplastics, polystyrene is the best suited as it has no 'memory', P.V.C. has a weak memory, whilst the acrylics have a strong one. The acrylics also need a different form of heating so they cannot be used in the same machine as the other two. The vacuum former works by heating a sheet of plastic which is held round the edges. When hot enough the mould is brought up to it and then the air is rapidly pumped out, the vacuum produced pulling the soft plastic into or over the mould. The shapes that can be made are limited because of the necessity of removing the now hard plastic from the mould. The advantage lies in the unlimited number of rapid reproductions that can be made. The flat sheet can be printed on by the silk screen process with special inks and then formed, making relief prints. It is easy to be merely pretty with plastics but these materials have tremendous possibilities if their qualities can be deeply understood.

Stone

Mankind has immortalised itself in the stone artifacts of its various civilisations. Today stone may have lost this importance but it is still a valid means of expression and traditional stones and methods still have their place. As probably more books have been written on this subject than any other craft this section will be confined to a more industrial handling technique.

In the same way that standard steel sections can be used, so too can the various stone — especially marble — sections and mouldings available in quantity from demolished Victorian residences.

Sculpture in marble by Brian Bishop.

Marble sculpture by Robert Walton.

Marble, or any other stone, is easy to cut with the correct tool which most large builders' merchants and fireplace manufacturers have for this purpose, a water-lubricated, resin disc saw. Generally such places are helpful in doing small jobs of this sort. As 'Araldite' will stick stone it is very easy to make constructions and reliefs using varieties of stone very effectively.

Fabrication Because extensive workshop facilities are not available this does not mean that work must be restricted to indoor small size pieces. 'Stone' by Michael Kenny was made by riveting aluminium sheet on to an aluminium frame which was also fabricated by riveting; a drill, hammer, dolly and sheet saw being the only tools needed. Some of Alexander Calder's very large stabiles are made in this way. Similarly, plywood (especially 2 mm.) and hardboard can be built on to a wooden frame. If the whole is treated and painted it is quite suitable for outdoors.

There is a strong tendency, when it is decided to use a particular material before first having an idea worked out, for the more obvious limitations of that material to stifle creativity. It is better to make a maquette and then choose the material or wait until an idea demands to be made in a particular material. The skills of one discipline brought to bear on the problems of another can often produce interesting and useful solutions, so do try to solve some technical problems without recourse to the experts.

'Stone' 1968 by Michael Kenny.

Spinning and Weaving

Mary Barker

Spinning

Before weaving can begin, some way must be found to turn fibres into yarn. Our ancestors interwove strips of bark, skins or reeds, to make windbreaks, fish traps and simple baskets. Although these have perished, early pottery often shows incised patterns reminiscent of twill, herringbone and other simple weaves. Subsequently they must have discovered that twisting fibres from wool, fur or plants, would make yarn. Spindle whorls and loom weights are found in excavations of Lake Dwellings and Stone Age remains. (Fig. 1(a) and (b).)

All fibres can be made into a thread by drawing them out into a thin line and putting in enough twists per inch to hold them together. Wool is easy to spin because each individual fibre has a certain degree of crimp and, if examined under a microscope, will show a scale structure. Fleeces vary from a soft, full handle such as South Down, to a silky, demi-lustre wool like a Lincoln, or a springy, resilient tweed type such as Cheviot.

Before twisting to make a yarn, the fibres must be teased open and separated to form a fluffy mass easy to draw out. With a good fleece this may be all the preparation needed. Otherwise a pair of carders are used to open the fibres. Carders are oblong pieces of wood, covered with bent wires. They have handles (Fig. 2) and although a pair are both the same, it is usual to mark them clearly right-hand and left-hand as the wire teeth wear differently in use. The teased wool is arranged on the left card, and then stroked gently by the right card until there is a straight fringe of fibres. These are then transferred from right to left card and the process repeated. When straightened, the fibres are taken off and rolled into a rolag, ready to be drawn out and the twist put in.

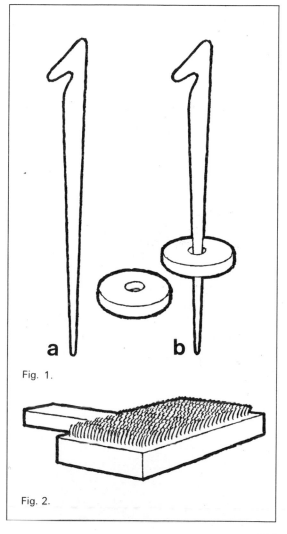

a   b

Fig. 1.

Fig. 2.

Spinning consists of three processes, drawing out the fibres, putting in the twist, and then winding on the spun yarn.

To spin with a spindle, let the rolag lie over the back of the left hand, and with the right hand draw out a thin roving. Attach this to a piece of yarn that has been tied to the spindle shaft, then wound below the whorl and fastened by a slip knot to the hook at the top of the shaft. Give the spindle a twirl in a clockwise direction, then pull out some more fibres as twist runs up towards the rolag. Continue drawing and twirling until the spindle hits the floor. It is then time to wind the thread neatly round the spindle.

These three actions take time so thought was given to speeding up spinning. Leonardo da Vinci shows in his sketch books his idea for solving the problem but the spinning wheel is thought to have first been made in Rhineland in the 16th century. The advantage of the wheel over the spindle is that all three processes, drawing, putting in the twist and winding on, all take place at once. Early spinning machinery used the same principles and developed slowly into the highly complicated industrial apparatus used today.

Dryad

Wool is easier to spin when it is in its natural grease as the fleece has been shorn from the sheep. If it is so dirty that it must be washed before spinning, a few drops of oil should be added before teasing the scoured fibres. It is possible to dye either the fibres or the yarn, but in both cases, grease and oil must be washed out first. Dyed fibres can be blended on the carders to give subtle coloured thread. By following the instructions on a packet of commercial dyestuff, quite successful results can be obtained. Some information on natural dyes and dyeing processes generally will be found under Tie-and-Dye, page 238.

Handspinning is slow so, after giving it a trial, it might be best to choose some mill spun yarn. There are special yarns made for weaving but knitting wool can be used for your first piece of work.

Weaving

To make cloth, one series of threads called warp is held taut from front to back of the loom. These threads are divided by some device to make an opening through which a continuous thread, weft, interlaces with the warp at right angles. Plain weave is the simplest interlacement, like darning, under one thread over the next (Fig. 3).

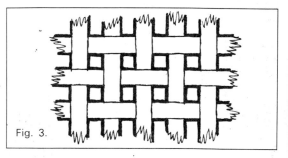

Fig. 3.

From prehistoric times, weavers have tried to find more convenient ways of separating the warp threads to make a shed for the weft shuttle to traverse. Some early looms consisted of a frame to hold the warp threads taut, with one shed obtained by darning a wide stick under the odd ends and turning it on its side. All the even ends had a loop of string called a leash, put round them individually. These leashes were then tied into bundles or to a rod so that they could be lifted to make the other shed. Fig. 4.

Today, a rigid heddle reed loom can be bought which makes plain weave. This rigid heddle consists of metal slats with a hole half way, held

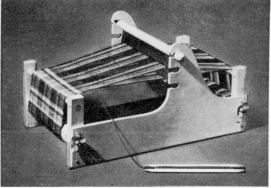

Dryad two-way rigid heddle loom.

A treadle loom has the shafts attached to pedals. There can be more than four shafts, but over eight the loom becomes awkward to use.

Four shaft Harris table loom.

in a frame. There are usually six slats to an inch with six spaces between. This will give twelve ends per inch. When the rigid heddle is raised, all the threads through the holes are lifted; when the heddle is depressed, all these ends are pushed down. By this simple means the two sheds giving plain weave are made. When extra decoration is needed, the threads have to be lifted almost like embroidery. It is possible to make delightful patterns in this way although of course it takes time.

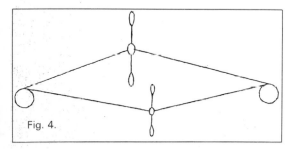

Fig. 4.

A four shaft table loom can weave pattern according to the way the threads are entered through its four shafts. This is called the draft. After the heddles are threaded, the ends must be pulled through the reed to space them out to the correct number of ends per inch.

The shafts are raised to form the shed, and with four shafts there are fourteen different combinations of lifts.

Design Before the warp can be wound, an accurate plan must be made for the finished article. In a way one works backwards by visualising the end product, and then analysing it. To weave a scarf on a heddle reed loom, first decide how long and how wide it is to be, whether striped vertically, horizontally, checked or just a plain colour warp with a contrast colour weft. When these decisions have been made, plan it out as follows:

Scarf — finished dimensions — 54 in. by 8 in. knotted fringe 3 in. each end.

Warp length	54 in.
Take up and shrinkage	5 in.
(3 in. per yard)	
Waste	18 in.
Total:	77 in. — say $2\frac{1}{4}$ yards.

Width	8 in.	
Sett	12 ends per inch	
Total number of ends	8 by 12	96
Double outside two ends for selvage		4
	Total:	100

The plan is to make a black and white scarf with check border at the edges and horizontal stripes. Colour order of warp

Black	4.	4.	4.	4.				16
White	2.	4.	4.	64.	4.	4.	2.	84
						Total:		100 ends

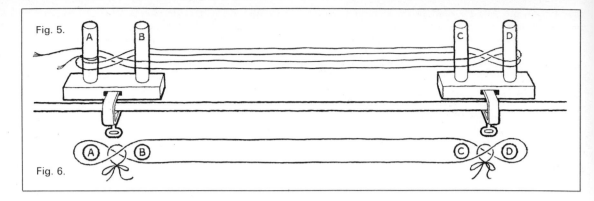

Fig. 5.

Fig. 6.

Warping The warp has to be wound with a cross at each end so that the threads are kept in order. To do this clamp two pegs about six inches apart each end of a table, A.B.C.D. The distance between A. and D. must be the length of the warp. Tie the thread to peg A. then wind in front of B. and C. and behind D.; on the return journey, the wool passes in front of D. and behind C. and B., in front of A. and so on (Fig. 5). From A. to D. is counted as one thread, back to A. the second end. Take care to follow the colour plan exactly. It is possible to upturn chairs on the table and use the legs instead of posts for warping. For long warps, there are special peg boards and warping mills to make this process swift and easy but there are still pegs each end to make the two crosses. When the correct number of threads has been wound, tie round the crosses with a strong contrast yarn, and remove the warp carefully from pegs A. and B. crocheting it into a chain until it is finally slipped off peg D. This chain keeps the warp even (Fig. 6).

Rolling on Warp The next stage is to spread the warp out to the correct width. A piece of apparatus called a raddle is useful for this (Fig. 7). It consists of a bar of wood with pegs or nails at one inch intervals or even half or quarter inch apart. The rod from the back of the loom is put through the loop of cross C.D. and the strong cord through the other loop C.B. Take care to check that this end of the crochet warp unchains. The threads are then divided into the spaces of the raddle in correct order of the cross. If the sett of the cloth is 12 ends per inch, 12 threads are put into each inch division, and so on. Tie the back rod to the canvas apron on the back roller of the loom, spacing out the cords so that they are straight. The warp chain

is then held firm in the left hand and given a few sharp taps with the side of the right hand. Any threads that have been loosened during raddling should be picked up here. It is most important to roll on the warp at even tension. Holding the warp chain firmly with one hand, turn the back roller with the other. A sheet of firm brown paper, one inch wider on each side than the warp, is rolled in to prevent subsequent layers of threads bedding down on each other. Thin sticks can be used

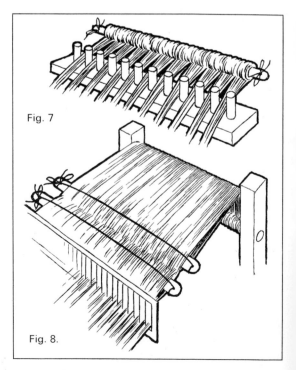

Fig. 7

Fig. 8.

instead. As the warp unchains, repeat the shake and tap routine keeping a watch for any loose ends.

When the second cross of the warp is reached, shed sticks are fastened each side with cords (Fig. 8), then the cross tie is undone and the warp loops tied by half bows in about one inch sections to keep them tidy. Looms vary in design and some way of supporting the shed sticks conveniently must be found. With the rigid heddle reed, the loops of the warp are cut and the ends threaded first through a slit then through a hole taking the next in order of the cross each time. The selvage is made by entering double ends through the first slit and hole, then thread ends singly until the last two which are doubled for the other selvage. The next step is to tie the threads in inch-wide sections round the rod attached to the front roller taking extreme care that the tension is even.

To begin weaving, raise the heddle reed, and pass the shuttle through the shed leaving two inches of weft outside the web. This weft end is then tucked round the outside selvage thread into the same shed. Always begin and end the weft thread in this way. If you put the end into the next opposite shed, the finishing off will show. To return to the original scarf design, the colour order of the weft must be first four white and then four black picks (the name for weft threads). This weft plan will give white, black and mixed checks at the borders with white and mixed stripes across.

Difference of four shaft loom Not only does the reed have to be entered as a separate process but also there are many alternative ways of threading the heddles. They can be arranged 4.3.2.1. or any other way to experiment, for instance, 4.3.2.1.2.3.4.1. The order in which the shafts are lifted will give pattern to the cloth. The squared paper diagram shows that when shafts one and three are raised alternately with shafts two and four, plain weave is obtained just like that made by the rigid heddle. However, lift the shafts in the following order in pairs, one and two, two and three, three and four, four and one; these two different ways of entering the heddles will give very different patterns. There are three choices to be made in designing for four shafts. First the order of threading the heddles called the draft, secondly the size of reed and how many ends to put through each dent, called ends per inch or sett, and lastly, the order of lifting the shafts. The best way to understand all this is to set up the loom with a narrow sample, three inches in straight draft and three inches in a different draft, and then try weaving with different lifting plans.

There are infinite variations on four shafts but at first the rigid heddle seems limited to plain weave. This need not be dull; besides all the colour combinations of stripes and checks, here are some ideas to try.

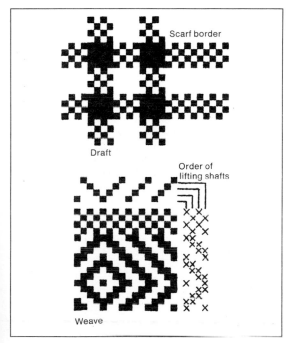

Scarf border

Draft

Order of lifting shafts

Weave

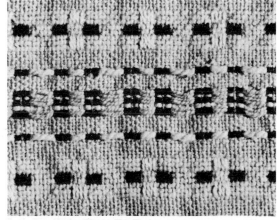

Enlargement of four shaft weave.

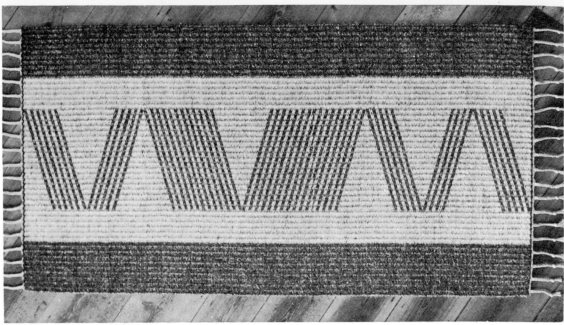

Peter Collingwood

Horsehair and wool rug woven in shaft-switching method by Peter Collingwood.

Cotton Melinex and cellophane wall hanging.

Vary the thickness of the warp by putting four ends through the slit and then only one through the hole. Try this in stripes.

Fill half an inch of the heddle reed as usual then leave half an inch empty. After weaving half an inch, put in a stick instead of the weft. Carry on weaving and then remove the stick. This will make an open lacy scarf.

Embroidery on the loom. With one colour warp, weave two inches in self colour weft, then use one pick of doubled weft, four picks of fine thread, say silk across wool. Thread a needle with a length of the doubled weft, put this through half inch of the open shed, then make a blanket stitch round the first thick weft pulling all the fine threads together. Repeat this stitch at intervals across the warp.

Pick up. Weave one inch as usual then, with a stick in front of the heddle, pick up four threads, leave four threads, right across the warp. Turn the stick on end and put the weft through. Pull out the stick and repeat the process, lifting up the four threads that were left down last time. Repeated several times, this will make a block pattern. The difficulty is that the take up of weft yarn will be different and tend to pull in the sides of the cloth. To avoid this, try using a row of plain weave between each pick up weft. This is called using a 'tabby binder', 'tabby' being the nickname for plain weave, and this tabby binder is often used when weaving an elaborate draft on a four shaft loom.

Great progress has been made in industrial textiles during the past decade. Mass production brings standardisation of things to buy but this will encourage people to create something of their own and find the pleasure the craftsman has in using his hands.

At first the fun of making is enough but soon proper pride in work well done will develop skill.

This skill is needed for quality of textile — all important in an age of change and rapid technological invention. Besides the hand weaver making original and beautiful things for himself, there must be the designer-craftsman creating ideas that will influence the whole field of textiles.

These are only a few suggestions as I do not want to spoil anyone's fun in exploring their own ideas. It can be discouraging when one of these ideas does not work, but try to find out what went wrong. Sometimes the difference between success and failure in weaving is very small; change the size of yarn, double up the sett, put in a few spaces or vary the beat; any one of these factors might make all the difference.

Tie-and-Dye   Anne Maile

Tie-and-dye is a fascinating and practical craft suitable for skilled and unskilled people of all ages. Cloth (usually white) is knotted, folded, bound, sewn or manipulated in various ways so that during the dyeing process certain parts resist the dye. The skill lies in planning these dyed and undyed areas to form pleasing patterns and colour schemes. After the dyeing is finished, whether with one, two or more colours, the sample is untied and ironed out flat. With the first dyeing the original white cloth is reserved in the resist pattern. The first colour is reserved, if extra binding or sewing is added before dyeing the second colour, and so on.

Origins The origins of tie-and-dye, also known as Plangi in some countries, as Bandhana in India, Shibori in Japan and Adire in Nigeria, are obscure. Tritik is the term given to the sewing methods in many countries. At different times it has been practised in most parts of the world, except Australasia. The earliest known records of the craft come from China, India and Japan (approx. 6th–10th centuries A.D.). Knowledge of the craft spread along the old 'Silk Road' and the old caravan routes from the Far East to the Mediterranean countries, It was a flourishing craft in Peru at the time of the ancient Incas, before the Spanish conquest in the 15th century A.D. Early peoples of Mexico and many countries in South America and the south-west region of the U.S.A. also practised the craft, possibly from the Middle Ages. Today, very beautiful Adire cloths come from Nigeria in West Africa but when they were first produced is not known.

The basic principle of tie-and-dye, with its dyed and undyed sections of cloth, could have been discovered accidently and then developed independently in various parts of the world. In the past the craft was carried out within the family circle or tribe, using the type of hand-woven cloth made in the district. Colours for the dyes were obtained from local plants like indigo, cutch, lichens, etc.; from roots such as madder; from barks came fustic, logwood, etc.; some dyes from beetles and insects, for instance lac, kermes and cochineal, and purple from the Purpura shell-fish. Minerals also provided colouring matter.

Equipment Tie-and-dye is a craft that can easily be carried out at home or in the classroom as the basic needs are simple. These are:

Dyes See p. 242.

Dyebath All receptacles of enamel, stainless steel and galvanised ware are suitable for both hot and cold dyeing, but for cold dyeing it is possible to use plastic, glass and pottery vessels.

Fabric Avoid crease resistant cloths

A. All kinds of cotton cloths, especially mercerised, dye well. Cambric, calico (bleached), drill, lawn, muslin, organdie, sheeting, towelling, cotton velvet or velveteen, etc. Unbleached calico should be washed several times in the washing machine or boiled with soda and soap powder or detergent. Leave cloth to cool in this liquid then rinse thoroughly.

B. Linens and viscose rayons.

C. Pure silks and chlorinated woollens.

Some of the dyes will colour the man-made fibres but as a rule they need different dyes from the ones dealt with here.

Thread All strong cotton and linen threads, yarn, twine, fine string, raffia, etc. Rubber bands can also be used. These are easier for younger children.

Tie-dyeing consists of the following processes:

Wash and iron cloth.
Mark out pattern if necessary and tie up the cloth according to the methods chosen.
Wet out tied-up sample if required and dye.
Rinse and dry.
Add more binding or sewing, or completely untie the sample and then re-arrange it and re-tie it, before dyeing the next colour.
After the final dyeing rinse well and dry.
Untie.
Rinse again. Dry partially and iron while still damp.

Tying-up Methods

Marbling Bunch up the cloth into a ball, or a longer length into a roll and bind firmly in all directions (Fig. 1a). A small amount of binding will allow more dye to penetrate, a more densely bound sample retains more white cloth. After the first dyeing, untie, then re-tie the cloth, bringing the undyed areas to the outside of the bundle. Dye the second colour. Repeat until a satisfactory texture has been achieved.

Binding must be done firmly so that the dye does not penetrate too easily and fastened off securely by tying two ends of thread together, or with a slip knot. A narrow binding produces a resist line, a solid band keeps out most of the dye in that area, and criss-cross binding gives a texture on the cloth. Fig. 1b.

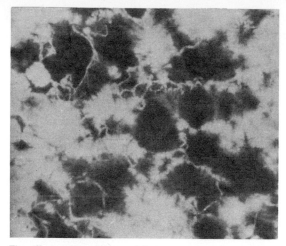

The effect achieved by marbling.

Knotting Fine fabrics are most suitable for this technique. All knotted patterns are improved if, after the first dyeing, the knots are untied, then tied up again as before and dyed the next colour. The knots can be tied loose enough for trouble-free untying but they will then need a little re-inforcing with binding or rubber rings to make sure of getting a resist.

Fold cloth in half lengthwise and tie into knots at intervals, twisting the cloth before tying (Fig. 2a).

Pick up the central point of a square of fine cloth, twist it and tie it into a knot. Pull out each corner in turn and tie into smaller knots (Fig. 2b).

For a repeat pattern over a length of cloth pick up points where planned and tie into knots.

Fig. 1.

Fig. 2.

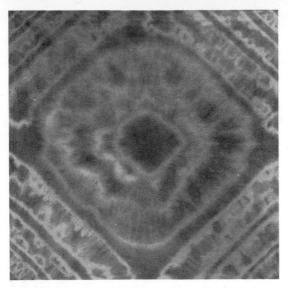

The effect achieved from knotting as in Fig. 2b.

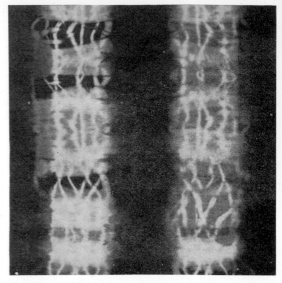

The effect achieved from pleating as in Fig. 1b or 3a.

Clump Tying Bind small objects, such as stones, beads, buttons, marbles, corks, peas, beans, rice, etc. into the cloth at random or to form some pre-arranged design. Do not cut the binding thread between each object, but bind with a continuous thread; it is easier to untie. Fig. 3c.

Stripes Gather, pleat or roll the cloth into a tube lengthwise and bind at intervals. This will give resist stripes across the fabric with bands of colour in between (Fig. 3a and 3b). Change some of the bindings before dyeing the second colour. For diagonal stripes, pleat the sample into a tube diagonally and bind it at intervals.

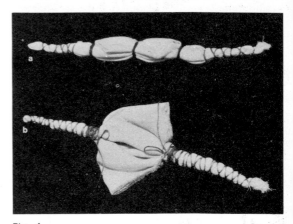

Fig. 4.

Folded Squares Fold a square of fine cloth into quarters, then across diagonally to form a triangle. Add binding. Dye the first colour. Untie and re-arrange before dyeing the second colour. Innumerable ways of folding squares can be devised, giving a wide range of exciting designs (Figs. 4a and 4b).

Circles Pick up a point of cloth and smooth it down to look like a closed umbrella. Begin the binding, near the point for a small circle and further away for a larger circle.

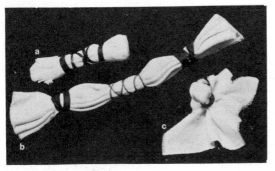

Fig. 3.

Spots For tiny spots pick up a minute point of cloth on a needle and bind just below it. Remove needle. A multi-spot is formed by picking up and binding together several points of cloth.

Sewing For these techniques the thread must be very strong or used double. Begin by making a good-sized knot at the end of the sewing thread and always knot any ends when the thread is cut, during the pulling up. Complete all the sewing on each sample before pulling up the threads, bunching the fabric as closely as possible and fastening off without slackening the thread. When untying, cut the thread at the fastening-off knot and the fabric will be released.

Running stitches on single cloth, whether one, two or more rows, can be used to create bands of texture resembling smocking, or to outline any shape drawn on the cloth. Stitches should be approximately $\frac{3}{8}$–1 inch. Small stitches do not give definite resist patterns.

Running stitches on double cloth can form bands of texture across the fabric or be used to outline any symmetrical shape, half of which is drawn against the fold of the cloth.

Oversewing across a fold or roll of cloth gives a most interesting band of pattern.

The outline of any shape drawn on the cloth can be oversewn, the size and density of the stitches determining the effect of the resist line so produced.

The area within any sewn shape can be bound or have small objects tied into it.

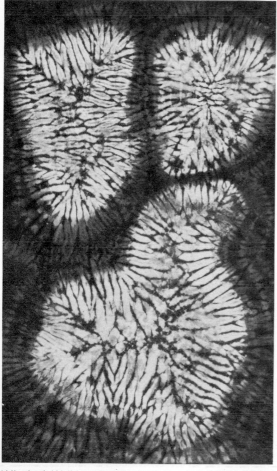

'Alluvion'. Wall hanging by the author in cotton.

'In Full Bloom' an example of sewing and dyeing.

Pleated Shapes Almost any symmetrical shape can be formed by pleating on double cloth. Draw half the shape against a fold of cloth. Pleat up the cloth along the pencil line. Add a binding to hold the pleats in place, then add further binding where required. This method is effective for large circles, diamonds, ovals, etc. If preferred, the pleating of the cloth can be done by weaving a safety-pin in and out along the pencil line. Close the pin when the shape is enclosed. Put a binding below the pin, then remove it. Repeat for each shape.

Dyeing It is advisable to wear an apron or overall and rubber gloves. Newspaper can be spread over any areas that might get splashed with dye. Drain dyed samples on newspaper before rinsing. Also, newspaper can be used to squeeze out excess water from rinsed samples.

A sample that is 'wetted out' (dipped in cold water, then squeezed) before being dyed, produces a much more definite resist than if put into the dye dry. Longer dyeing usually gives a deeper colour. Aim to get good strong colours. These show up the resist pattern to advantage. Allow for the colour being much paler when the sample is dry. Always move the sample about in the dye liquor during dyeing.

'Around and About'. Wall hanging by the author. A pleated shape dyed on silk.

Light fastness. The degree to which the dyes are liable to fade in sunlight is denoted by:

Fair — will fade somewhat after a while.
Good — may fade slightly.
Very good — should not fade.

Levelled off spoon 'scoop' measures have been used for amounts given in the dye recipes. Decide how much dye liquor is required to cover the sample then work out the quantities of dyes and chemicals from the following standard recipes.

Dyeing Methods

Dylon, Multipurpose, Dylon Liquid, Drummer, Rit, Tintex, etc. will dye fabrics A, B, C (see p. 238), and a few man-made fibres. Light fastness — fair. Varies for different fabrics.

Paste dye from 1 packet of dye (which dyes ½ lb. dry weight of cloth) with a little water, add 1 tablespoon salt, vinegar as directed, and 2–3 pints boiling water. Use 1 cap measure of liquid dye plus salt or vinegar to 2 pints boiling water.

Direct Dyes for fabrics A and B. Some will dye C fabrics. Light fastness — varies from fair to very good for the best brands.

Paste 1 teaspoon dye with a little cold water, add 1 pint hot water, and 2 tablespoons salt. Dye just below the boil for 5–60 minutes, according to depth of colour required and thickness of bundle. Rinse. Repeat for each colour.

Acid Dyes for fabrics C. Light fastness varies from fair to very good for the best brands of dye.

Paste ½ teaspoon dye with a little cold water. Add 1 pint of hot water, 1–2 tablespoons Glauber's Salts and 1 teaspoon acetic acid 30 per cent (or 1 tablespoon vinegar). Dye just below the boil for 5–45 minutes, according to thickness of bundle and depth of colour required.

The dyes above can be dyed cold but the colours are much paler than when dyed hot. Use less water. After mixing, bring dye liquor to the boil to make sure all the dye powder has been dissolved. Alternatively, after pasting, mix dyes with boiling water. Rinse well until water is clear, or resists will become stained after the sample is untied.

'February Fill-Dyke'. Another silk wall hanging by the author. This pattern could easily be adapted for a cushion cover.

'Industry'. A wall hanging in wool, dyed by the author. Compare this bold effect with the more delicate silk and cotton hangings.

Whether dyed hot or cold, when all the dyeing is completed, rinse thoroughly. Dry. Untie. Rinse and dry quickly. Iron while damp, covered with newspaper so that the colour does not 'spread'. The samples can be untied whilst they are still wet but there is a danger of the resists becoming stained.

When laundering fabrics dyed with these dyes give them a warm wash only, plus a little soap powder or detergent and dry quickly.

Reactive Dyes for fabrics A and B. Paler colours on C. Light fastness good–very good. Fabrics dyed with these dyes can be boiled.

Procion M and Dylon Cold Water Dyes can be intermixed and dyed cold or warm.

Other reactive dyes, Cibracron, Remazol, Levafix E, etc. should be dyed warm from 30°C.–40°C. (68°F.–104°F.), or for greater penetration – up to 70°C. (150°F.).

In the dyebath dissolve 1–2 teaspoons dye with 1 pint warm water. In a separate bowl dissolve 4 level tablespoons salt and 1 level tablespoon

soda in 1–2 pints hot water. 1 small tin Dylon Cold = 2 teaspoons dye. When the sample is ready, and *not* before this, combine the two solutions, stir and begin dyeing immediately. Dye for ½–1 hr., moving it about constantly for the first 15 minutes and then at intervals.

Rinse the sample until the water clears. Place in boiling water, plus a little detergent, for 5 minutes, moving sample about occasionally. Rinse well.

Untie the sample when wet or when it is dry. Rinse after untying and if possible give the sample a hot wash and final rinse.

When two or more colours are being dyed, give a very hot wash or very hot rinse in between each if possible, otherwise leave the sample to soak in the rinse water, changing it occasionally. The unfixed dye should be removed in order to get the full yield of the next colour. Exciting effects are produced if the sample is untied after each colour, re-arranged and tied up again before dyeing the next colour. Each dyeing remains intact.. This enables the pattern to be built up in different sections of the cloth with successive dyeings. Once the soda has been added, the dye becomes

'Daybreak'. Cotton wall hanging by the author, bought by Reading Education Committee.

'Fission' Cotton wall hanging by the author, bought by Kingston Education Committee.

ineffective in a very short time. Use immediately on adding the soda.

To store, place any mixed up dye in one bottle and the salt/soda solution in another. To use, take equal quantities of each as required. Like this, the dye can be used after a week, or even longer if the bottles are tightly corked.

Indigo and Caledon Vat Dyes are excellent for tie-and-dye but as they are insoluble in water they need to be vatted before they can be used to dye fabric.

Permanganate of Potash and Iron Rust (ferrous sulphate) are cheap to buy and can be used as dyes.

Tie-dyed fabrics are personal and unique. They are particularly distinctive made up into all kinds of garments and articles for the home.

Inspiration may be found through examining examples of other people's work. The Commonwealth Institute in London has samples of West African and Indian work. A wide variety of tie-and-dye can also be seen at the Victoria and Albert Museum, the British Museum and the Horniman Museum. The libraries at these museums all contain the CIBA Review No. 104 'Plangi Tie and Dye Work' which gives a short history of the craft. Further reading is suggested on page 245. But when all is said and done there is nothing like trying out your own experiments!

Bibliography

Bookbinding
Bookbinding for Beginners | John Corderoy | Studio Vista
Introducing Bookbinding | Ivor Robinson | Batsford
Modern Design in Bookbinding | Edgar Mansfield | Peter Owen

Brass Rubbing
Beginner's Guide to Brass Rubbing | Richard J. Busby | Pelham Books
Monumental Brasses | Herbert W. Macklin | Allen & Unwin
Creative Rubbings | Laye Andrew | Batsford

Cane, Rushes and Raffia
Canework | Charles Crampton | Dryad
Baskets and Basketry | Dorothy Wright | Batsford
Introducing Rushcraft | K. Whitbourn | Batsford
Raffiawork | — | Dryad

Clay and other Shaping Materials
A Potter's Book | Bernard Leach | Faber
The Technique of Pottery | Dora Billington | Batsford
Beginner's Book of Pottery | H. Powell | Blandford
Making Pottery | Judith and Roy Christie | Penguin
Pottery without a Wheel | Keith Tyler | Dryad
The Pottery Handbook of Clay, Glaze and Colour | Harold Powell | Blandford
Pottery: The Technique of Throwing | John Colbeck | Batsford
Creative Clay Craft | E. Röttger | Batsford
Modelling | Maria Petrie | Dryad
Terracotta: Glass, Sand and Stone | W. D. Nicol | O.U.P.
Art of Papier Mâché | Carla and John B. Kenny | Pitman

Collages
Creating in Collage | Natalie d'Arbeloff and Jack Yates | Studio Vista
The Technique of Collage | Helen Hutton | Batsford
Starting Fabric Collage | Frances Kay | Studio Vista
Fabric Pictures | Eugenie Alexander | Mills & Boon

Copper Enamelling
The Craft of Enamelling | K. Neville | W. G. Ball
The Technique of Enamelling | Geoffrey Clarke, Francis and Ida Feher | Batsford
Practical Enamelling and Jewelry Work | Brian Newble | Studio Vista
Make your own Enamels | Jutta Lammèr | Batsford

Dolls
Make your own Dolls | Ilse Ströbl-Wohlschläger | Batsford
Dolls in National Costume | Iola Barlow | Batsford
Book of the Teddy Bear | M. Hutchings | Mills & Boon
Costume Dolls and How to Make Them | W. Craven | Pitman
How to Make Foreign Dolls and their Costumes | J. Hallen | World's Work
Dolls and How to Make Them | M. Hutchings | Mills & Boon
Toying with Trifles | M. Hutchings | Mills & Boon
Real Book of Making Dolls and Dolls Clothes | C. Roberts | Dobson
Paper Toys for Infants | Sayers & Gardener | Blackie
Making and Dressing Figures | A. V. White | Routledge
Dolls of the World | G. White | Mills & Boon
The Doll Book | Worrell | Van Nostrand

Embroidery
Mary Thomas's Embroidery Book | Mary Thomas | Hodder & Stoughton
Dictionary of Embroidery Stitches | Mary Thomas | Hodder & Stoughton
Creative Stitches | Edith John | Batsford
The Craft of Embroidery | Alison Liley | Mills & Boon
Simple Stitches | Anne Butler | Batsford
The Young Embroiderer | Jan Beaney | Kaye & Ward
Inspiration for Embroidery | Constance Howard | Batsford
Let's Start Designing | Pat Scrase | Studio Vista
Embroidery Design | Enid Mason | Mills & Boon
Embroidery and Fabric Collage | Eirian Short | Pitman
Patchwork | Averil Colby | Batsford
Ecclesiastical Embroidery | Beryl Dean | Batsford
Church Kneelers | Joan Edwards | Batsford
Blackwork Embroidery | E. Geddes and M. McNeill | Mills & Boon

Fabric Printing
An Introduction to Textile Printing | I.C.I. | Butterworth
Fun with Fabric Printing | Kathleen Monk | Mills & Boon
Screen Printing on Fabric | Valerie Searle and Roberta Clayson | Studio Vista
Printed Textiles | Pat Albeck | O.U.P.
Introducing Textile Printing | Nora Proud | Batsford
Simple Fabric Printing | P. and S. Robinson | Mills & Boon
Fabric Printing | J. Lauterburg | Batsford

Foil
Modelling with Foil | J. R. Milsome | B.P.C. Publishing
Fun with Coloured Foil | Manfred Burggraf | Batsford

Gem-cutting and Polishing
Collecting and Polishing Stones | Herbert Scarfe | Batsford

Glass
Glass | John Burton | Pitman
Modern Glass | Geoffrey Beard | Studio Vista
Stained Glass | James Paterson | Pitman

Leather
Leather Goods Manufacture | G. C. Mosley | Pitman
Leatherwork | I. P. Roseaman | Dryad

Metal
Creative Metal Craft | Heinz Ullrich and Dieter Klante | Batsford
Metalwork Theory and Practice | J. R. Bodford | John Murray
Metalwork | Sandham and Willmore | Arnold
Metalwork | Keeley | Arnold
Small Scale Aluminium Casting | Joseph | Macmillan
Metalwork Designs of Today | Brian Larkman | John Murray
Metal Forging and Wrought-Iron Work | John Cross | Mills & Boon

Mobiles
Making Mobiles | Ann and Christopher Morey | Studio Vista
Mobiles | William D. Bland | Pitman
Make your Own Mobiles | T. M. Schegger | Oak Tree Press

Model Making
The Craft of Model Making | Thomas Bayley | Dryad
First Models in Cardboard | G. Roland Smith | Dryad
Simple Models | Josephine Mold | Cambridge University Press
Scrap Happy — A New Approach to Model Making | H. L. M. Hoskins | Denholm House Press

Musical Instrument Making
Making and Playing Bamboo Pipes | Margaret Galloway | Dryad
Musical Instruments Made to be Played | Ronald Roberts | Dryad

Natural Materials
Decorative Straw Work | Lettice Sandford and Philla Davis | Blandford
Fun to Make from Odds and Ends | Ursula Blair | Nelson

Paper
Sculpture in Paper | Bruce Angrave | Studio Vista
Make it in Paper | Michael Grater | Mills & Boon
One Piece of Paper | Michael Grater | Mills & Boon
Paper Folding & Paper Sculpture | Kenneth Ody | Arco
Creative Paper Crafts | Ernst Röttger | Batsford
Cut Paper Work | C. Russell Cox | Dryad
Creative Corrugated Paper Craft | Rolf Hartung | Batsford
Papercraft | Dona Meilach | Pitman
New Dimensions in Papercraft | S. Yamada and K. Ito | Pitman
Simple Origami | Eric Kenneway | Dryad
Fun with Coloured Paper | Jutta Lammèr | Batsford

Plastics
Plastics as an Art Form | T. R. Newman | Pitman

Polyester Resin, Glass Fibre, Casting and Cold Cast Metal	—	Tiranti
Methyl Chloride in the Fabrication of Styrofoam	—	DOW Chemical Co. (U.S.A.)
Glass Fibre for Amateurs	C. M. Lewis and R. H. Warring	Argus Press
Sculpture in Plastics	Nicholas Roukes	Watson-Guptill

Printmaking
Introduction to Printing	Herbert Simon	Faber
Introducing Surface Printing	Peter Green	Batsford
Simple Printmaking	Cyril Kent and Mary Cooper	Studio Vista
Making Colour Prints	John Newick	Dryad
Printmaking: A Medium for Basic Design	Peter Weaver	Studio Vista
Printing for Fun	Koshi Ota	Museum Press
Relief Printing	James Van Hear	Pitman
Introducing Linocuts	Jane Elam	Batsford
Introducing Woodcuts	Gerald Woods	Batsford
Etching	Julian Trevelyan	Studio Vista
Introducing Lithography	Gerald Woods	Batsford
Lithography	Henry Cliffe	Studio Vista
Simple Screen Printing	A. Kinsey	Dryad

Puppets, Model Theatres and Masks
Exploring Puppetry	Stuart and Patricia Robinson	Mills & Boon
The Complete Puppet Book	Educational Puppetry Association	Faber
Puppetry Today	Helen Binyon	Studio Vista
How to Make Puppets and Teach Puppetry	Margaret Beresford	Mills & Boon
Puppet Theatre — Production and Manipulation	Miles Lee	Faber
Marionettes	Donald Seager	Studio Vista
Simple Puppetry	Sheila Jackson	Studio Vista
Puppetry (Experience with Materials)	W. D. Nicol	O.U.P.
Shadow Puppets	Olive Blackham	Barrie & Rockliff
Space Age Puppets and Masks	M. C. Green and B. R. H. Targett	Harrap
Masks and How to Make Them	Richard Slade	Faber
Three Model Theatres	Roy Smith	Nelson
Build your own Model Theatre	Anthony Parker	Stanley Paul
Juvenile Drama	George Speaight	Macdonald

Sculpture
Starting with Sculpture	Robert Dawson	Studio Vista
Direct Metal Sculpture	Dona Meilach and Donald Seiden	Allen & Unwin
The Creation of Sculpture	Jules Struppeck	Henry Holt (U.S.A.)
New Materials in Sculpture	H. M. Piercy	Tiranti
Sculpture of the World	Sheldon Cheney	Thames & Hudson
Carving in Plaster of Paris	Edward Phelps	Dryad

Sewing
Singer Sewing Book	Mary Brooks Picken	McGraw-Hill
The Dressmaking Book	Adele P. Marjolis	Mills & Boon
Creative Sewing	E. Olive Pounds	Hamish Hamilton

Stage Costumes and How to Make Them	Julia Tompkins	Pitman
Fibres and Fabrics	Brenda Piper	Longmans
Making Clothes for Young Children	Gillian Lockwood	Studio Vista
Needlework for Juniors	Barbara Snook	Batsford
Techniques of Dressmaking and Soft Tailoring	E. Lucy Towers	University of London Press
Making Baby Clothes	Barbara Snook	Batsford
The Complete Book of Home Needlecrafts	Dora Seton	Evans

Spinning and Weaving
The Technique of Weaving	John Tovey	Batsford
The Weaver's Craft	L. E. Simpson	Dryad
Simple Weaving	Hilary Chetwynd	Studio Vista
Weaves and Pattern Drafting	John Tovey	Batsford
Creative Design in Wall Hangings	Lili Blumenau	Allen & Unwin
The Technique of Woven Tapestry	Tadek Beutlich	Batsford
The Techniques of Rug Weaving	Peter Collingwood	Faber
The Use of Vegetable Dyes	V. Thurstan	Dryad

Tie-and-Dye
Tie-and-Dye as a Present-Day Craft	Anne Maile	Mills & Boon
Dyes and Dyeing	Pat Gilmour	Society of Education through Art
Tie-and-Dye	—	Dylon International

Wood
Creative Wood Craft	Ernst Röttger	Batsford
Simple Designs in Wood	P. F. Lye	Allman
What Wood is That?	Herbert L. Edlin	Thames & Hudson
The History and Practice of Wood Carving	Frederick Oughton	Allman
Design your own Craftwork	W. E. Brooke and K. Barkley	John Murray
Woodwork Design	A. W. Lewis	Methuen
Foundation of Design in Wood	F. O. Zanker	Dryad
Wood Sculpture	Ron Cartmell	Allman
Woodcarving for Beginners	Charles Graveney	Studio Vista
The Complete Book of Woodwork	Charles Hayward	Evans
Making Furniture	Charles Hayward	Evans
Wooden Toy Making	Winifred Horton	Dryad
Making Toys in Wood	Charles Hayward	Evans

General
Creative Crafts	Karl Hils	Batsford
Handicrafts for All	Peter Arkwright	Arco
Beginning Arts and Crafts	R. Seville	Evans
Creative Arts and Crafts	Henry Pluckrose	Oldbourne
The Artist's Handbook of Materials and Techniques	Ralph Mayer	Faber
Introducing Crayon Techniques	Henry Pluckrose	Macdonald
Introducing Acrylic Painting	Henry Pluckrose	Batsford
An Introduction to Polymer Painting	Harold Workman	Blandford

Materials and Suppliers

The following notes are a brief guide to where most of the craft materials mentioned in the book are obtainable but it will be realised that a large number of department stores, art, craft and stationery shops will also be able to supply many of the materials needed. A list of addresses begins on page 248.

Cane, Rushes and Raffia
Cane, side cutters, pliers, bodkins and wooden bases: craft shops, Dryad, Northern Handicrafts.
Plastic rotacane: Nottingham Handicraft Co., Dryad.
Rushes are not easy to locate unless you are willing to gather and prepare your own but local enquiries may lead to a source of supply.
Seagrass, seagrass needles and shuttles, stool frames: Dryad, Northern Handicrafts.
Natural raffia: craft shops, garden shops, Eaton Bag Co., Dryad.
Synthetic raffias: Eaton Bag Co., Dryad, Northern Handicrafts, Harrods.

Clay and other shaping materials
Clay, glazes, materials for glazes, oxides, colours, tools, wheels, kilns and accessories: Wengers, Catterson-Smith, Mills & Hubball, Podmores, Tiranti, Dryad, Potclays.
Modelling clays and tools, Plasticine: Tiranti, Dryad.
Synthetic modelling clay, hardener, etc.: Newclay Products, E. J. Arnold.
Plaster of Paris: Boots the Chemists.
Moulds for slip casting: Flexitools.
Prepared papier mâché: Galts, Gloy.

Foil
Light-weight kitchen foil: stationers, general stores, Woolworths.
Aluminium sheeting: Hardware shops.
Neo-fol: art suppliers, Reeves, F. G. Kettle.
Enamel paints and adhesives: model-makers' suppliers and do-it-yourself shops.

Glass
Glass: glass manufacturers and merchants.

Resins and resin-based adhesives: C.I.B.A.
Colours: Ceramic manufacturers.

Leather
Dryad carry a comprehensive range of materials, fittings and tools for the leather-worker.
Suede and leather: Watch for the advertisements of firms such as McRae Leather of Haslemere.
Vilene: drapers and fabric departments.
Foam rubber: Woolworths, plastic shops.
Spirit stains: craft shops and general stores.
Rubberised linen: drapers.

Metal
Everything for metalwork: Buck & Hickman.
Model engineering, castings, drawings, fittings and materials for metalwork: Bassett Lowke, Bonds of Euston Road, Stuart & Turner.
Metal finishing: Wm. Canning.
Brass, copper and all non-ferrous metals: Wm. Gabb.

Aluminium ingots: British aluminium.
Wrought iron: N. Hingley & Sons.
Stainless Steel: Taylor Stainless Metals.
Silver and silver soldering materials: John Matthey.
Small tools, micrometers, gauges, etc.: Moore & Wright.
Files: Nicholson File International.
Hollow sections in metal (round, square and rectangular): Stewart & Lloyd.
Firebricks: Hardware stores.
Sand: Builders' merchants, sand and ballast merchants.
Hardening compounds for metalwork: Kasenit Ltd.

Natural materials
Coral and shells: Eaton Bag Co., Sarogny Art Products.
Dried flowers, grasses, seed pods: Seafield E. Grant.
Florists' sundries: Constance Spry.

Paper
Papers: F. G. Kettle, Dryad, Hunt & Broadhurst, Samuel Jones, Paperchase, Dennisons.

Plastics
Polystyrene blocks: Margros.
Perspex acrylic sheet, tube, rod, etc.: F. J. Bly (Plastics), Invicta Plastics, I King.
Perspex offcuts: Dryad.
Fibreglass: Fibreglass, Tiranti, Trylon.
Adhesives: C.I.B.A., Margros.
Foam rubber: plastic shops, do-it-yourself shops, Woolworths.

Wood
Wood, plywood, hardboard, chipboard, etc.: timber merchants.
Tools: toolshops, ironmongers, department stores.
Tools for woodwork and woodcarving: Dryad.
Clamps for woodcarving, cramps for laminating: Flexitools.

Bookbinding
Tools, apparatus, leathers, cloths, boards, adhesives, brushes, gold leaf and accessories: Dryad.
Vellum and parchment: H. Band.
Gold leaf, burnishers, etc.: Geo. Whiley.
Papers: Hunt & Broadhurst, Dryad.

Brass rubbing
Detail paper: Winsor & Newton, stationers, artists' colourmen.
Shelf paper: Woolworths, W. H. Smith, Boots.
'Heel ball' or cobbler's wax, Astral wax: Philips & Page.
Brass-rubbing sticks: Reeves.
Waxes and paper: Tiranti.

Collages
Mounting boards: Stationers, artists' colourmen.
Vilene: drapers, fabric departments.
Papers: Hunt & Broadhurst, Dryad, F. G. Kettle, Samuel Jones, Paperchase.
Cellophane, tissue papers: F. G. Kettle, Barnums, Reeves, Dryad.
Gummed papers: Dryad, Northern Handicrafts, Samuel Jones.
Wallpaper: Sample books of discontinued ranges from wallpaper shops.
Fabric pieces: Melwar.
Buttons and beads: The Bead Shop, A. Taylor, Ells & Farrier (will supply 'sweepings', i.e. bags of loose assorted beads).
Glitter, sequins, beads: Barnums, haberdashery departments.

Copper enamelling
Enamelling kits, kilns, blanks and shapes, sheet copper, enamels in all forms (lumps, powders, threads and crackle), jewellery findings, tools and accessories: Enamelaire.
Copper shapes, enamels: Harrods, craft shops, Arts & Crafts Unlimited.
Gum arabic: Craft shops, Dryad.
Ready ground enamels: W. G. Ball.

Embroidery
Threads, fabrics, embroidery frames, etc.: Harrods, Thomas Hunter, Mace & Nairn, Royal School of Needlework, Needlewoman Shop, Dryad, Westwood Sewing Machines.
Silk fabrics, cambric, lawn, calico, sheeting: Liberty, Emil Adler.
Specialists in embroidery fabrics: Richmond Brothers.
Beads and sequins: The Bead Shop, Ells & Farrier (will supply bags of 'sweepings', i.e. loose assorted beads).
Metallic threads and cords, and all materials for ecclesiastical embroidery: Louis Grossé.
Clip-on magnifying glasses: Quicks.

Fabric printing
Cambric, lawn, calico, sheeting: Emil Adler, John Lewis, drapers.
Cotton and rayon fabrics: Bradley Textiles (will supply job lots).
Cotton materials: Joshua Hoyle, Limericks, Tootal.
Terylene/organdie: Dryad, John Lewis.
Fabric printing inks, dyes, flocking powder, mordant, etc.: Dryad, T. N. Lawrence.
Cork lino: carpet shops and departments.
Wide selection of aids to screen making, fabric printing, etc.: Screen Process Supplies.
General supplies: T. N. Lawrence, Arts and Crafts Unlimited.

Gem-cutting and polishing
Lapidary equipments, stones, rocks and minerals, jewellery mounts, sundries: Gemrocks, Gemstones, Arts and Crafts Unlimited, Peter and Margaret Roberts.

Glovemaking
Gloving leather and suede, patterns, thread: Dryad, some needlework shops.

Improvising dolls
Stockinette: Dryad, Needlewoman.
Dowelling: timber merchants, general stores, do-it-yourself shops.
Stuffing: art needlework shops. Woolworths, plastic shops (foam rubber chips).

Mobiles
Invisible nylon thread: anglers' supply shops.
Copper wire: Dryad, general stores.
Aluminium wire: general stores, garages.
Embroidery materials: Needlewoman, art needlework departments.
Papers: Hunt & Broadhurst, F. G. Kettle, Paperchase, Dryad.
Glitter: Barnums, Constance Spry.
Beads and sequins: The Bead Shops, Ells & Farrier, Barnums.

Model making
Model-making materials: E. J. Arnold, Newclay Products.
Model engineering: Bassett Lowke.
Balsa supplies: Solarbo.

Musical instrument making
Tools: ironmongers.
Wood: timber merchants, do-it-yourself shops.
Metal: metal merchants.
Drumheads: H. Band, musical dealers.
Teachests: tea warehouses such as Twinings.
Bamboo (for Pipes): Dryad.

Plain sewing
Tools, threads, fastenings, trimmings: Singer Sewing Machine Co.
Sewing machines: Singer Sewing Machine Co., department stores, specialist shops.

Carbon paper (for dressmakers): Singers.
Fabrics: Department stores, specialist shops such as Emil Adler.

Plaster and polystyrene plaques
Plaster of Paris: Boots the Chemists.
Polystyrene: shops specialising in plastic goods, do-it-yourself shops, Margros.

Printmaking
All printing supplies: E. J. Arnold, A. Brown of Hull, T. N. Lawrence.
Printing table equipment, including stops, registration bars and table 'skin': Macclesfield Engineering.
Silkscreen printing equipment: E. T. Marler.
Screenprinting inks: John T Keep.
Rubber printing sheets: Sutcliffe Moulded Rubber.
Lithographic supplies: Algraphy, A. Gilby & Sons.
Etching supplies: Hunter Penrose.
Linocutting tools and supplies: Dryad.
Cork lino: carpet shops.
Tools for wood engraving and boxwood blocks: Dryad.
Inks: E. J. Arnold, Winstone.
Papers: E. J. Arnold, Hunt & Broadhurst, Dryad.

Puppets, model theatres and masks
Lead weights: fishing supply stores, gunsmiths, hardware shops, John Lewis.
Plastics: do-it-yourself shops, specialist plastic shops.
Screw eyes, etc.: hardware shops, Woolworths.
Thread: fishing supply stores, general stores.
Puppets, working plans and all materials for the puppeteer: Waldo S. Lanchester.
Materials for 'Penny Plain Twopence Coloured' toy theatres: Pollocks.

Sculpture in various media
Sculptors' tools and accessories: Tiranti.
Plaster tools: Tiranti.
Plaster of Paris: Boots the Chemists.
Superfine White Industrial Plaster: builders' suppliers.
Stone: stonemasons.
Adhesives: C.I.B.A., hardware stores.
Fibreglass mat: Fibreglass Ltd., Tiranti, Trylon.
Clay and other modelling materials: ceramic suppliers, Newclay.
Clamps: Flexitools.
Steel rod: metal suppliers.
Glass fibre: Fibreglass Ltd., Tiranti, Trylon, some hardware and plastic shops.
Perspex: Invicta Plastics, I. King, Dryad.
Sand: builders' merchants.
Expanded polystyrene: Margros, decorators' supply shops, general stores, specialist plastic shops.
Waxes: Poth Hille.
Car styling wax: Williams, Campbell.

Spinning and weaving
Spindles, spinning wheels, bobbins, carders: Dryad.
Fleece: Dryad, Ebenezer Prior.
Looms and accessories: Dryad, London School of Weaving, Harris.
Yarns of all kinds: Dryad, London School of Weaving, Hugh Griffiths.

Tie-and-dye
Cambric, lawn, calico, sheeting, etc.: Emil Adler, John Lewis.
Cotton and rayon fabrics: Bradley Textiles (will supply job lots), fabric shops and departments.
Cotton materials: Joshua Hoyle, Limericks, Tootal.
Dyes, etc.: Bayers Dyestuffs, Candle Makers' Supplies, Cornak Chemicals, Dylon, Hoechst Dyestuffs, Mayborn Products, Pronk Davis & Rusby, Skilbeck Bros.

Some useful addresses

Every effort has been made to ensure that at the time of going to press the following information was correct. It will be appreciated, however, that addresses do change and manufacturers are continually revising and improving their products. The majority of firms mentioned provide a mail order service but, if not, they will usually give advice on where or how their products may be obtained.

Emil Adler, 46 Mortimer Street, London, W.1.	Various silk fabrics, cambric, lawn, calico, sheeting, etc. Threads by Brooks and large reels of Sylko.
Fred Aldous Ltd., Lever Street, Manchester.	Suppliers of all kinds of craft materials.
Algraphy Ltd., Willowbrook Grove, London, S.E.15.	Lithographic suppliers.
E. J. Arnold & Son Ltd., Butterley Street, Leeds 10.	Model-making materials, plastic modelling media, printing supplies, paints, papers, inks, etc.
Arts and Crafts Unlimited, 49 Shelton Street, London, W.C.2.	Comprehensive range of craft materials including enamelling products, lapidary equipment and supplies for all kinds of printing and dyeing.
W. G. Ball Ltd., Anchor Road, Longton, Stoke-on-Trent	Enamels for copper and steel ground ready for use.
H. Band & Co., Brent Way, High Street, Brentford, Middx.	Vellum and parchments for bookbinding, writing and illuminating. Lampshade material and drumheads
Bassett-Lowke Ltd., 18–25 Kingswell Street, Northampton.	Model engineering, castings, drawings, fittings and materials for metalwork.
Bath & Portland Stone Firms, Vincent House, Vincent Square, London, S.W.1.	Stone for sculptors.
Bayers Dyestuffs Ltd., Kingsland House, Paradise Road, Richmond, Surrey	Will supply 3 lb. quantities only of Sirius Supra (direct), Isonal (Acid) and Levafix E (reactive).
The Bead Shop, 53 South Molton Street, London, W.1.	Specialists in beads and sequins.
F. J. Bly (Plastics) Ltd., 22 Laycock Street, Upper Street, Islington, London, N.1.	Perspex acrylic sheet, tube, rod, etc.
Bonds of Euston Road Ltd., 357 Euston Road, London, N.W.1.	Model engineering, castings, drawings, fittings and materials for metalwork.
Boots the Chemists (most branches)	Superfine dental plaster, plaster of Paris, beeswax, etc.
Bradley Textiles Ltd., 15 Stott Street, Nelson, Lancs.	Cotton and rayon fabrics. Will supply job lots.
British Aluminium Co. Ltd., Norfolk House, St. James's Square, London, S.W.1.	Aluminium ingots.
A. Brown, Perth Street West, Hull.	Papers, paints, inks and other printing materials. General art supplies.
J. Bryce Smith Ltd., 117 Hampstead Road, London, N.W.1.	Papers, painting and drawing materials and other art and craft equipment.
Buck & Hickman, 2–8 Whitechapel Road, London, E.1.	Suppliers of everything required for the practice of metalwork.
Candle Makers Supplies, 101 Moore Park Road, London, S.W.6.	Range of waxes and dyes and sundries for batik, tie-and-dye and candle making.
Wm. Canning & Co. Ltd., Great Hampton Street, Birmingham 18.	Metal finishing.
R. M. Catterson-Smith Ltd., Exhibition Grounds, Wembley, Middx.	Potters' wheels and kilns, ovens and furnaces for various crafts.
C.I.B.A. (A.R.L.) Ltd., Duxford, Cambridge.	Araldite resins, adhesives, fillers, strengtheners, etc. Good technical information service.
Cornak Chemicals Ltd., Swinton Works, Moon Street, London, N.1.	Will supply 4 oz. or 1 lb. tins of the following dyes: direct – Chlorantine, acid – Cibalan, reactive – Cibacron.
Dennison Manufacturing Co. Ltd., Colonial Way, Watford, Herts.	Crepe paper. Imitation stamens and green cotton-covered tray wire.
Dryad, Northgates, Leicester.	Suppliers of an extremely wide range of craft equipment and materials from spindles and natural fleece to ebony stain and flocking powders and mordant. Their catalogue is a worth-while investment.
Dylon International Ltd., 139 Sydenham Road, London, S.E.26.	Suppliers of dyes. Procion M in 4 oz. and 1 lb. tins. Dylon dyes, Multi-purpose, liquid and Dylon Cold, in small, 4 oz. and 1 lb. tins. Helpful literature available particularly with reference to tie-and-dye.
Eaton Bag Co. Ltd., 16 Manette Street, London, W.1.	Natural and synthetic raffia, grass matting, coral and sea shells.
The Educational Supply Association Ltd., Pinnacles, Harlow, Essex.	Papers, painting and drawing materials and other art equipment. Also plastic sheeting.
Ells & Farrier, 5 Princes Street, London, W.1.	Wide variety of beads in all shapes and sizes, sequins and bead trimmings by the yard. Bags of 'sweepings' (loose assorted beads).
Embroiderers' Guild, 73 Wimpole Street, London, W.1.	Many services to members including lectures, demonstrations, advice, exhibitions, 1-day schools. Books and patterns for sale. Library. Certain facilities available to the public.
Enamelaire Ltd., 61B High Street, Watford, Herts.	Manufacturers and suppliers of enamelling kilns, a comprehensive range of pre-stamped copper blanks and shapes, sheet copper, enamels in all forms (lumps, powders, threads and crackle), jewellery findings, tools, accessories, etc.
Fibreglass Ltd., St. Helens, Lancs.	Fibreglass.
Flexitools, Albrighton, Wolverhampton.	Useful equipment for schools and home craftsmen such as clamps for sculpture and woodcarving, cramps for laminating and moulds for slip castings.
F. Freidlein, Kudu House, 60 Minories, London, E.C.3.	Ivory for carving.
Wm. Gabb Ltd., 127 Bar Street, Hockley, Birmingham 19.	Suppliers of brass, copper and all non-ferrous metals.
James Galt & Co. Ltd., Brookfield Road, Cheadle, Cheshire	Finger paints, instant papier mâché, various teaching aids and apparatus.
Gemrocks Ltd., Halton House, 20/23 Holborn, London, E.C.1.	Gem-cutting and polishing machines, precious and semi-precious stones, rocks and minerals, jewellery mounts, sundries and books relating to minerals and rocks and the making of jewellery.
Gemstones, 35 Princes Avenue, Hull, Yorks.	Lapidary equipment designed primarily for schools, evening classes, etc.
A. Gilby & Sons Ltd., Devonshire Road, Colliers Wood, London, S.W.19.	Lithographic suppliers.
Gloy, Eighth Avenue Works, London, E.12	Paste and gum, prepared papier mâché.

Hugh Griffiths,
Brookdale,
Beckington,
Bath, Somerset.
Weaving yarns of all kinds.

Louis Grossé Ltd.,
36 Manchester Street,
London, W.1.
Metallic threads and cords and all materials for ecclesiastical embroidery.

'Harris' Looms,
North Grove Road,
Hawkhurst, Kent.
Range of looms and accessories.

Harrods Ltd.,
Knightsbridge,
London, S.W.7.
Art needlework department stocks a good selection of embroidery fabrics and threads, etc. Copper enamelling supplies.

N. Hingley & Sons Ltd.,
Netherton Ironworks,
Dudley, Worcs.
Suppliers of wrought iron.

Hoecht Dyestuffs Ltd.,
65a Station Road,
London, E.4.
Will supply large quantities of all dyes. (Remagol is their reactive dye.)

Joshua Hoyle & Sons
(Manchester) Ltd.,
12 Bow Lane,
London, E.C.4.
Cotton materials available through county suppliers. (Many other manufacturers will do this.)

Hunt & Broadhurst Ltd.,
Botley Road,
Oxford.
All kinds of papers.

Thomas Hunter,
Northumberland Street,
Newcastle on Tyne 1.
Range of embroidery materials including threads and felt.

Hunter Penrose Ltd.,
London, E.C.1.
Etching supplies.

Invicta Plastics Ltd.,
Oadby, Leicester.
Suppliers of Perspex.

Samuel Jones & Co.,
Camberwell,
London, S.E.5.
Fancy and gummed papers, etc.

Kasenit Ltd.,
7 Holyrood Street,
Bermondsey, London, S.E.1.
Hardening compounds for metalwork.

John T. Keep & Sons Ltd.,
Victor Paint Works,
Theobalds Road,
London, W.C.1.
Makers of poster colours, paints, acrylic medium, screen printing inks, etc.

F. G. Kettle,
127 High Holborn,
London, W.C.1.
Good stock of papers of all descriptions.

I. King,
27 Houlton Street,
St. Pauls, Bristol 2.
Perspex factors.

Waldo S. Lanchester,
The Puppet Centre,
Stratford upon Avon, Warwicks.
Materials for the puppeteer; puppets, working plans, books, etc.

T. N. Lawrence & Son Ltd.,
2–4 Bleeding Heart Yard,
Greville Street,
Hatton Garden, London, E.C.1.
Printing papers and equipment for linocutting, print-making, fabric printing, etc. including tools, inks, rollers, blocks, mallets, flocking powder and mordant.

John Lewis & Co. Ltd.,
Oxford Street,
London, W.1.
Excellent haberdashery department. Range of fancy braids and trimmings, white cotton-covered millinery wire, some embroidery materials.

Liberty & Co., Ltd.,
Regent Street,
London, W.1.
Silk and cotton fabrics.

Limericks,
89 Hamlet Court Road,
Westcliff-on-Sea, Essex.
Cotton materials.

London School of Weaving,
136 Kensington Church Street,
London, W.8.
Looms and yarns.

Macclesfield Engineering Co.,
Bridge Street,
Macclesfield, Cheshire.
Printing table equipment, etc. including stops, registration bars and table 'skin'.

Mace & Nairn,
89 Crane Street,
Salisbury.
Embroidery fabrics and threads. Very good mail order service.

Margros Ltd.,
Monument House,
Monument Way West,
Woking, Surrey.
Acrylic paints, media and other products, including adhesives, polystyrene blocks and electric modelling tools.

E. T. Marler Ltd.,
14 Greville Street,
Hatton Garden,
London, E.C.1.
Suppliers of silkscreen printing equipment.

John Matthey & Co. Ltd.,
73–83 Hatton Garden,
London, E.C.1.
Silver and silver soldering materials.

Mayborn Products Ltd.,
Dylon Works,
Sydenham, London, S.E.26.
Makers and suppliers of a wide range of dyes and necessary chemicals, e.g. cold water dyes, Procion, etc.

McRae Leather Ltd.,
Hill Court,
Station Road,
Haslemere, Surrey.
Suede and nappa leather.

Melwar,
1115 Chester Road,
Stretford, Manchester.
Bundles of cloth. Catalogue free on request.

Mills & Hubball Ltd.,
Victoria Rise,
Clapham Common,
London, S.W.4.
Range of equipment and materials for the potter, including clay, glazes, colours, tools and accessories. Information on pottery making also available.

Moore & Wright Ltd.,
14–28 Norton Lane,
Meadow Head, Sheffield 11.
Small tools, micrometers, gauges, etc.

Newclay Products Ltd.,
Overston House,
Sunnyfield Road,
Chislehurst, Kent.
Modelling clays, hardeners, model-making materials, etc.

The Needlewoman Shop,
Regent Street,
London, W.1.
Very wide range of materials for the needlewoman including threads, fabrics, frames, books, etc.

Nicholson File International,
20 Ridge Park,
Purley, Surrey.
Files for metalwork.

Northern Handicrafts Ltd.,
Cheapside,
Burnley, Lancs.
Good range of handicraft materials. Mail order service.

Nottingham Handicraft Co.,
Melton Road,
West Bridgford, Notts.
Range of handicraft materials including plastic rotacane for basketry.

Paperchase,
216 Tottenham Court Road,
London, W.1.
Very good selection of papers.

Philips & Page, Ltd.,
50 Kensington Church Street,
London, W.8.
Astral wax for brass rubbing.

Podmore & Sons Ltd.,
Shelton,
Stoke on Trent, Staffs.
Suppliers of equipment, tools and materials for pottery and metal enamelling.

Pollocks Toy Museum,
Scala Street,
London, W.1.
Makers of the original 'Penny Plain, Twopence Coloured' Toy Theatre, for which they can supply materials.

Potclays,
Copland Street,
Stoke on Trent, Staffs.
Clays.

Poth Hille,
37 High Street,
London, E.15.
Suppliers of waxes.

Ebenezer Prior Ltd.,
Dyson Street,
Bradford, Yorks.
Fleece.

Pronk, Davis & Rusby Ltd.,
44 Penton Street,
London, N.1.
Suppliers of 1 oz., 4 oz. and 1 lb. tins Fibrajax (direct dye) and Lanajax (acid dye), etc.

Quicks,
256 St. Margaret's Road,
St. Margaret's, Middx.
Clip-on magnifying glasses in three strengths (medium is best for embroidery). These glasses are easier to use than the type which hangs round the neck.

Peter and Margaret Roberts,
Atholl Road,
Pitlochry, Perthshire.
Lapidary equipment and supplies for the amateur.

Reeves & Sons, Lincoln Road, Enfield, Middx.	Makers of a very wide range of artists' materials and suppliers of Neo-fol plates, brass rubbing sticks and tissue paper in good colour among other things.
George Rowney & Co. Ltd., 10–11 Percy Street, London, W.1.	Artists' materials of all kinds.
Royal School of Needlework, 25 Princes Gate, London, S.W.7.	Threads, metallic threads, fabrics and patterns for embroidery.
Sarogny Art Products, 11 Craneford Way, Twickenham, Middx.	Seafern, coral and shells.
Screen Process Supplies Ltd., 24 Parsons Green Lane, London, S.W.6.	A wide selection of aids to screen making, fabric printing and materials for more sophisticated screens, on which they offer advice and information. Supplies include squeegees, photo opaque paint, profilm and tracing film.
Seafield E. Grant, Tollgate, Warwick Road, Stratford upon Avon, Warwicks.	Dried flowers, grasses and seed pods from all over the world.
Singer Sewing Machine Co. Ltd. (branches all over the country)	Sewing cottons, machine embroidery thread, haberdashery, as well as their comprehensive range of sewing machines.
Skilbeck Bros Ltd., Bagnall House, 55–57 Glengall Road, London, S.E.15.	All chemicals, dyestuffs and ingredients for helizarin pigment colours and aniline dyestuffs in small quantities. Gelatine in flake or powder form. Potassium Bichromate crystals. This firm has a very efficient technical service and will provide recipes and advice.
Solarbo Ltd., Commerce Way, Lancing, Sussex.	Balsa supplies.
Constance Spry Ltd., 98 Marylebone Lane, London, W.1.	Paper, ribbons, glitter and florists' sundries.
Stewart & Lloyd Ltd., Lloyd House, Colmore Circus, Birmingham 4.	Hollow sections in metal (round, square and rectangular).

Stuart & Turner Ltd., Henley on Thames, Oxon.	Model engineering castings, drawings, fittings and materials for metalwork.
Sutcliffe Moulded Rubber Co. Ltd., Ossett, Yorks.	Rubber printing sheets.
A. Taylor, 42 Brewer Street, London, W.1.	Buttons in all shapes and sizes.
Taylor Stainless Metals Ltd., Slough, Bucks.	Stainless steel.
Alec Tiranti Ltd., 72 Charlotte Street, London, W.1.	Art and craft books, artists' materials, modelling materials, fibreglass, potters' supplies and tools, brass rubbing waxes and paper, etc. Sculptors' tools and materials.
Tootal Broadhurst Lee & Co. Ltd., 56 Oxford Street, Manchester 1.	Inexpensive cotton fabrics.
Trylon Ltd., Wollaston, Northants.	Fibreglass. Technical advisory service.
Wengers Ltd., Stoke on Trent.	All materials and equipment for pottery.
Westwood Sewing Machines, Reffels Bridge, Linkfield Lane, Redhill, Surrey.	Good range of threads and all supplies for embroidery. Every effort made to provide the more unusual materials.
Geo. M. Whiley Ltd., 54–60 Whitfield Street, Tottenham Court Road, London, W.1.	Gold powder, gold leaf, gold and silver foil, burnishers, etc.
Williams, Campbell & Co. Ltd., Britannia Works, West Drayton, Middx.	Car styling wax.
Winsor & Newton Ltd., Wealdstone, Harrow, Middx.	Artists' materials, fabric printing inks, craft supplies, etc.
Winstone Ltd., 150/2 Clerkenwell Road, London, E.C.1.	Printing inks.

Suppliers in Canada

ALBERTA

Alberta Drafting & Blue Print Co. Ltd.,
524–6 Avenue S.W.,
Calgary, Alberta.

Caldraft Ltd.,
615–8 Avenue S.W.,
Calgary 2, Alberta.

Graphic Arts Western Ltd.,
4525–1 Street S.E.,
Calgary 24, Alberta.

Hughes Owens Co. Ltd.,
601–8 Avenue S.W.
Calgary 2, Alberta.

Burlington Art Shop Ltd.,
10317 Jasper Avenue,
Edmonton 15, Alberta.

Delta Paint & Decorating Centre,
12504-118 Avenue,
Edmonton 41, Alberta.

Framecraft 7711,
7711-85 Street,
Edmonton 82, Alberta.

Hughes Owens Co. Ltd.,
10326–101 Street,
Edmonton 15, Alberta.

BRITISH COLUMBIA

Angelo's Arts Ltd.,
1417 Charlotte Street,
North Vancouver, B.C.

Bing's Art Materials
6696 Hastings Street E.,
Burnaby 2, B.C.

Broadway Art Shop,
3027 Broadway Street W.,
Vancouver 13, B.C.

Central Stationery
4178 Main Street,
Vancouver 10, B.C.

Hansen's Toys & Art Supplies,
1130 Robson Street,
Vancouver 5, B.C.

Hughes Owens Co. Ltd.,
569 Richards Street,
Vancouver 2, B.C.

MacEwen Arts
432 Homer Street,
Vancouver 3, B.C.

Maxwell Artists' Materials,
366 Hastings Street W.,
Vancouver 3, B.C.

Reid's Art Materials,
5847 Victoria Drive,
Vancouver 16, B.C.

MANITOBA

Fraser Art Supplies Ltd.,
348 Donald Street,
Winnipeg 2, Manitoba.

Hughes Owens Co. Ltd.,
464 Hargrave Street,
Winnipeg 2, Manitoba.

THE MARITIMES

Canadian Color Centres Ltd.,
K-Mart Mall W.,
ss Fairville B1
Saint John, N.B.

Hughes Owens Co. Ltd.,
69 Dock Street,
Saint John, N.B.

Hughes Owens Co. Ltd.,
123 Water Street,
St. John's, Nfld.

Halifax Art Centre Ltd.,
6243 Quinpool Road,
Halifax, N.S.

Hughes Owens Co. Ltd.,
1685 Hollis Street,
Halifax, N.C.

Mahon's Stationery Ltd.,
7001 Mumford Road,
Halifax, N.C.

Unicorn Gift Shop,
Woodlawn Shopping Centre
Halifax, N.S.

ONTARIO

Crafts Gallery,
40 George Street,
Brantford, Ontario.

Ancaster Gifts, Toys, Hobbies,
293 Wilson Street,
Ancaster, Ontario.

The Art Centre,
64 King Street,
Hamilton 10, Ontario.

Bennett's Family Hobby Centre,
891 King Street W.,
Hamilton 15, Ontario.

Burlington Hobbies & Crafts
494 Brant Street,
Burlington, Ontario.

Hughes Owens Co. Ltd.,
41 King William Street,
Hamilton 21, Ontario.

The Book Shop
The Shopping Centre,
Kingston, Ontario.

Hughes Owens,
515 Sussex Street,
Kingston, Ontario.

J. C. Jaimet & Co. Ltd.,
42 King Street, W.
Kitchener, Ontario.

Anderson Art Store,
471 Dundas Street,
London, Ontario.

Robert Holmes Ltd.,
240 Dundas Street,
London, Ontario.

Evans & Kert Ltd.,
Billings Bridge Plaza,
Ottawa 8, Ontario.

Hughes Owens Co. Ltd.,
515 Susser Drive,
Ottawa, Ontario.

Mall Gallery,
17 O'Connor Street,
Ottawa 4, Ontario.

Wallack's Art Shop & Gallery Ltd.,
202 Bank Street,
Ottawa 4, Ontario.

G. B. Galway & Sons,
Peninsula Shopping Centre,
St. Catharines, Ontario.

Hobby Shop,
236 St. Paul Street,
St. Catharines Ontario.

Mitton Hobby Shop,
147 Mitton Street N.,
Sarnia, Ontario.

D. & D. Hobby Shoppe,
27 Cedar Street,
Sudbury, Ontario.

Wolfe's,
133 Durham Street, S.,
Sudbury, Ontario.

Gallery of Fine Arts,
1202 Victoria Avenue,
Thunder Bay, Ontario.

Naylor's Color Shop,
84 King Street S.,
Waterloo, Ontario.

G. B. Copeland's Bookstores & Stationery,
1292 Lincoln Road,
Windsor 15, Ontario.

Paintcraft,
1465 Ottawa Street,
Windsor 14, Ontario.

Albert's Art Shoppe,
60 Avenue Road,
Toronto 5, Ontario.

Copper Crafts,
120 Bedford Road,
Toronto 5, Ontario.

Curry's Art Store Ltd.,
756 Yonge Street,
Toronto 5, Ontario.

Family Hobby Craft,
145 Lakeshore Road E.,
Toronto 2, Ontario.

Grumbacher Artists' Materials,
723 King Street W.,
Toronto 2-B, Ontario.

Hughes Owens Co, Ltd.,
470 Yonge Street,
Toronto 1, Ontario.

Jessica's Art Mart,
593 Markham Street,
Toronto 4, Ontario.

Lewiscraft,
284 King Street W.,
Toronto 2-B, Ontario.

Loomis & Toles Ltd.,
214 Adelaide Street W.
Toronto 4, Ontario.

Three Arts Store,
298 Brunswick Avenue,
Toronto 4, Ontario.

Toronto Art & Drafting Centre,
880 Ellesmere Road,
Scarboro, Ontario.

Toronto Hobby Centre,
23 Eglinton Square,
Scarboro, Ontario.

QUEBEC

Art-Tec,
269 Sherbrooke Street W.,
Montreal 18, Quebec.

Boutique Enrg (LA),
1378 Sherbrooke Street W.,
Montreal 25, Quebec.

Omer Deserres Ltd.,
343 Ste. Catherine Street,
Montreal 18, Quebec.

Thomas R. Fisher Ltd.
1218 Drummond Street,
Montreal 25, Quebec.

Garo LaMaison De L'Art Enrg,
305 Ste. Catherine Street E.,
Montreal 18, Quebec.

Hughes Owens Co. Ltd.,
2050 Mansfield Street,
Montreal 2, Quebec.

Konrad's Art Shop,
6430 Victoria Avenue,
Montreal 26, Quebec.

Montreal Decorators Supply Co. Ltd.,
196 Ste. Catherine Street W.,
Montreal 18, Quebec.

Town Art Centre,
2870 Lucerne Road,
Montreal 16, Quebec.

Universal Hobby & Art Supply,
824 Decarie Street,
Montreal 28, Quebec.

SASKATCHEWAN

Annes Art & Craft Supplies,
1941 Scarth Street,
Regina, Saskatchewan.

Perry's Art Centre,
3008-13 Street,
Regina, Saskatchewan.

Handicraft Supplies Ltd.,
229-2 Street E.,
Saskatoon, Saskatchewan.

James Art Studio,
246-3 Avenue S.,
Saskatoon, Saskatchewan.

Raye's Art Centre,
13, 1901-8 Street E.,
Saskatoon, Saskatchewan.

Suppliers in Australia

A.C.T.

J. B. Young Ltd.,
Civic Centre,
Canberra.

NEW SOUTH WALES

Arbee Handcraft Centre,
127 York Street,
Sydney.

QUEENSLAND

Queensland Supply Co.,
389 George Street,
Brisbane.

SOUTH AUSTRALIA

L. W. Hutton & Co. Ltd.,
206 Rundle Street,
Adelaide.

TASMANIA

Arbee Handcraft Centre,
137A Liverpool Street,
Hobart.

VICTORIA

Arbee Handcraft Centre P/L.,
354 Lt. Bourke Street,
Melbourne.

WEST AUSTRALIA

Basnett Garland P/L.,
47 King Street,
Perth.

Index

Accessories, leather dress 54
Acid dyes 242
Acrylic sheets, in sculpture 82
Acrylics, hard 227, 228
Adams, Robert 226
Adhesives
  bookbinding 116
  collages 123, 124
  glass appliqué, etc. 48
  leatherwork 53
  model making 160
  resin-based, use in glass
    constructions 49
  tiles and mosaic pictures 33
  use in preparation of papier
    mâché pulp 22
  woodwork 89
Adire 238
Afromosia 94
Albums, binding 114
Aluminium
  annealing 66
  enamelling 126
American Museum of National
    History 219
Aniline dyes 138
Annealing, metalwork 66
Antique glass 47
Anvil 64
Appliqué, glass 48
Armatures 223
Arrowhead stitch 173
Ash 94
Assisi work 175
Attachments, jewellery 126
Awl 115

Back stitch 103, 168, 169, 173
  spaced back stitch 104
Backing boards, bookbinding 114
Balalaika 187
Balloon-based masks 214
Band nippers 115
Band stitches 168, 171
Bandhana 238
Basic Sewing 101-113
Basil (sheepskin) 51
Basketry 11-16
  borders 12, 14
  bye-stakes 12
  canes, various kinds 11
  foot-trac 12
  foot-trac border 12
  Indian coiled basketwork 16
  making a basket 12-14
  materials 11
  methods of weaving 12
  new weaving cane, joining 13
  pairing 12
  randing 12
  soaking cane 12, 14
  stakes 11
  technical terms 11-12
  tools 11
  upsetting 12
  waling 12
  weavers 12
  wooden bases 12
Basting 103
Beads, for embroidery 167
Bed, lathe 68
Beech 94
Bench knife, small and large 115
Bench
  metalworker's 59
  woodworker's 89
Benchwork, metal 59
Bending, forge work 65
  features 65
  wood 92
Bias (crossway) binding 108-109
Binder hammer 116
Binding, bias 108-109
Binding for tie-and-dye 239

Bindings, glove 144
Biscuit firing, pottery 43
Bishop, Brian 226, 229
Blackwork 176
Blades
  hacksaw 59
  slotting 60
Blanket stitch 104, 123, 170
Block printing, fabrics 132-134
  recipes 137
Blockboard 85-86
Blocking press 115
Blocks, collage relief 196
Blown glassware 46
Board shears 115
Boards
  backing and cutting, book-
    binding 114
  bookbinding generally 117
  man-made 85, 86
  pressing, bookbinding 115
Bodkin
  bookbinding 115
  sewing 102
Bone folders 115
Bookbinding 114-120
  adhesives 116
  boards 117
  brushes 116
  cloths and fabrics 117
  equipment and tools 114-115
  finishing, including gold leaf
    finishing 119
  leathers 116
  lining materials 117
  materials 116
  paper 117
  principles of construction 118
Bookcloths 117
Borax, use as a flux 62, 63
Bottle dolls 146, 147
Box pleat 107
Braid stitch 168, 171, 173
Brass
  annealing 66
  enamelling 126
Brass Rubbing, materials and
    methods 121-122
Brazdys, Antanas 227
Brazing 62
Bridle joint 90
British Film Institute 218
British Instructional Films Ltd., 218
British Museum 219, 244
British Puppet and Model Theatre
    Guild 218
Broad chain stitch 173
Broderie Anglais 178
Brooklyn Museum 219
Brushes, and care of 116
Built-up work, leatherwork 54
Bullion knot or stitch 172, 173
Burnishing of prints with a simple
    press 197
Buttonhole
  scissors 102, 104
  silk 167
  stitch 104, 168, 170, 173
Buttonholes 104
Bye-stakes, canework 12

Cabinet construction 91
Cable chain stitch 170, 173
Cable stitch 168, 169
Cabochon unit, lapidary 139
Calder, Alexander 154, 230
Calfskin
  bookbinding 116
  leatherwork 51
Canework 11-16
  borders 12, 14
  bye-stakes 12
  canes, various kinds 11
  foot-trac 12
  foot-trac border 12

Indian coiled basketwork 16
joining 13
making a basket 12-14
materials 11
methods of weaving 12
pairing 12
randing 12
soaking cane 12, 14
stakes 11
technical terms 11-12
tools 11
upsetting 12
waling 12
weavers 12
wooden bases 12
Canvas work 177
Cape goatskin 116
Cape leather 142
Car styling wax 225
Carcass construction 91
Card cutter 115
Card dolls 149
Carders 231
Carpenter's try square 87, 116
Carton masks 213
Carton or small bottle dolls 147
Carving
  cuttle fish bone 73
  wood 96
Case hardening, metalwork 66
Casting
  cement 223
  foundry work 66
  pottery 35
  sculpture 221
Cellulose lacquer 93
Cement casting 223
Centre lathe work 68
Centre punch 61
Centre tools 115
Chain stitches 168, 170, 173
Chained feather stitch 169
Chamois leather 142
Chartres Cathedral 48
Chequered chain stitch 170
Cheviot fleece 231
Chevron stitch 168, 171, 173
Chicken wire doll 149
Childhood, Edinburgh Museum of
    219
Chip board 86, 117
Chisels
  forge work 64
  woodcarving 96
  woodwork 87
Chucks 69
CIBA Review 244
Ciment fondu 82, 223
Clamp, bookbinder's (nipping
    press) 115
Clamps
  G 115
  toolmaker's 59
  vice 59
Claves 190
Clay and Synthetic Modelling
    Materials 17-43
  coiling 20, 27
  decoration 23
  developing a ball 25
  developing a basic shape 26
  durability 21
  earthenware 23
  grog and other additives 23
  hardener 18
  jewellery making 18
  kneading 24
  lugs and handles 30
  modelling 17
  nature of clay and prepared
    clay 23
  Newclay 18
  papier mâché 17, 21
  pinched dish 25
  Plasticine 17

porcelain 24
reconstituting clay 24
reinforced clay 18
shaping clay 24
slabs 30
stoneware 23
tiles 31
wedging 24
Clay-based masks 215
Clay pressing 223-224
Closed buttonhole stitch 170, 173
Closed feather stitch 169, 173
Cloth bag masks 213
Cloth filling stitch 173
Cloth masks 214
Cloud filling stitch 173
Clump tying, tie-and-dye 240
Cobbler's wax 121
Cochineal 238
Coiled basketwork, Indian 16
Coiled
  figures 28
  pots 28-29
Coiling
  modelling 20
  pottery 27
Cold water dyes 243
Collage relief blocks 196
Collages 123-125
  fabric 123
  paper 124
  three-dimensional 124
Collingwood, Peter 236
Colours
  enamel 126
  enamelled glass 48
  glass 46
  pottery 38-39
  screen printed fabrics 136
  stained glass 48
Colours (dyes) from natural
    sources 238
Columbian Pine 84, 94
Combination unit, lapidary 139
Common Ground Ltd. 218
Commonwealth Institute 244
Composite embroidery stitches
    172-173
Concert guitar 184
Coney skins 142
Construction
  bookbinding 118
  woodwork 87-93
Continental glovemaking 143
Controls for string puppets 207-
    208
Cooper Museum for the Arts of
    Decoration, New York 219
Coping saw 87
Copper annealing 66
Copper Enamelling 126-131
  kits 126
  materials 126
  method 126-131
Copper
  shapes 126
  sheet 126
  foil 126-127
  wire 126-127
Coral knot or stitch 168, 172, 173
Cords for embroidery 167
Corn dollies 71
Corrugated modelling wire 20
Coton à broder 167
Couched filling stitch 172, 173
Couched stitch 168
Couching 168, 169, 173
Counted thread work 173
Coventry Cathedral 48
Crested chain stitch 170, 173
Cretan stitch 168, 171, 173
Cretan filling stitch 173
Crewel wool 167
Crochet-backed gloves 142
Crompton, Rebecca 164
Cross-cut handsaw 87

Cross halving 90
Cross stitch 173
Cross stitch work 174
Crossed buttonhole stitch 170, 173
Crossway (bias) binding 108-109
Curling, papercraft 77
Curtains for a puppet stage 218
Cushion, gold 115
Cut-edge work, leatherwork 53
Cut texture, papercraft 78
Cut work 178
Cutch 238
Cutter, card 115
Cutting boards for bookbinding
   114
Cutting
   gems 139
   glass 47
   paper 77
Cutting out
   leather 54
   leather gloves 143
Cuttle fish bone, carving 73
Cylinder doll 149

Darts 106
da Vinci, Leonardo 232
Deal, white and red 94
Decoration
   clay and similar models 23
   copper shapes, with enamels
      127
   glass 47-48
   gloves 144
   pottery 37-40
Descriptive printmaking 196
Design
   embroidery 182
   weaving 233
   woodwork 93
Designation of drills 61
Detached buttonhole filling stitch
   173
Detached buttonhole stitch 173
Detroit Institute of Art 219
Dies, metalwork 62, 65
Direct dyes 133, 242
Dish moulds 34
Doeskin 142
Dolls, Improvising 145-153
   card doll 149
   carton or small bottle doll 147
   chicken wire doll 149
   cylinder doll 149
   dolly peg doll 148
   felt doll 153
   knitted doll 153
   newspaper doll 150
   paper bag doll 146
   plastic bottle doll 146
   rag doll 153
   sock doll 150
   stockinette or vest doll 150
   wire doll 147
   wired newspaper doll 147
Dolly peg doll 148
Double chain stitch 170, 173
Double knot stitch 172, 173
Double oversew stitch 144
Double running work 176
Dovetail saw 87
Dowelled joint 91
Dowelling 90
Draft, weaving 233
Drawing down, forge work 65
Drawfiling 61
Drawn fabric work 174
Drawn thread work 174
Dress, child's and variations
   110-111
Dress fabrics 109
Dress patterns 113
Dressmaking (see Basic Sewing)
   101-113
Drifting, forge work 65
Drilling speed 61
Drills
   designation 61
   electric pistol 61

flat 61
hand 61
twist 61
Drumheads 189
Drummond, K. R., bookseller 218
Drums 189
Dyebath 238
Dyes and dyeing
   aniline 138
   natural 238
   pigment or direct 123
   preparation and methods, tie-
      and-dye 242-244
   weaving 232

Earthenware 23
Educational Puppetry Association
   218
Educational Supply Association
   218
Electric/acoustic guitar 187
Electric kiln, pottery 42
Electric pistol drills 61
Electric sewing machines 112
Electric soldering iron 63
Embossing leather 54, 57
Embroidery frames 166
Embroidery on the loom 236
Embroidery, Modern 163-183
   articles to embroider 164
   Assisi work 175
   blackwork 176
   canvas work 177
   counted thread work 173
   cross stitch work 174
   double running or Roumanian
      work 176
   drawn fabric or pulled work 174
   drawn thread work 174
   Hardanger 174
   history and general 163-165
   needleweaving 176
   patterned darning 176
   stitches 167-173
   tools and materials 165-167
Embroidery scissors 166
Enamel
   generally 126
   on steel 126
Enamelling
   copper 126-131
   glass 48
   steel 126
End papers 117
Engineer's parallel vice 59
Engraving glass 47-48
Etching glass 48
Expanded polystyrene
   as a material in model making
      160
   as a sculptural material 81, 82,
      227-228

Fabric collages 123
Fabric Printing 132-138
   aniline dye 138
   block printing 132
   inks 132
   lino cutting 132
   pigment dyes or direct dyes 133
   potato cuts 134
   printing on cloth 132
   recipes 137
   screen printing 135
   steamer 138
   thickening 138
Fabrics
   bookbinding 117
   dress 108-109
   embroidery 166
   furnishing 109
   knitted 109
   tie-and-dye 238
Face plate, lathe 69
Facetting machines 140
Facings, glove 144
Fagg, Stella 228, 229
Feather stitch 123, 168, 169, 173
Feed, automatic, lathes 70

Felt doll 153
Felted fabrics 117
Ferrous metals, heat treatment of
   65
Fibreglass 82, 223, 227
Fibres, natural and synthetic 108
Figured (decorated) glass 47
Figurines, foil 44
Files and filing
   cuts, grades and lengths 60
   drawfiling 61
   handles 60
   pinning 61
   techniques of filing 60
   tension 60
   woodcarving 96
Fillets 113
Filling stitches 171, 173
Films for puppeteers 210
Filo Floss 167
Findings, jewellery 128
Finishing stove (gas, electric or
   butane gas) 115
Finishing tools, bookbinding 115
Fireproofing scenery and
   costumes 218
Firing
   biscuit, pottery 43
   enamelled copper 127
   glaze, pottery 43
   moisture and shrinkage of clay
      43
   pottery generally 42
Fishbone stitch 168, 171, 173
Fittings, leatherwork 52
Flamenco guitar 185
Flat drills 61
Flat frame construction 90
Flat glass 47
Flat seam, machined 106
Flat stitches 171, 173
Flatters, forge work 65
Fleeces
   characteristics 231
   preparation for spinning 232
Flexible moulding materials 223
Float glass 47
Flock 133
Flux
   brazing 62
   soldering 63
Fly stitch 168, 169
Foam rubber, use as a sculptural
   material 81
Foil 44-45
   as a craft material 44
   copper 126, 127
   figurines 44
   moulding, cutting and
      decorating 44
   rubbings 44
   tooling 44
   tools 44
Foil-based masks 215
Folders, bone 115
Folk guitar 187
Foot-trac, canework, definition,
   method and order of working
   12
Forge work
   anvil 64
   forge 64
   techniques 65-66
   tools 54-65
Forming methods
   paper 78-79
   wood 92
Foundry work 66
Four shaft loom 233, 235
Foyle's Bookshop 218
Frame, for screen printing fabric
   134
Frame construction, flat and open
   90
Frames, embroidery 166
French knots 172, 173
French press 115
French seam 105
Fresca 167

Fullers, forge work 65
Fungus 72, 74
Furnaces for foundry work 67
Furniture
   current trends 94-95
   modular/unit furniture 95
Fused glass 50
Fustic 238

G clamps 115
Gabo, N. 227
Gathers 107
Gelatine method of screen
   printing fabric 134
Gelatine-Potassium method of
   screen printing fabric 135
Gem-Cutting and Polishing
   139-141
   combination or cabochon units
      139
   facetting machines 140
   method 139
   tumbling or barrelling 139
Gilding metal, use for enamelling
   126
Glaire 119
Glass 46-50
   antique glass 47
   appliqué 48
   blown glass 46
   coloured glass 49
   constructions in glass 49
   cutting glass 47
   decorative treatments 47-49
   enamelling 48
   engraving 47
   etching 48
   flat glass 47
   float glass 47
   fused glass 50
   press glass 47
   sandblasting 48
   slab glass 47
   stained glass 48
   use in collage 124
   use in copper enamelling 131
   use with pottery glaze 41
   wheel engraving 48
Glauber's salts 242
Glaze firing 43
Glaze spraying 41
Glazing, pottery
   adapting a glaze 41
   application 41
   broken glass 41
   ready-made glazes 41
   recipe for glaze 40-41
Glovemaking 142-144
   assembly 143
   bindings 144
   Continental glovemaking 143
   cutting out 143
   decoration 144
   equipment 143
   facings 144
   patterns 142
   pressing 144
   stitching 144
Glove puppets
   materials and methods 204-206
   stage 217
Glover's needles 143
Glover's tape measure 143
Gloving leathers 142
Glue
   bookbinding 116
   collages 123-124
   leatherwork 53
   papercraft 76
   woodwork 89
Glue-stencils 199
Goatskin
   for leatherwork 51
   native tanned, natural and dyed
      116
   Niger (Morocco) 51
   South African 116
Gold cushion 115
Gold knife 115

Gold leaf finishing, bookbinding 119
Gonzalez, Julio 225
Gouges
  bookbinding 115
  woodcarving 96
Grain gloving 142
Greenwich Maritime Museum 159
Grog 23
Ground enamel 126
Grout 33
Guilloche stitch 168, 173
Guillotine 115
Guitars, method of making 184-187

Hacksaw
  blades 59
  junior hacksaw 59
Halving, cross 90
Hammer, binder 116
Hammers for forge work 64
Hand drills 61
Hand sewing machines 112
Hand vices 59
Hand-made paper 117
Handsaw, cross cut 87
Handles
  metalwork files 60
  pottery 30
Hardanger work 174
Hardener for use with reinforced clays 18
Hardening of ferrous metals 66
Hawaiian guitar 187
Headstock, lathe 68
Heavy chain stitch 170
Heddle reed loom 233
Heddles 233
'Heel ball' 121
Helizarin pigments 137
Hemming 104
Hepworth, Barbara 98
Herringbone ladder filling stitch 173
Herringbone stitch 104, 168, 171
Hides, for leatherwork 51
Hogskin 142
Holder, type 115
Holbein stitch 172
Honeycomb filling stitch 172
Hooks and eyes 105
Horniman Museum 219, 244
Hutton, John 48

Imitation peccary 'poskin' 142
Improvising Dolls 145-153
Incised decoration, pottery 37
Incision printing 194
Indian coiled basketwork 16
Indigo dye 238, 244
Inks, fabric printing 132
Instruments, Musical 184-190
Interlaced band stitch 172, 173
Interlacing stitch 172, 173
Inverted pleat 107
Iron, knocking-down 115
Iroko 94
Ivory carving 230

Jasperware 35
Jersey fabric 109
Jewellery
  attachments 126
  ceramic 18
  copper enamelled 126
  findings 128
Joints, woodwork 89, 91

Kenny, Michael 230
Kermes 238
Kiln
  copper enamelling 126-127
  experiments in fusing glass 50
  firing pottery 42
  pottery generally 41-42
Kingston-upon-Hull Museum 219
Kip sides, leatherwork 51

Knife
  bench, small and large 115
  bookbinder's 115
  gold 115
Knife pleats 107
Knitted doll 153
Knitted fabric 109
Knives for bookbinding 115
Knocking down iron 115
Knotted buttonhole stitch 170
Knotted stitches 172, 173
Knotting, tie-and-dye 239

Lac 238
Lace stitch filling 173
Lace thread 167
Laced running stitch 169
Lacquer, cellulose 93
Lambskin, wool 142
Laminboard 85, 86
Lamination, wood 92
Lanchester Puppets 218
Lap joint 90
Lapidary 139-141
Lapped seam 106
Lathe (centre) work 68
Lathe parts 68
Leaded coloured glass 48
Leaf stitch 168, 171, 173
Leash 232
Leather 51-58
  adhesives 53
  as a craft material 51
  bookbinding 116
  care of leather 51
  dress accessories 54
  finishing 57
  fittings 52
  glovemaking 142
  off-cuts 51
  reinforcements and padding 53
  techniques 54-56
  tooling or embossing 57
  tools 51
  types of leather 51, 116
  types of leatherwork 53
Leaves 73
Lentils 124
Letterpress 115
Lichens 238
Lincoln fleece 231
Line pallets 115
Line stitches 168, 169
Linen press 115
Linen thread 167, 238
Lining materials for bookbinding 117
Linings for gloves 142
Linocuts 132, 197
Lino cutting 132
Lithography 195
Liverpool Cathedral 80
'Log Cabin' patchwork 181
Logwood 238
London Science Museum 159
Long and short stitch 171, 173
Loom weights 231
Looms
  four shaft 233
  rigid heddle 233
  treadle 233
Loop stitch 104, 168, 171, 173
Looped stitches 173
Lugs, pottery 30
Lumps, enamel 126
Lying press 114
Lyons Museum 219

Machine embroidery
  for a mobile 157
  use in fabric collage 123
Madder 238
Magazines, binding 114
Magic or chequered chain stitch 168, 173
Making Models 159-162
Making Musical Instruments 184-190
Mallet, wooden 87

Maltese cross stitch 172, 173
Man-made boards 85-86
Man-made fabrics 108
Man-made fibres 238
Mandolin 187
Maquettes 223, 226
Maracas 190
Marble 229-230
Marbled papers 117
Marbling
  decoration of pottery 40
  tie-and-dye 239
Marimba 189
Marionettes 206-210
  stage for 217
Maritime Museum, Greenwich 159
Masks 212-215
McPharlin, Paul, Collection of Puppets 219
Metal oxides
  use in colouring enamel 126
  use in colouring glass 46
  use in pottery 38
Metal sculpture 225
Metal spraying 227
Metallic threads for embroidery 167
Metals
  copper enamelling 126-131
  ferrous, heat treatment of 65
  generally 59-70
  non-ferrous, heat treatment of 66
  silver soldering 63
  suitable for model making 160
Metalwork 59-70
  benchwork 59
  brazing, hard soldering and soft soldering 62-63
  centre lathe work 68-70
  cutting technique 59
  drills and drilling 61
  filing 60
  forge work 64-66
  foundry work 66-68
  taps and tapping 62
  tools 59-62
Metalworker's bench 59
Microcrystalline wax 225
Mild steel 227
Milk bottle tops 124
Mitchell, William 80
Mitre joint 90
Mobiles 154-158
  examples and stringing 154-158
  history 154
  materials 154
Model Making 159-162
  adhesives 160
  general 159
  materials 160
  techniques 162
  tools 160
Modelling
  coiling 20
  corrugated modelling wire 20
  decoration 21
  durability 23
  hardener 18
  knitting a joint 18-19
  making a start 19
  Newclay 18
  papier mâché 17,21
  plasticine 17
  Reinforced clay 18
  tools 19
  variety of materials 17
Modern Embroidery 163-183
Modular furniture 95
Monotypes 198
Monumental brasses 121
Mordant 133
Morocco leather 51, 116, 120
Mortise and tenon joint 90
Modelling wax 223-225
Mosaics 33
  adhesives 33
  grout 33
  tesserae 32

Moscow State Puppet Theatre 217
Moulding materials 221-225
Moulds
  plaster, for pottery 33
  press 33, 224
Mull 117
Munich Museum 219
Musée de l'Homme, Paris 219
Music, binding 114
Musical Instrument Making 184-190
  guitars 184
  simple percussion 188
  wind instruments 188

Nails 92, 124
Nappa leather 142
Native tanned goatskin 116
Natural fibres, fabrics from 108
Natural dyes and dyeing 232, 238
Natural hide 51
Natural Materials 71-74
Natural raffia 15
Natural sheepskin 51
Needles
  embroidery 165
  glovemaking 143
  plain sewing 102
Needleweaving 176
Needlework Development Scheme 164
Negative prints 196
Net embroidery 179
Newclay 18
  for model making 160
  tiles 32
Newspaper doll 150
Newspaper and wire doll 147
Non-ferrous metal, heat treatment of 66
Niger goatskin 116
Nippers, band 115
Nipping press 115
Nylon fabric 109
Nylon fabric gloves 142

Oak 84, 85, 94
'Oasis' morocco leather 116, 120
Obraztsov, Sergei 219
Offset printing technique 197
Oil, burning on to metal sculpture 227
Oilstones 116
Oiska 167
Okey's Plate Powder 52, 116
Open buttonhole filling 170
Open chain stitch 170, 173
Open Cretan stitch 171
Open firing technique in copper enamelling 127-128
Open fishbone stitch 171
Open frame construction 90
Open seam 105
Ornamental pallets 115
Overcasting 104
Overlaid seam 106
Oversewing 104
  tie-and-dye 241
Oxides, metal
  use in colouring enamel 126
  use in colouring glass 46
  use in pottery 38

P.V.A. 89
P.V.C. 228
Padding, leatherwork 53
Painting
  wood 93
  wooden toys 95
Pairing, canework
  definition 12
  method 13
Pallets, line and ornamental 115
Paper 75-79
  as a craft material 75
  basic forms in papercraft 78-79
  basic techniques of papercraft 75-78
  bookbinding 117

collages 124
hand-made 117
masks 79, 214
mobile 154
sculpture 79
stencils 135, 199
Paper bag doll 146
Paper bag masks 213
Paper dress patterns 113
Paper plate masks 214
Papier mâché
characteristics 21-22
decoration 23
modelling 17
model making 160
preparing pulp 22
Paperbacks, binding 114, 118
Paraffin wax 225
Parallel vice, engineer's 59
Paring leather 55
Paring stone 115
Particle board 86
Pasta 124
Paste
for bookbinding 116
use in leatherwork 53
Patchwork 181
Patterned darning 175
Patterns
dress 113
glovemaking 142
leatherwork 55
weaving 233-237
Pearl cotton 167
Pebbles 26-27, 73
Peccary 142
Peep-shows 211
Peg doll 148
Pekinese stitch 168, 169, 173
'Penny Plain, Two Pence
Coloured' 212
Percussion instruments 188-190
Perlita 167
Persian, sheepskin 51
Perspex 227-228
Photo opaque paint 135
Photograph albums, binding 114
Piece moulds and moulding 223
Piercing saw 60
Pig-grained sheepskin 51
Pigment dyes 133
Pigments, Helizarin 137
Pigskin 51
Pilot holes, metalwork 61
Pinched dishes 25
Pine, Columbian 84, 94
Pinking shears 105
Pinning, metalwork 61
Pins 102
Pipes, musical 188
Pistol drills, electric 61
Pitt Rivers Museum 219
Pittard's gloving leathers 142
Plain seam 105
Plain sewing 102
Plain weave 232
Plane, smoothing 87
Plangi 238, 244
Planographic printing 195
Plaster, use and suitability for
sculpture 221
Plaster moulds, pottery 35
Plaster moulds, sculpture 223
Plaster of Paris
collages 124
mixing 33, 191
moulds for pottery 33
**Plaster and Polystyrene
Plaques** 191-192
Plaster plaques, material and
method 191
Plastic bottle doll 146
Plastic sheet 223, 228
Plasticine
masks based on 215
use in modelling 17
Plastics 80-83
generally 80
themosetting 82, 225

Plate glass 47
Plate (paper) masks 214
Play production, puppets 216
Pleats 107
Plectrum, guitar 187
Pliers 126
Plough, bookbinding 114
Plywood 85, 86
Polishing and cutting gems 139
Pollock's Toy Museum 212, 219
Polyester resin 227
Polystyrene, expanded
as a material in model making
160
as a sculptural material 81,82,
227-228
Polystyrene plaques, material and
method 192
Polyurethane 93
Porcelain 23
Portfolios, binding 114
Portuguese stem stitch 169
Potato cuts 134
Pottery 23-43
applied decoration 37
applying colour 39
biscuit firing 43
casting with slip 35
clay and prepared clay 23
coiling 27-29
colours 38
definition 23
developing a ball 25
developing a basic shape 26
dish mould 34
earthenware 23
firing 42
glaze firing 43
glazing 40 41
grog and other additives 23
incised decoration 37
kilns 41
kneading 24
lugs and handles 30
making a start 25
marbling 40
moisture and shrinkage 43
mosaics 32
pinched dish 25
plaster moulds 35
porcelain 24
preparation of slip 40
reconstituting clay 24
sgraffito 39
shaping the clay 24
slabs 30
slip decoration 39
sprigging 35
stoneware 23
throwing 36-37
tiles 31
wax resist 39
wedging 24
Power tools 89
Press
blocking 115
fasteners 105
French 115
linen 115
lying 114
moulds, use in pottery 33
nipping 115
pin 114
standing 115
Pressed glass 47
Pressing boards, bookbinding 115
Pressing, clay 223-224
Pressing gloves 144
Printing
block 132
burnishing/simple press 197
colour 197
fabric 132-138
incision 194
planographic 195
relief 193
screen printed fabric 134, 136
silkscreen 200
stencil 194

Printing inks, fabric 132
Printmaking 193-201
collage relief blocks 196
colour printing 197
descriptive printmaking 196
glue-stencils 199
incision printing 194
linocuts 197
monotypes 198
paper stencils 199
planographic printing 195
printing by burnishing and with
a simple press 197
relief printing 193
silkscreen printing 198, 200
stencil printing 194
stencils 198
wax resist 200
woodcuts 197
Prints, negative 196
Prix stitch 144
Profilm 135
Pulled work 174
Punch, centre 61
Punching
leatherwork 53
metal, forge work 65
**Puppets, Masks and Model
Theatres** 202-219
bookshops 218
films 218
fireproofing 218
glove puppets 202-204
masks 212-215
museums 219
peep shows, toy theatres
211-212
play production 216
rod puppets 210
shadow puppets 202-204
societies 218
string puppets or marionettes
206-210
stages 216-218
Purpura shellfish 238
Push-on puppets 212

Quilting 180

Raddling 234
Raffia
natural and synthetic 15
uses 16, 236
Rag doll 153
Raised chain band stitch 168, 170,
173
Raised honeycomb filling stitch
173
Raised honeycomb stitch 168, 173
Randing, canework
definition 12
method 13
Rasps 96
Reactive dyes 243
Red deal 94
Registration
block printing of fabrics 133
colour printing 197
planographic printing 195
screen printing fabric 136
silkscreen printing 200
Reinforced clay 18
Reinforcements for leatherwork 53
Relief blocks, collage 196
Relief modelling 21
Relief printing 193
Resin-based adhesives
glass appliqué and constructions
48-49
woodwork 89
Resin casting 223
Resin, polyester 227
Resin, self-coloured 227
Resins, thermoplastic 82
Rigid heddle loom 233
Roan (sheepskin) 51
Roblick, Freda 80
Rod puppets 210
stage for 217

Rolag 231, 232
Rolling on warp 234
Rolls, bookbinding 115
Rosette chain stitch 171, 173
Rosette stitch 168
Rothestein, Michael 196
Roumanian work 176
Royal College of Art 48
Rubber, foam, use as a sculptural
material 81
Rubbings
brass 120-122
foil 44
Running stitch 103, 168, 169, 173
Running stitch method, tie-and-
dye 241
Rushes (and seagrass) 15

Saddle, lathe 69
Sand for foundry work 67
Sandblasting, glass 48
Satin stitch 168, 171
Saw
bookbinding 116
coping 87
piercing 60
sheet 60
tenon or dovetail 87
Scarf, woven, plan for 233
Science Museum, London 159
Scissors
bookbinding 116
embroidery 166
glovemaking 143
sewing and dressmaking 99, 102
Scoring
paper 75
curved score 76
Scrapbooks, binding 114
Screen printing 134-138, 200
Screw-cutting 69
Screws and nails 92
Scroll stitch 168, 169, 173
Sculpture in Various Media 220-230
casting and building up 221
exercises 220-221
fabrication 230
introduction 220
metal sculpture 225
paper 79
plastics 80-83, 227
stone 229
tools 221, 225, 228, 230
wood 96, 98
Seagrass, tools and method for
seating a stool 15
Seams
French 105
lapped or overlaid 106
machined flat 106
plain or open 105
Seeding stitch 168, 171, 173
Sequins
for collages 123
for embroidery 167
Setting down, forge work 65
Sewing
basic sewing 99-113
gloves 144
leather 56, 57
stitches 103-104
Sewing frame, bookbinding 115
Sewing keys, bookbinding 115
Sewing machines 112
Sewing method, tie-and-dye 241
Sewing needles 102
Sgraffito decoration of pottery 39
Shadow puppets 202-204
stage for 217
Shadow work 179
Shafts 233
Shaping clay 124
Shaping Materials 17-23
Sharpening devices 52, 116
Sheaf stitch 169, 173
Shears and scissors
board 115
bookbinding 116
pinking 105

Shed 232-235
Sheepskin
  gloves 142
  leatherwork 51
Shells 73, 124, 154
Shibori 238
Shot-blasting 227
Shot, enamel 126
'Shower of leaves' mobile 155
Silkscreen printing techniques
    198-201
  fabric printing by 135
Silver
  soldering 63
  use for enamelling 126
Single oversew stitch 144
Skiver 51, 116
Slab glasses 47
Slabs, pottery, construction of 30
Slate frame 166
Slide-in rod puppets 212
Slip
  decoration of pottery 39
  preparation of 40
Slip casting
  moulds 33
  use and method in pottery 35
Slip hemming 104
Slotting blades 60
Smocking 107, 180
Smoothing plane 87
Snips 126
Sock doll 150
Soft embroidery cotton 167
Soft soldering 63
Soft toys 146
Soldering
  fluxes 63
  irons, tinman's and electric 63
  silver 63
  soft 63
South African goatskin 116
South Down fleece 231
Spaced back stitch 104
Spaced buttonhole filling stitch
    170
Spaced buttonhole stitch 173
Spanish guitar 185
Spanish knotted feather stitch 172
Spindle, to spin with a 232
Spindle whorls 231, 232
Spinning and Weaving 231-237
  design in weaving 233
  difference of four shaft loom 235
  looms 233
  rolling on warp 234
  warping 234
  weaving 232
  spinning 231-232
Spinning machinery 232
Spinning wheel 232
Spiral mobile 154
Spirit stains, use in leatherwork 58
Spokeshave 115
Spots, tie-and-dye 241
Spray painting in screen printing
    of fabric 136
Spraying
  glaze 41
  metal 227
Sprigging 35
Stab stitch 144
Stages for puppets 216-218
Stained glass 48
Stains, spirit, use in leatherwork 58
Staite glove patterns 142
Stakes, canework 12
Standing press 115
Steam bending of wood 92
Steamer, for fabric printing 138
Steel, enamelled 126
Steel sculpture 225
Steel sections 226, 229

Stem stitch 168, 169, 173
Stencil printing 194
Stencils 135, 198
  glue 199
  paper 135, 199
  Profilm 135
Stitchbook, embroidery 163
Stitches, embroidery 167-173
Stitches, embroidery, use in fabric
    collage 123
Stitches, glovemaking 144
Stitches, plain sewing 103-104
Stitching gloves 146
Stitching leather 56
Stockinette or vest doll 150
Stone, carving, in sculpture
    229, 230
Stone, paring 115
Stoneware 23
Stool, seating with seagrass 15
Stove, finishing (gas, electric or
    butane gas) 115
Straight edge 116
Stranded cotton 166
Strands, enamel 126
Streatly-Russell patterns for
    gloves 142
String puppets 206-210
  stage for 216
String weaving, for a mobile 157
Stringing a mobile 156
Stringing puppets 206-210
Stripes, tie-and-dye 240
Stropping board 52
Strops 116
Styrofoam 82
Suede
  glovemaking 141
  leatherwork 51
Superfine White Industrial
    Plaster 221
Surform 96
Swage blocks, for forge work 65
Swages for forge work 65
Synthetic fibres, fabrics from 108
Synthetic raffia 15

Tacking 103
'Tabby' 237
Tabby binder 237
Tailstock, lathe 68
Tambour frame 166
Tapestry (canvas work) 167
Taps, metalwork 62
Tea chest bass 189
Teak 84, 85, 94
Tempering of ferrous metals 66
Tenon saw 87
Tenor guitar 187
Tenor ukelele 187
Tension files 60
Terrosa Ferrata 223
Tesserae
  adhesives 33
  grout 33
  making a picture 33
  mosaic making 32
Tête de bœuf stitch 172, 173
Theatres, toy 212
Thermoplastics 227
Thermoplastic resins 82
Thermosetting plastics 82, 227
Thimble, use of 102
  importance in embroidery 165
Thonging, leatherwork 53
Thorn stitch 168, 169, 173
Threaded back stitch 173
Threads
  embroidery 166
  glovemaking 143
Three rod plain border,
    canework 14
Throwing, pottery 36, 37

Tie-and-Dye 238-244
  dyeing 242-244
  equipment 238
  fabric 238
  origins 238
  pleating 242
  sewing method 241
  thread 238
  tying-up methods 239-241
Tile cutter 32
Tile frame 32
Tiles, pottery 31
  adhesives 33
  grout 33
  how to make 32
Tinman's soldering iron 63
Toft, Thomas 40
Tongs, blacksmith's 65
Tooled leatherwork 54
Tooling
  foil 44
  leather 57
Toolmaker's clamp 59
Tools
  bookbinding 114, 115
  canework 11
  copper enamelling 126
  cutting glass 47
  decorative treatment of glass
    47, 48
  embroidery 164-167
  foil 44
  forge work 64
  leatherwork 51, 52
  metalwork 59-62
  modelling 19
  model making 160
  seagrass 15
  sewing 99
  sculpture 221, 225, 228, 230
  woodwork 87-89
Touch forms 96
Toy Museum, Rottingdean 219
Toy theatres 212
Toys, wooden 95
Tramming 177
Treadle loom 233
Treadle sewing machines 112
Tridias Toyshop 212
Trimmings, sewing 113
Tritik 238
Try square 87, 116
'Tub', bookbinding 114
Tucks 107
Tumbling, lapidary 139
Turned-over-edge work, leather 54
Turning between centres,
    lathework 69
Tweezers 126
Twist drills 61
Twisted chain stitch 168, 170, 173
Twisted embroidery silk 167
Twisted lattice stitch 172, 173
Tying-up methods, tie-and-dye
    239
Type and type holder 115

Ukelele 187
Unit furniture 95
Up and down buttonhole stitch
    170, 173
Upsetting, canework
  definition 12
  method 13
Upsetting, forge work 65

Vacuum forming 227, 228
Vellum 117
Vest doll 150
Vice
  clamps 59
  engineer's parallel 59
  hand 59

woodworker's 89
Victoria and Albert Museum
    219, 244

Waling, canework
  definition 12
  method 13
Warp 108, 232
Warping 234
Waste mould 223
Watersnakes, leatherwork 51
Wave stitch 168, 173
Wax
  car styling 225
  cobbler's 121
  microcrystalline 225
  modelling 223-225
  paraffin 225
Wax resist
  pottery decoration 39
  silkscreen printing 200
Weavers, canework 12
Weaving 232-237
  design 233
  difference of four shaft loom
    235
  rolling on warp 234
  warping 234
Weaving method, basketry 12-13
  joining canes 13
Weaving string, for a mobile 157
Wedging clay 24
Wedgwood jasperware 35
Weft 108, 232
Welding, forge work 65
Whalebone 124
Wheatear stitch 168, 170, 173
Wheel engraving, glass 48
Whipped back stitch 169
White deal 94
Wind instruments 188
Wire
  copper 126, 127
  corrugated modelling wire 20
  dolls 147, 149
  frame masks 214
  modelling on 20
Wired newspaper doll 147
Wood 84-98
  adhesives 89
  as a material 84-85
  availability 85
  carcass or cabinet construction
    91
  carving 96
  characteristics and properties 84
  construction 87-92
  cost 94
  current trends 94
  finishing 93
  flat frame construction 90
  forming 92
  joining 89, 92
  lamination 92
  man-made boards 85
  open frame construction 90
  sculpture 96-98
  steam bending 92
  tools 87
  toys 95
  use 93, 94
Woodcuts 197
Wooden bases for basketry 12
Wooden toys 95
Woodworker's bench 89
Wool
  characteristics and preparation
    for spinning 231-232
  crewel and tapestry 167
  lambskin 142
Workers Film Association Ltd. 218

Zinc spraying 227